PROPOSE YOUR BOOK

PROPOSE YOUR BOOK

HOW TO CRAFT PERSUASIVE PROPOSALS
FOR NONFICTION, FICTION, AND
CHILDREN'S BOOKS

PATRICIA FRY

ALLWORTH PRESS
NEW YORK

Allworth Press books may be purchased in bulk at special discounts for sales promotion, corporate gifts, fund-raising, or educational purposes. Special editions can also be created to specifications. For details, contact the Special Sales Department, Allworth Press, 307 West 36th Street, 11th Floor, New York, NY 10018 or info@skyhorsepublishing.com.

19 18 17 16 15   5 4 3 2 1

Published by Allworth Press, an imprint of Skyhorse Publishing, Inc.307 West 36th Street, 11th Floor, New York, NY 10018. Allworth Press® is a registered trademark of Skyhorse Publishing, Inc.®, a Delaware corporation. www.allworth.com

Cover design by Mary Belibasakis

Library of Congress Cataloging-in-Publication Data is available on file.

Print ISBN: 978-1-62153-467-9
Ebook ISBN: 978-1-62153-477-8

Printed in the United States of America.

CONTENTS

INTRODUCTION

At some point during the process of writing a book, you may realize that you need a book proposal. Maybe you've finished writing your memoir, travel guide, business book, cookbook, mystery, or historical novel and you're seeking publication. You approach a publisher or an agent who says, "Please submit a complete book proposal."

Perhaps you're just thinking about writing a children's book, a how-to, or an inspirational book and you've recently joined a local writers' group or attended a writers' conference. Surely, during a workshop, a presentation, or even casual networking, the term *book proposal* will come up.

You wonder, "What is this thing called a book proposal?" And some of you will resist finding out for as long as you can. You'll go ahead and write your book to please yourself. When you start receiving rejection slips from publishing houses every time you submit the finished manuscript, you may realize that you should have written a book proposal. You eventually learn that, in some cases, this formality can make the difference between a publishing contract and that dreaded rejection letter.

Not only is a book proposal required by most publishers of fiction, nonfiction, and children's books today, you (the author) should consider it a mandatory part of the book writing/publishing process. Why? A complete book proposal can help you to make better decisions on behalf of your book project, and thus experience greater success.

If you've resisted the task of writing a book proposal or if those you've submitted have been rejected, this book is for you. If you've just entered into the world of authorship and you're faced with the prospect of writing a book proposal, keep reading.

Propose Your Book is designed to take the mystery out of the book proposal. I know how overwhelming writing that first one can be. I was introduced to the book proposal over three decades ago and I didn't take too kindly to the idea. After dodging the bullet for as long as I could, there came a time when it was inevitable. I had to bite that very same bullet and write my first book proposal. I've since written dozens of my own book proposals and I've coached many other authors through the process of writing theirs.

Keep in mind that today's book proposal is not the same document required by publishers in the 1980s and '90s. Over the years, as the publishing industry has changed, the book proposal has taken on a new significance and form. The online courses I taught throughout the early 2000s, and the subsequent book I wrote featuring tips for writing a book proposal (2004), are no longer in alignment with industry standards.

While there are hundreds more publishing options and opportunities for authors today, there is also an enormous increase in competition. What does this mean for you, the hopeful author? It means that you need all of the ammunition you can muster in order to succeed with your project. Educate yourself about the publishing industry and enter into it only after you are entirely and completely prepared.

In order to succeed in the highly competitive publishing business, it's imperative that you strive to keep up with the trends and requirements of the industry. Part of that requirement for most authors involves writing a book proposal.

If you're stressed just thinking about this daunting task, the information and suggestions in this book may provide the antidote you need. Herein, you'll learn to successfully meet the challenges of writing the all-important and necessary book proposal with elevated understanding and purpose.

Part One

The Book Proposal Explained

The first step in the process of writing a successful book proposal is to understand what it is and what it's supposed to do. Don't skip over or simply skim these four chapters. They are designed to teach you the basic premise of the book proposal and reveal all of the necessary elements. We'll also suggest some impressive enhancements you can incorporate into your book proposal for both fiction and nonfiction.

What Is a Book Proposal and Why Do You Need One?

Before I confuse you with the particulars of a book proposal, let me provide some important essentials. If you plan to transition from writer to published author, it is critical that you understand something about the publishing industry and how to successfully navigate within its parameters.

While writing is a craft—a creative activity—publishing is a serious business. You may write from the heart, but a publisher will consider even a book of poetry from a business standpoint. A publisher is not interested in the fact that it made you feel good to write this book, that it took you ten years (or three months) to write it, that your great uncle was a writer, or even that you have an MFA degree. Well, he may be mildly interested at a human level, but the main thing he wants to know about your project is, will it make him some money?

A publisher (and a literary agent) will view your book as a product. And so should you. As an author, you must consider yourself the CEO of your book from the very beginning. Why? The answer is two-fold:

- Publishing is a fiercely competitive business. In order to succeed as a published author, you must adopt a business stance. And the earlier in the process you can do this, the better.
- You know more about your project than anyone else and you care more about it. Who is more qualified to take charge and make decisions on behalf of your book?

Being the CEO of your book means taking full charge of your project. Immerse yourself in a study of the publishing industry. To experience a level of success any other way is unlikely and unreasonable, and the proof is in the pudding. At last count, statistics showed that over seventy-eight percent of all books fail in the marketplace each year. Across the board, the reason is at least partially lack of author knowledge about the industry or a refusal to apply what he or she has learned.

A book can fail for many reasons. Maybe it's poorly written, has no measurable audience, or no one bothered to promote it. No matter the reason why a fiction or nonfiction book doesn't perform well in the marketplace, the author is always at fault. Here are some common mistakes authors make:

- They don't take the responsibility as CEO of their books seriously.
- They don't write the right book for the right audience.
- They don't hire a good book editor.
- They don't view their book as a product.
- They neglect to promote their book—in fact, they often don't even realize they need to.

When authors study the industry and apply what they learn, they have a much better chance of succeeding.

What Is Success?

While we're on the subject, let's discuss the concept of success. What is your perception of success? What is your goal for your novel, memoir, children's book, or informational book? Do you dream of retiring on the proceeds? Do you plan to use the book as a tool for expanding your accounting, marketing, catering, family counseling, graphic arts, or interior design business, for example? Or would you like to establish a career as an author? Maybe you simply have something to say and you crave an audience, or you are trying to prove something to someone through a book by showing them, "I am competent (talented, clever, smart)" —fill in the blank.

I tell people that I write books, articles, blog posts, newsletters, etc., because I can't not write. My motivation for writing is passion. I'm addicted to the process. I justify the time I spend writing by producing useful and entertaining products that I can sell. Thus, I make a living doing what I love. My goal has always been to establish and maintain a career as a writer, while offering readers something of value.

People write for all sorts of reasons. What's yours? Here's an equally important question: What is the purpose of your proposed book? Are you writing in order to help people, to teach a concept or activity, to provide information, or is your book designed as pure entertainment? Some authors write books because they want to share something from their lives—a story of recovery or rehabilitation, details of a once-in-a-lifetime trip or experience, or a tribute to a remarkable family member, for example. Others want to make a difference through their writing. They hope to change lives and change minds.

Avoid the Bulldozer Book

I caution those of you with a desire to change others through your writing. Certainly, what we read can alter our way of thinking. The danger lies in the author's expectations as well as his or her perceived readership. Address readers who are seeking greater riches, a fresh perspective on life, or help with anger management, for example, and you'll sell copies of your related book. Try to force your ideas and values on those who don't want to change, and you'll miss the mark. The book might still fly—but you may have to alter your original marketing strategies to make it happen.

Some years ago, I wrote a book on fathering and fatherhood. It was designed to motivate disinterested and disengaged fathers to step up to the parental plate. Of course, I couldn't find a publisher. And if I'd self-published, I probably wouldn't have sold many copies. Why? First of all, statistics show that men purchase only something like thirty or forty percent of the books sold in the United States, and I'd bet that few of those are self-help books on parenting. Certainly, fathers who don't want to take responsibility for their children are not going to read a book like this one. What was I thinking?

Before launching out to produce a book, clearly define your reason for writing it and the book's purpose. And then consider human nature. You might want to help, but you won't get very far if the targeted reader isn't receptive. Even though you think people should stop smoking, eat more greens, think positive thoughts, or conserve water, some of them like things just the way they are. Your motive for writing the book might be pure and good. But, if you truly want to make a difference and make some money, you'll need to look beyond your altruistic desires and perhaps design a book that's more palatable to your target audience. It just makes good business sense.

Once you have an inkling that your perceived book's purpose may be flawed, don't give up. Take another look at your idea. Turn it inside out, upside down, and sideways. If you are attached to the material and the concept, maybe you can preserve it in another form—one that is more likely to attract an eager audience. In the case of my book on fatherhood and fathering, I might reinvent it as a celebration of fatherhood and fathering featuring lovely stories from devoted dads and charming photos of fathers with their children and package it as a gift book. I'd envision wives, mothers, and even grown daughters and stepdaughters buying it for the dads in their lives. I might not reach my original audience, but the book would certainly serve to reinforce positive behavior, and perhaps influence the future fathers coming up in these families.

If you hope to produce a successful nonfiction book, it's critical that you review your reasons for writing it and the book's purpose. Are they valid or frivolous? Are you being realistic or naive? Decide now, because these are some of the questions you'll be asked by the literary agents and publishers you approach.

Educate Yourself

The next step in the process of producing a successful book has little to do with the actual planning or writing of it. This highly recommended phase is designed to educate and enlighten you—the hopeful author—with regard to publishing. Before entering this fiercely competitive field, you need to understand something about the publishing industry. And the best way to educate yourself is through the following:

- Read books by professionals in the industry. I recommend starting with *Publish Your Book: Proven Strategies and Resources for the Enterprising Author* by Patricia Fry (Allworth Press). There are other excellent books listed in the resource section of this book.
- Subscribe to appropriate publishing-related newsletters. Many of them are free. (See "Resources for Authors" in Part Seven of this book.)

- Join national organizations and local clubs related to writing, publishing, and book marketing as well as your book's theme/genre. Then participate!
- Attend writers' conferences. You'll pick up a lot of information by attending workshops and networking with other authors.

When you know something about the publishing industry, you'll understand what the agent or publisher is looking for when they review your book proposal and why. If you prepare a proposal from a writer's perspective without considering the publisher's position, you're likely to miss the boat and lose out on the contract. If you forge ahead and self-publish without having developed a meaningful book proposal, you may flounder and fail in this fiercely competitive industry.

Here's a reality check: the process of writing a book does not prepare you for the serious business of publishing. Sure, you know people from your writers' group who have published books. You read stories in the daily news about local authors. You see authors appearing with their books on every TV talk show. There are ordinary people everywhere who have published books on a wide variety of topics and in all genres. This is no time to adopt an "if they can do it, I can do it" attitude. What you may not know is that the authors who appear to have become extremely or even somewhat successful probably did not make a haphazard leap from writer to published author. They did what I suggest you do—they studied the publishing industry before getting involved. And then they approached publishers from a more professional perspective.

Publishing is a business. Publishers are in business to make money. Across the board, they choose projects based on the book's potential in the marketplace. Publishers accept books they think will sell—that large segments of readers will purchase. A publisher will look at your book from an entirely different angle than you do. That's why I stress to authors, "*Learn how a publisher thinks.*" In order to be successful, authors must shed the emotional veil they wear during the writing process before entering into the business of publishing.

Certainly, publishers sometimes give in to intuition when choosing a manuscript for their lists—they occasionally go with a hunch. Most often, however, they're calculating in their decisions. The acquisitions procedure has become almost a science for many publishers. While authors tend to follow their hearts where their books are concerned, publishers generally make decisions based on knowledge, statistics, and experience. While the author comes from an emotional place, the publisher uses his head.

It's true that just about every publisher and every editorial staff has made mistakes. We've all read about hugely successful bestselling books being rejected by many publishers before hitting it big. And publishers have been known to invest in books that bombed. So the science of acquisitions isn't fail-safe, but those publishers who stay afloat in these precarious, changing times do so mainly because of their business sense.

If you are seriously seeking a publisher for your marvelous book, you'll have a better chance of acceptance if you strive to understand the business and comply. One way to comply, of course, is to write a strong book proposal, because most publishers and agents today will request one for fiction, nonfiction, memoirs, and even children's books. Not only that, you, as CEO of your book, will gain a much more secure foothold within the industry once you've gone through the process of writing a book proposal.

Your Business Plan

So what is this mysterious book proposal, exactly? Ever hear of a business plan? Potential business owners typically prepare one before buying a restaurant, opening a smoke shop, or starting a computer repair business, for example. When you launch a book, you are entering into a highly competitive business. At that point, your book is no longer your baby—a beautiful creative tome, a heartfelt memoir, or a solid self-help treasure. It is now a product that requires keen marketing strategy in order to make those coveted sales. It's no easy task to shift from writer to businessperson, but developing a book proposal (or business plan) can help.

Think about this: You wouldn't open a hardware store, gift shop, or pet grooming service without creating a business plan. You'd want to know, for example, who are your customers, what services/products do they want/need, where do they reside/shop/hang out, and who are the major suppliers in this field? You'd want to know something about your competitors—what do they offer, what do they charge, who are their customers, and how do they attract them?

If you've ever established a business, you may be familiar with a business plan. If not, this could be a new concept for you. Developing a business plan is sort of like investment planning or event planning. You have a goal in mind and you insert the information pertinent to reaching that goal. In this way, a business plan and a book proposal are similar, although a business plan has a slightly different style and focus than a book proposal. The business plan is more of a fact-finding and number-crunching exercise designed to prove or disprove the viability of a proposed business or product. The book proposal, while there's a similar objective, has a more personal edge—it's designed to make a case for your book as well as for you, the author.

If the task of developing a book proposal seems a little intimidating, just stay focused on the fact that you're the CEO of your book, and your entry into the world of publishing should be somewhat successful. If you reject this title and this concept, you could be in a world of hurt.

We've already established that your book is a product. When you approach traditional publishers, you are asking them to invest in your product. Naturally, before making a decision, they want to see your business plan.

There's certain information a publisher needs in order to help him determine the potential for your book. He wants evidence verifying that this book is wanted/needed by a large segment of readers. He's keenly interested in who they are, how many of them there are, where they are, and how they can be reached. He wants to know something about you as it relates to the topic/genre of your proposed book. Why would anyone buy a book on this topic or in this genre written by you? He wants proof that you understand and accept your responsibilities as the author of this book, especially when it comes to promoting it.

The fact that you are reading this book and that you have made it this far indicates that you're either quite savvy when it comes to the book proposal or you're willing to learn. Because understanding and acceptance are of primary importance, you, dear author, are on the road to publishing success. Keep reading.

What's the Purpose of the Book Proposal?

The majority of publishers request a book proposal as a first step in their potential relationship with an author, and they have certain criteria for authors to follow. While these criteria are generally the essence of a book proposal, different publishers may have different requirements within these standards. But there's another reason for writing a book proposal. For you, the author.

Why does the author need a book proposal? Before writing a nonfiction book, if you hope to be successful, you must determine whether this book is a good idea, whether you are the right person to write it, whether there is a substantial audience for the book, and what you can and are willing to do toward promoting the book. As the CEO of your book, writing a complete book proposal (or a business plan) is an important part of that responsibility.

First, you must be sure your project has potential, and the earlier in the process you determine this, the better. Way too many authors enter writing mode and there they stay—even when attempting to transition into the world of publishing. Remember this: Publishing is not an extension of your writing. Publishing requires a whole different thought process, mindset, skills, tools, information, and knowledge than writing does. Devising a complete and well-thought-out book proposal will help you to begin the necessary shift from creative to business mode.

If the author hopes to land a traditional publisher, he or she will most likely be required to prepare a book proposal for his nonfiction book, novel, or even children's book. Your proposal gives your agent what he or she needs in order to represent your book idea to acquisitions editors at publishing houses.

Before a publisher invests in a project, he or she wants to know that it is a viable product, and the information you provide in the book proposal will help him or her determine this. It is up to you, the author, to create a clear picture of your project for the agent, acquisitions editor, or publisher.

Through the book proposal process, you may realize you need to modify your initial vision for your book. You may determine, for example, that there are an abundance of books similar to the one you want to write, but you discover that there are aspects of the topic that have not been adequately covered. A shift in focus just might be the ticket to landing a major publisher.

I used to teach an online book proposal course. A few years ago, one of my students, during the execution of her book proposal, realized that she needed to change the direction of her scientific children's book. Through research, she discovered that her original vision was not quite right for her publisher of choice. With this new focus in mind, she completed her proposal and emailed it to the publisher. Within the hour, she received a telephone call and a contract. Had she submitted her original pitch, she might have blown that opportunity. She took her responsibility as CEO of her book seriously and it paid off, big-time.

The purpose of the book proposal is to pitch an idea the publisher can't refuse and back it up with proof in a straightforward fashion. You want to pique his interest; encourage him to consider your project; make him love it as much as you do; and help him to see the value in it without hype, exaggeration, and deceitful measures. Here are a few examples of things you do *not* want to say to a publisher:

- "All of my friends and family love this book." This statement is typical of a first-time author and absolutely meaningless to a publisher. In fact, it could be a red flag. It shows the publisher how shortsighted the author is and that he or she probably lacks an understanding of the whole marketing process. (Testimonials or endorsements from professionals in your field or genre might impress the publisher, however.)
- "If you don't publish this book, there's something wrong with you" or, even worse, "you'll be sorry." (Publishers do not take kindly to threats. I heard of one author who threatened to kill himself if the publisher didn't issue him a contract.)
- "This book will make you a lot of money." (Okay, this is definitely the message you want to relay to the publisher. But don't make this statement unless you can back it up with honest-to-goodness proof or solid facts and statistics.)
- "This is the only book I will ever write." (Publishers like to know that, if this book does well, you have others in the pipeline. They prefer working with authors they've found to be credible, who can produce, who know how to market, and who are easy to work with.)

Just What Is Meant by *Advance* and *Royalties*?

A book proposal may get you some money. Most large and many medium-size publishers offer an advance, from $100 to $10,000. First-time authors typically receive $500 to $1,000. Few small publishers are able to offer an advance. However, this should not keep you from approaching them. Some have proven, over the years, that they definitely have what it takes to launch a successful book.

So what is an advance? It's payment against future royalties. Publishers provide this payment to help offset the author's costs and loss of income from other sources while he's working on a book for them. Once the book is published, the publisher keeps the royalties from book sales until the advance amount is paid back. At that time, the author will begin to receive the agreed-upon percentage of book sales (royalties).

There are more opportunities out there for authors than ever before. Not only are hybrid self-publishers cropping up everywhere; traditional publishers are offering many varied packages for authors. Some publishers make outright purchases. They might pay $500 to $5,000 for a book manuscript, which means there would be no royalties. Some publishers ask authors to invest with them in their book project. Generally royalty amounts are larger in these instances.

What percentage of royalties can you expect? As you will learn, there are no standards in publishing. Every publisher is different and so are their terms. Royalty amounts might be as small as 1.5 percent to 50 percent. Some e-book contracts allow for royalties of 70 percent. But most often, for print books, you'll be offered somewhere between 5 and 10 percent. Some publishers pay royalties on the retail price and others pay on the wholesale price. Then there are different percentages for book club and other unique sales.

As you can see, in publishing it is a mix of apples and oranges, with a few grapes and strawberries added. So what you learn about one publisher might not apply to the next. Just like authors, parents, teachers, cabdrivers, gymnasts, and children, publishers are individuals with personal tastes. And they each have unique requirements.

Give 'Em What They Want

You will discover as you proceed through this book that all book proposals are not cut from the same cloth. The content of your book proposal will depend on the genre, topic, and style of your book, as well as your personality. Different publishers, even those within the same genre, will often request different information from their potential authors. Facts or perspectives that may be highly important to one publisher might not matter much to another. That's why most professionals recommend that you create a complete book proposal covering all of the elements for your nonfiction or fiction book. This way you're prepared to present the exact information each publisher or agent requires. Some publishers are super picky about the format of your proposal. Others don't even mention it in their submission guidelines. Some want to see a formal presentation, others request something more casual.

You've no doubt heard that there are many more manuscripts and proposals being rejected by traditional publishing companies than accepted. Actually, it's always been that way, but your chances of getting traditionally published today are even slimmer than ever before. Popular statistics show that only three in 10,000 submissions are accepted.

It's tough! Dreams are shattered every day. But understand that not all of those other 9,997 submissions were anywhere near worthy of publication. Sure, some were excellent and even better. But a large number of them were submitted by uninformed authors who didn't bother to educate themselves about the publishing industry, and thus did not follow the publisher's guidelines. Some don't even know that submission guidelines exist. Others may take a look at them, but decide not to follow them.

Impatience is often a handicap for authors. Some are in such a rush to get published that they send publishers (sometimes the wrong publisher) whatever they happen to have on hand. It might be a published article they plan to develop into a book, a convoluted description of a proposed book, page after page of rave reviews from friends and family, or the entire first draft of their manuscript, rather than what the publisher has asked for. Often the author doesn't even take the time to find out what the publisher wants. And this is a huge mistake.

I've met would-be authors who complain that all they receive from publishers are rejection slips and they wonder why. I'll ask, "Have you prepared a book proposal?"

The author may respond, "What's a book proposal?" or "No, I decided not to bother with that. It's obviously too much work and I just don't have the time."

I might ask, "Are you following each publisher's submission guidelines?"

The author typically says, "Huh?" or she crinkles up her nose and asks, "What's that?" Yet others tell me, "Naw, I couldn't see the point."

Are submission guidelines really that important? Only if you hope to land a publisher for your book. Not writing a book proposal, even though you want to land a publisher, is like showing up for a tennis match without a racket or stepping up to the plate without a bat (or a fork).

Please Appease the Publisher

The point is, publishers are busy people. Some of them receive thousands of queries, proposals, and/or manuscripts each year. Those who receive fewer per year—say 100 to 800—are still dealing with eight to over sixty submissions per month. And publishers only publish a tiny percentage of the manuscripts they receive. One statistic says a typical publisher accepts three percent of queries or proposals received.

I'm not telling you this to discourage you. I want you to be aware of the competition you're facing, so you'll take the steps necessary to get noticed. While there are around 300 traditional royalty publishers in the United States today, there are also many thousands of people writing and attempting to publish their books. Some of them are establishing their own companies, thus raising the total number of publishing companies into the thousands. Add to this the increase in "self-publishing" companies (a variant of the vanity press). There are many publishing opportunities and options out there, but still large numbers of authors join you in their burning desire to have their books published traditionally.

If you hope to land a publisher for your book, it's critical that you provide the information he requires in the way he wants to receive it. Do your best to help the publisher choose your project from among all of the other excellent proposals stacked on his desktop. (Read more about locating, choosing, and working with agents and publishers in Part Six.)

Understand and Comply with Submission Guidelines

Submission guidelines are not some evil concept designed to scare you out of your wits. Each publisher and agent knows what elements and information they need in order to make the right choices for their companies. It's a time-saver for them when authors follow their guidelines. Those authors who do not often find themselves on the receiving end of many rejection slips.

Not all submission guidelines are the same. In fact, they are often unique to each publisher and agent. In your Internet travels, you might find a few that seem similar. But don't let that fool you. There are also many wildly creative submission guidelines. While some publishers are lax about the way material comes to them—they might accept an excellent manuscript that shows up on their doorstep—others won't even untie a bow around a submission package if their guidelines say, "No bows and whistles."

Here's the drill; before submitting anything to an agent or publisher, please consider the following:

- Locate each publisher's or agent's submission guidelines. (Tips for finding them below.)
- Study the guidelines for your publishers/agents of choice.
- Follow each set of guidelines explicitly. (If you're not sure how to decipher or respond to a portion of the guidelines, ask the publisher or agent or contact a professional.)

(You can email me at anytime: PLFry620@yahoo.com)

Here's a sampling of what you'll find when you start exploring submission guidelines:

- Many publishers and agents request a full-blown book proposal, often with some very specific requirements.
- Other publishers' guidelines are sparse and leave inexperienced authors with a lot of questions. (Keep reading; this book will answer many of them.)
- Still others have explicit instructions for authors to follow. They want only certain parts of a proposal submitted in a specific way.
- Some publishers post their current project needs on their submissions pages. They may be seeking a good young adult adventure series, torrid romance stories, recovery memoirs, etc. And they may advertise at their site that they no longer accept Western adventures or children's picture books.
- Some guidelines are designed to advise authors as to basic story construction. You can learn a lot from these publishers.
- A few publishers provide an online questionnaire in place of the typical submission guidelines.
- I found one publisher who requires that authors create an account with them in order to submit their manuscripts. There's no money involved. I believe the publisher just wants you to show that you're committed.

Note: If you have printed out a particular publisher's guidelines in advance, before submitting your proposal, always check to make sure the guidelines are still valid. While some publishers rarely update their websites, making it awkward for authors who strive to appear professional in their approach, other publishers frequently post changes. You want to use the most current guidelines available.

It's important that you open your mind and attempt to see your project from the publisher's point of view—which can be miles and miles apart from that of the typical author. The more in alignment you become with the publisher's way of thinking, the more apt you are to present a proposal he can't resist.

I'm often asked: what's the best way to send the proposal? Again, let the guidelines lead the way. Most will state whether the publisher wants to receive the submission via email or through the post office, whether to send it as an attachment or in the body of an email, whether to use staples or paper clips, etc.

Always keep a copy of anything you submit to a publisher or agent. Never send originals. Most publishers today admit that they discard those submissions they are not interested in, and this goes for manuscripts as well as proposal packages.

How to Locate Submission Guidelines

Publishers commonly post their guidelines at their websites. Often, you'll find a link in the bar across the top of the home page or along one side that leads to the guidelines. Sometimes the link is at the bottom of the home page.

You might find the direct link under "submission guidelines," "author's guidelines," "writer's guidelines," "guidelines," "for authors," "submit," or "manuscript submissions." Sometimes you have to use your imagination to discover the right link to click. And occasionally the link is not obvious at all. It's hidden within a pull-down menu, for example. If you can't find the guidelines at first glance, click on "contact us" or "about us." There have been times when I located the link only after clicking a link to another page at the site. For example, I might click on "publishing" or "books" and find a link to the guidelines on that page. The point being, you must be creative and tenacious when it comes to locating those sometimes-elusive guidelines.

If you still can't find the guidelines, do a regular Internet search using the company name and the words "submission guidelines." As a last resort, email or call the publishing house.

How do you locate the publisher's contact information? Seems elementary, I know, but you would be surprised at how often I get questions like this. Some people just don't know how to conduct research. Okay, here you go: locate the publisher's website and click "contact us," or "write to us," or "we want to hear from you . . ." If you don't find an email address, phone number, or street (or PO box) address, turn again to the Internet.

There are many online directories, including those for publishers. Type in "directory of publishers" or "publisher directory." Search the directory for a particular publisher. It's possible you'll find the address there. Or use a print directory such as *Writer's Market* or *Literary Market Place* (available in the reference section of your library and online for a fee).

There are some publishers without submission guidelines, but it's rare. In this case, you should send a query letter describing your fiction or non-fiction book. The publisher, if interested, will likely provide any further instructions in a return email or letter.

While the book proposal requirements are still pretty much as they have been for the last five years or so, the query letter has morphed into something quite different. This letter used to be an introduction to a book project. It included a brief synopsis and a little about the author in a scant one to one-and-a-half pages. Now, some publishers are asking for query letters of five or six pages and more—a sort of mini–book proposal. The only things missing from this "letter" are the sample chapters and chapter summaries. (Read more about the query letter in Part Six.)

The Psychology of a Book Proposal from the Publisher's POV

Most authors believe that publishers are interested most of all in a book that's well written. They want to see a good story or a well-organized nonfiction book. Well, yeah, but this is not their chief concern. The publisher is primarily interested in his bottom line.

Publishers, like plumbers, insurance agents, mechanics, and retail store owners, are in business to make money. Your job as an author is to submit a well-researched, well-organized, well-written book proposal demonstrating the profit potential for your book. It helps if you can also convince the publisher that you understand your responsibilities as marketing agent for this book. The way to get the publisher's or agent's attention is by submitting a promising project represented in the most logical and professional manner.

This is a good place to mention that it does no good and, in fact, is harmful to authors to make false promises and conjure up bogus facts, statistics, and figures in an attempt to sway a publisher. Most publishers have been in the business long enough to know a good project from a bad one and to sense whether an author is being truthful or not. A publisher is quick to recognize red flags in the author's approach and the materials he or she submits. With so many excellent packages and professional authors to choose from, it is easy to reject those that raise any questions, whatsoever.

Why Does the Publisher Want to Know That?

In chapters 3 and 4, we'll cover each aspect of the book proposal. Here, I'd like to give you a brief lesson on the why's and what-for's of the proposal. It's important that you gain clarity on the following seven points. The main concern for the publisher, and it should also be for you, is whether or not this book is a viable product. The book proposal will help the publisher (and you) to answer this question. Here's the rundown revealing the psychology of the book proposal from the agent's, publisher's, or acquisitions editor's point of view.

These points are listed in no particular order. The fact is that different publishers may apply greater importance to one or two of these points over the others. What is critical to one may not be to another. The main take-away in this section for you should be to start thinking like a publisher so you're more apt to appeal to his or her sensitivities. The publisher wants to know:

1. **Can the author write?** Your query letter, cover letter, and synopsis are designed to tell the publisher whether or not you have a good story (for fiction), or a good concept (for nonfiction), and if you can actually write this type of book. Can you tell a cohesive story? Can you logically organize a how-to or informational book? Is your use of grammar up to snuff? Is the overall presentation appealing and cogent?

Publishers and agents receive numbers of projects and some of them are darn good. Those that are poorly written, disorganized, sloppily presented, incomplete, or not in compliance with what the publisher accepts are quickly discarded. Those that are professionally executed, are on a topic or in a genre the house publishes, and conform to the proposal requirements will have a much greater chance of making their way to the top of the heap for consideration.

When you can put yourself in the publisher's shoes and begin to think like him, you'll realize the importance of presentation. I'm not talking about (and publishers generally do not appreciate) bells and whistles, polka dots, and paisley. They crave a straightforward, well-written, complete package presented in an orderly fashion.

If you are not accustomed to the world of business and have never worked on projects that require a system and a clean, organized presentation, get some help with your proposal. If you don't know a professional author, consult a friend or relative who's been in business or who has worked within the corporate world.

If your writing is lacking, take steps to remedy this. When I evaluate a less-than-perfect proposal or manuscript, I recommend one of three things, depending on the level of imperfection I observe in the writer's work. If it is fairly well written with just a few editorial sins—repetitive, too wordy, continually off topic, weak transitions, etc.—I may suggest the author hire a good book editor before submitting the proposal.

If the story has numerous flaws and inconsistencies and the writing is poor, I might suggest that the author take a writing course and/or take time out to study more about writing in this particular genre.

If the writing is atrocious, I will gently recommend that the author join a writers' critique group, participate for a year or more, share his or her work often, and listen and learn.

If you're not sure if your book is good or whether you can write well enough to land a publisher, get some honest feedback before approaching one. Publishers are not in the business of teaching. Most do not have sympathy for the new writer who hasn't taken time to learn something about his craft.

I've met people who can write lovely prose—who can make a story sing, but who can't write directions or instructions worth a lick. I've known professional business writers who cannot grasp the concept of storytelling. So even those who can write well in one area or genre could be quite clumsy in another.

If you want a chance with your publisher of choice, you must play by his rules. Hone your writing skills before approaching him. And you'd better make sure your presentation and the product you're offering are top notch.

2. **Is there a market for this book?** As I said before, publishers are in business to make money. As he looks over your proposal, he is viewing it from an economic perspective. He wants to know, is this book wanted and/or needed by a large segment of society? Are these people apt to read it? If it's fiction, is it a popular genre? If it's nonfiction, does it have information readers want? If the publisher typically produces books in this genre or on this topic, he already knows something about the readership. But he will look to you—the author—for additional convincing.

He wants you to show him through statistics, for example, that there is an audience for this book. The more you know about your audience and their needs, and the more closely you can meet their needs through your book, the greater the chance this publisher will be interested in your promising project. Back up your argument with facts. Publishers turn off to an author's hype and unsubstantiated claims about their proposed books. And they'll turn down proposals containing exaggerations and unwarranted, unproven embellishments.

Publishers appreciate forward-thinking authors with creative ideas for exploring new topics, new angles for old topics, and for imaginative additions to their books designed to attract a larger audience. Find ways to legitimately show the publisher the money and you're more likely to get a contract.

This is one of the most important parts of your book proposal, as far as most publishers are concerned, and it should be important to you, too. That's why you need to know:

- Who is your audience? Never, never say everyone. Don't even think it. Your book has a target audience and it is up to you to identify it. Does your book contain information or is it in a genre that is wanted/needed by numbers of readers? If your book has no relevance to anyone except you and maybe a few family members, how in the heck will you market the thing?
- How many people does your audience comprise? In other words, what percentage of people own pets, travel abroad, cook vegetarian, or read historical novels, for example?

Answer these questions sufficiently in your proposal and you're more apt to pique the interest of an appropriate publisher. When you sit down to write the book, write for this very audience.

Too often, an author writes for him- or herself. Some of my clients and students admit that they wrote a book they wanted to write with no regard for their ultimate readers. They believed that if they liked this style of book or the subject matter, others would, too. Absolutely no research or study went into their *product* before they sat down to write.

After the fact, when they realized they'd written within a narrow niche, some of them scrambled to change the focus of their books or they attempted to identify their books under a more popular genre. A few even attempted to do so without rewriting. *What?* Calling science fiction a romance novel does not make it so, and this is deceitful.

If you decide you've made a mistake in writing your book, and want to switch to another genre, do so legitimately. Study the genre and then do a rewrite. Write what you want, if you wish—humor, mysteries, animal stories, how-to books—but do so always with your audience in mind. This is an important part of an author's responsibility: to keep readers in mind throughout the entire writing, editing, and proofing process.

Okay, so now you know that you must correctly identify your audience for a potential publisher and estimate their numbers with some accuracy. Why? So he knows whether or not this book will fit into his list, and so that he can estimate the sales potential. (We'll discuss how to locate statistics in chapter 4.)

3. **How will you locate and engage your audience?** Before sending off your book proposal, make sure you've included everything the publisher needs to know in order to make a good decision. If you don't, you're only sabotaging yourself and your chances at publishing success.

Here's the deal: you can tell the publisher who your potential readers are. But he'll also want to know how you will go from point A to point B—where are these readers and how will you engage them? Where do they hang out? Where do they buy their books? What prompts them to buy books? Is it from Amazon's recommendations? From reviews at their favorite blog sites? You need to know your audience and their book-buying habits.

A publisher will feel a greater sense of confidence with your project if you can provide him with a roadmap to potential readers. Prove to him that you have pinpointed avenues to at least 10,000 readers and he'll start seeing dollar signs before his eyes. Do you know what those dollar signs can lead to? You got it—a publishing contract and maybe an advance.

I realize I've mentioned the publisher's bottom line and his interest in money and high book sales several times so far. That's because I know how hard it is for some of you to comprehend this concept. I've been asked to edit or evaluate book proposals for some of my students and workshop attendees. Even after I spent hours preaching and nagging on this issue, it's obvious that some of these authors still failed to comprehend. They handle the marketing section of their proposal as an afterthought and focus mainly on the wonderful story they've written. Don't make this mistake.

If you still can't wrap your mind around the concept of commerce—if you're still in la-la land where the idea of marketing your book is concerned—get help. Take a business course, join a forum on book marketing, and read books on book promotion. I recommend *Promote Your Book: Over 250 Proven, Low-Cost Tips and Techniques for the Enterprising Author*, by Patricia Fry (Allworth Press).

4. **Why are you the right person to write this book?** Do you have expertise in the topic? Is your slant on the topic or story unique or especially clever? You must convince the publisher or an agent not only that this book is a good idea, but also that you are the best person to write it. If you plan to publish the book yourself, you still need to address this question. Are you the best person to write this book? Why?

Why is this important? Think about it; let's say that you want to buy a book on showing a particular breed of dog. Does it matter to you who wrote such a book? Of course it does. Wouldn't you put more faith in an author who has judged dog shows for twenty years than someone who has simply attended a few shows and just acquired her first dog? However, you might enjoy reading this author's humorous account of her first dog show.

Publishers may pay more attention to nonfiction books by authorities and experts on the subject. But they're also interested in fascinating, timely books by authors who may have experienced the event or lived the story.

How does a first-time writer break in? There are ways to gain credibility in your field or genre. For example, you can become known as an author of fiction or children's stories by writing stories in your book's genre and submitting them to magazines, ezines, and popular blog sites and websites—lots and lots of them. Establish a blog and post frequently. I have written five books in my Klepto Cat Mystery series in less than two years, and they are selling quite well as Kindle books. So my pitch to a publisher of cozy mysteries would definitely include these facts, along with some sales figures to sweeten the pot.

While attempting to convince the publisher that you're the right person to write your book, brag a little (or a lot). List your affiliations and influences related to the book you're pitching. Debbie Puente was offered a publishing contract for her book on custard desserts partly because she worked for a kitchen store chain at the time. Before writing the book, Puente received confirmation from the chain store buyer that she would stock Puente's book in all United States stores. This was a major factor in Puente landing a publishing contract.

Do you have expertise or experience in the topic or genre of your book? What can you tell the publisher that would entice him or her to take a second look at your proposal? Will your name as the author sell copies of the book? Do you have a strong connection to an influential organization, company, or individual? This is the type of information that will impress a publisher.

5. **What can you contribute to making your book a success?** In other words, what is your platform? What connections and skills do you have that will help you promote and sell this book?

Where is the psychology in this point? Let's say that a publisher (or an agent) receives two or three proposals that he really, really likes, but he can only pursue one of them. How will he make the decision? Which one will he choose?

Can you guess? It's the one that he believes will make him the most money. And a measure for publishers and agents is the author's platform (following, way of attracting readers) and his or her understanding of and experience in book promotion and marketing.

Now the book proposal does not call for yes and no answers. It requires careful thought, study, and research, and boy is this study and research important—especially in this highly competitive publishing climate. Also important is any information that elevates the author in the publisher's eyes.

Caution: don't blow in the wind. In other words, be able to back up any information you offer or promises you make. Avoid peppering your proposal with wild possibilities you have not tried and probably won't pursue. Learn what it actually takes to promote a book and go to work adopting some of those skills along with a marketing mindset. You must understand what will impress a publisher. I've known authors who have the right stuff—they just don't realize it and/or don't know how to use it or describe it.

Here's an anecdote from my own files. I had a talented client with a wildly promising project. She had a dynamite book idea and a great start on her book proposal. But when she got to the platform and promotions portion of her proposal, I noticed that it was rather weak. Thelma (not her real name) was an artist and her book idea featured a unique program incorporating the process of creating art with an aspect of personal improvement. In an effort to help her flesh this aspect of her book proposal out and give it much-needed power and authority, I asked Thelma to describe the response she'd received from people who had attended her sessions related to the unique process she outlined in her book.

She said, "Well, I've never actually taught this program."

I asked her to include comments from people who had used her program on their own. She said that no one had ever used it, as far as she knew.

I asked if she had ever taught any aspect of art, thinking we could use anecdotes from some of her teaching experiences. She had not.

But she did have some grandiose ideas for workshops in major cities across the states. I suggested that she tell the publisher about the workshops she planned—where they would be, what celebrities would attend, how many people she had signed up, etc.

She said she had no specific plans for workshops, yet.

That's when I recommended that she hold off writing the book—that she shelve the proposal for now and spend the next few months planning and presenting a workshop in which she would teach the system she represents in her book. And then she would have something concrete to use in convincing the publisher or agent of her book's value.

She could even put together a booklet to sell to workshop participants. Don't you think it would impress a publisher if the author could say, "I conducted a workshop in Los Angeles with Queen Latifah as our celebrity guest? We had 140 people enrolled and sold seventy-five copies of the booklet I created for the event. Here are positive comments from thirty-five attendees."

The point is, publishers will want to know certain things about authors. What are some of those things?

- What can you bring to the table as far as promoting your book?
- Why would anyone want to read a book written by you?
- Do you have a following—people who know you as an expert in your field, a celebrity, or a writer in that genre?
- Do you have connections—people who can help you to get the exposure you need?
- How will you attract readers?

I heard it said the other day that platform isn't the number of people you know as much as the number of people who know you. Thus the huge interest among authors in Facebook, Twitter, and other social media sites. We need "friends," and "followers." In some ways it's easier than ever to attract them—the opportunities are certainly out there.

What is the publisher thinking when he skims through your proposal in search of your credentials and marketing aptitude? You may not know this, but, should he publish your book, he can spend only limited time and money marketing it. It's the way of publishers today. An in-house publicist might be assigned to your newly published book for a period of three months or less. She probably has a system of sending out a certain number of press releases to their list. She might solicit interviews, podcasts, radio spots, and other appearances using their list and any connections you've supplied. She'll most likely have your book listed on Amazon and other online bookstores. She'll send out a few review copies, add your book to their catalog, which goes out to booksellers, then—this might surprise you—she'll move on to the next project.

Now, you're on your own. The publisher is relying on you to promote your book using the connections, ideas, and skills you shared in your proposal.

The thing that many new authors don't realize is that, while publishers used to take charge of marketing the books they produced, now they navigate toward authors they can partner with—those who can bring a fair share of assets to the table. And those assets had better translate somehow into book sales.

6. **What else is out there like your book?** What is your competition? How does your book fit into the marketplace? This is another important element that the publisher will consider and that you should strongly

consider before ever writing your book. If we're talking fiction, choose a genre that's popular, and stay true to that genre throughout the writing process. Romance stories have been popular for a long time. Now a lot of people are buying cozy mysteries, as well. If you decide to write a romance or a cozy mystery, for example, make sure you learn what this genre involves—what are the parameters? And then write the book within these boundaries.

Let's say you want to approach a certain publisher, but you've written a crime story and he publishes chick lit and light humor. You might reason, "Yeah, I have women in my story—there's a female cop and a few strippers. I could pass this off as chick lit." Don't even go there. First, you won't fool the publisher. Second, by trying to fool him, you may burn very important bridges.

The publisher wants to know how your book fits into the scheme of things within his company and the market he serves.

For nonfiction, is there a need and desire for your book? What books are out there on this topic? How many of them cover the topic in the same way you plan to? If there's an overabundance of books on this topic, you want to discover this early on so you can rethink your project. When you present your proposal to the publisher, you should be able to say something like, "While there are several books on this topic, none of them provide a workbook option," or "I've found the major books in this field lacking in these areas, which I cover in my book."

When you put together your book proposal, you'll be required to study your competition—those books that may compete with yours—and complementary books, as well. This section, when properly executed, is designed to convince the publisher that this book brings something new presented in a unique and useful way to a particular audience who is eager for this information. Through your honest and thorough comparison, you should be able to sell the publisher on the value and need for your well-thought-out book. If not, perhaps you should rethink your book.

7. **How will you promote this book?** Now this is more important than you might think. Still, many authors believe that landing a publisher will absolve them from anything to do with marketing and promotion. This is so not true! In fact, when a publisher requests only portions of

a book proposal or he just wants a query letter, he almost always asks specifically for your marketing plan.

The psychology behind this portion of the book proposal is pretty obvious. Again, the publisher wants a project that will make him some money. And you—the author—are a huge part of this happening. If you have a decent (or amazing) book that is wanted by a large segment of people who are fairly easy to locate and approach, if you're well known within this genre or topic, and if you have the skills, connections, aptitude, time, energy, willingness, and ideas to promote this book, man, you are looking good to the publisher.

Obviously, anything you can offer by way of proof and confirmation that you can successfully promote this book will definitely please any publisher. Please notice that I used the words "proof" and "confirmation." (Learn more about how to compile a marketing plan and present it to an agent or publisher in chapter 4.)

It's All Up to You

You already know that a book proposal is a sales pitch. It's a business plan. Now you understand something about what the publisher actually wants and how he views your proposal package. He may ignore your education section, skim over your lengthy synopsis, and seek out each tidbit that identifies your project as a potential moneymaker for his company.

If it seems as though I'm beating this into the ground, let me explain. You may be a rare author who understands marketing. Perhaps your left brain is in control or you're like me—you work from a center portion of your brain—a balance of the creative and the logical. But so many authors I meet are right-brain thinkers. They come from an artistic place, and have no background in anything as grounded as marketing and promotion. They're more comfortable within the realm of creativity and shun anything that requires a business mindset.

I know this author pretty well. He or she can read thousands of pages explaining the concept that publishers are primarily looking to make money. They hear this discussed at their writers' club meetings and the conferences they attend. But they pretty much ignore it. They avoid actually taking it in. They just can't comprehend how extremely important it is.

Thus, the creative author and the business-minded publisher might never find a balance in their understanding of one another.

So what happens to these authors, who can't open their minds to the reality of a publisher's point of view? They typically go with a self-publishing company and become one of the high percentage of authors who fail each year.

Elements of a Basic Book Proposal— Editorial Portion

There are two fundamental aspects to a book proposal—the editorial (writing) and the business (marketing). In this chapter, I focus on the editorial sections (synopsis and chapter summaries). Chapter 4 follows with the marketing pieces (the market and promotion). Please note that the order in which we present the sections of the proposal may not be the order that works for you or your unique project. Different agents and publishers may ask for just certain sections organized in a specific order. This guide is an example of one way to arrange a complete book proposal.

Just make sure that your proposal is clear, concise, and accurate, and that it includes everything a publisher needs in order to make that all-important decision to publish.

What about the tone for your proposal? Should it be upbeat, serious, or have a business edge to it? Here's what most publishing professionals suggest: if your book is on a serious topic—it's a business book, for example, and you've used a serious tone in the book—then certainly, use a more serious tone in your proposal. If it is a fun project involving humor or a playful theme, keep your voice light. A memoirist would adopt a tone to reflect the attitude of his or her story. Avoid the temptation to overindulge in a playful or dire demeanor while compiling the proposal. Remember that this may be a representation of your proposed book, but it is still a business proposal. A total lack of professionalism might be just the distraction you don't need to put before your publisher of choice.

The Cover Letter

While the cover letter is the first piece of your book proposal to be seen by an agent, acquisitions editor, or (in smaller publishing houses) the publisher himself, it may be the last part of the proposal you actually write. Why? It's easier to pull the cover letter together after you've written the synopsis, the about-the-author, marketing plan, and so forth. And the contents of the cover letter can change from proposal to proposal, depending on the requirements of each agent or publisher you contact.

The cover letter is not to be confused with the query letter. The query letter, which we will cover quite completely in chapter 16, is generally the first thing you would send to a publisher or an agent. This is how you initially introduce yourself and your project. The cover letter, on the other hand, accompanies the book proposal. It is your introduction to the proposal package.

The cover letter encompasses one page and, if being sent via the post office, includes the date, address block, and salutation. When sent as part of an email, the cover letter is not as formal. Just be sure to include all of your contact information, including phone number, in either case. It is not unheard of for a publisher or agent to call an author who makes a good impression.

Indicate in the letter that this is a book proposal for (your book title). You might be surprised at how many authors neglect this obvious step. It's another example of the author's disregard for her audience. Don't assume what the publisher or agent knows. Either use an attention line at the top of the letter stating, "Book Proposal for *Everything Blue*," or start the cover letter by writing, "Enclosed (or attached) is a book proposal for my memoir, *Everything Blue*."

Inform the publisher or agent if this is a simultaneous or multiple submission—that you are sending the proposal to more than one agent or publisher at the same time. As a general rule, it is okay to send query letters simultaneously, and some publishers and agents are okay with simultaneous proposal packages. But few will tolerate simultaneous manuscript submissions. If this is an exclusive submission (you have not sent this proposal package to anyone else), provide an exclusivity statement and an expiration date. In other words, "This is an exclusive submission through July 21, 2016."

Note: When suggesting an expiration date, give the agent or publisher enough time to review your project. You'll generally find their wait time listed on the publisher's or agent's submission guidelines. Their waiting period might differ for proposals, query letters, and manuscripts.

Let's say this publisher claims to respond to book proposals within six to eight weeks. If you don't hear from him by the eight-week mark, consider following up with a tracer letter or email asking about the status of your project. If you have given him an expiration date, remind him of it. (See more detailed information about wait periods and simultaneous submissions in chapter 16.)

Early in the cover letter, remind the agent or acquisitions editor if the proposal was requested. Say, for example, in your introductory paragraph, "In an email dated January 13, 2015, you asked to see the complete proposal for *An Elementary Guide to Rocket Science*."

Note: If you're sending your *requested* proposal through the mail, write or type "Requested Material" on the outside of the package. And make sure it is addressed to the exact person who requested it. Now, don't play games here. Don't assume that you can use this technique as a ruse to get your foot in the door. Agents and publishers can be picky about the authors they work with. They've seen enough difficult ones who have drained them of time, energy, and good humor. If they see signs that an author might be deceitful, they're apt to slap a rejection on him before they finish reading the cover letter.

Next, describe your story, your vision for your children's book, or coffee-table book, or nonfiction manuscript, in one or two brief paragraphs. Be sure to give the book's title. Is this book (or will this book be) part of a series? Do you plan illustrations, photographs, or other graphics? Are copies or samples of the artwork included in the proposal package? Is the book completed? If not, what is the proposed completion date?

Give a brief bio, including your expertise or experience in this topic or genre and a little about your publishing history. Have you published anything before? If so, give just an overview. There's no need to elaborate in the cover letter, as everything is detailed in the body of the proposal. In fact, when writing the cover letter, you'll want to pare the information down so just the pertinent material fits on one page.

Note: This is good practice for marketing your book, as you will be required, at times, to talk and write about your book in a nutshell.

Since the cover letter is the first thing an agent or publisher sees when he or she opens your proposal package, you want it to represent your project loud and clear. Notice that I said "loud *and* clear." Clarity is important. Complete concepts are important. Another thing that's important is that the agent or publisher actually reads your cover letter and is persuaded to continue on to the proposal.

Once you've written your cover letter, you'll no doubt discover that it's kind of long and maybe not as lively or enticing as it could be. Tighten the paragraphs, then go back and cull a few priceless descriptive terms and phrases from your synopsis to use in the cover letter. You may eventually use some of them on your book jacket cover, at your Amazon page, and during interviews, podcasts, radio spots, speaking engagements, and so forth.

Next, let the agent or publisher know if the manuscript is complete and how many words it comprises. If it is not, what is your estimated date of completion? Some authors say, "I will deliver the completed manuscript five months after signing your contract."

Generally, you will be able to use the same cover letter for every publisher and agent with minor personalization. However, some have specific requirements, even for the cover letter, so be sure to check each company's submission guidelines. One publisher, for example, asks authors to answer the question, "Why do you think we should publish your book?" It may not hurt to answer this question in all of your cover letters, if you have room to do so. I'd respond by indicating how nicely my book would fit into their list (do your research to verify this, first). I'd say something about wanting to partner with a company that holds character values in high esteem (if this is true). I might also touch on the fact that we both have the same interest in educating (or entertaining) a certain audience.

I end my cover letters (or query letters) by putting a positive suggestion into the agent's or publisher's mind. I might say, "I look forward to working with you on this worthwhile project." I might express my willingness to cooperate, by saying, "Please let me know if you need anything further."

End with, "Sincerely," and your name. If you are sending the proposal package through the mail, leave a space below "Sincerely" and sign your name.

No matter how the publisher requests your proposal be sent (through the post office, in the body of an email, or as an attachment), always include your contact information in the cover letter—physical address, email address, phone. Where applicable, include a link to your website and/or blog. If your website and blog do not reflect the nature of your book, I would leave it off.

The Title Page

The title page is a formality. It's a nice lead-in to the body of your proposal. What is a title page? Just look at the (generally) first page of any book. The title page is right facing and the copyright page is on the back side of it.

To create a title page for your proposal, first identify this package as a book proposal. Centered toward the top of the page (or off to the left is okay), type "A Book Proposal for . . . (title of book)" or simply, "Book Proposal."

Under that, about one quarter of the way down the page, type the title and the subtitle in sixteen- or eighteen-point type. Use Times New Roman or another easy-to-read type. Nothing fancy, please. I like to use sixteen-point type for the title and fourteen for the subtitle.

Under that, type "by" and your name. Here, you would also include the names of any co-authors and illustrators. Use twelve- or fourteen-point type.

At the bottom of the title page, type the final word count for your manuscript (not for the book proposal). If your manuscript isn't completed, estimate the number of words. Type, for example, "proposed word count—60,000" or "estimated word count—75,000." If the book is not complete, the word count might change depending on the publisher's requirements. If you're sending your proposal to a publisher who produces books in the 60,000 to 70,000-word range, then tell him your book will be 65,000. If he is seeking novellas and you are willing to keep your story to 15,000 to 20,000 words, then let this be known.

What if you have written the book and it encompasses just 40,000 words or as many as 100,000 when the publisher wants books strictly within a range of 50,000 to 75,000? Be up front with the publisher, but be flexible. Here's how I'd handle it: I'd slip a note into my cover letter to this publisher or write him a separate email stating that I have a completed manuscript on how to write a book proposal, which currently runs 40,000 words. I'd suggest that if he likes the concept and the manuscript, of course I'd be willing to add a section featuring actual book proposals that worked, or maybe give an example of a synopsis in the chapter focusing on synopses and a sample marketing plan for the marketing chapter, etc., in order to add richness to the book while meeting his word count requirements. If my manuscript is way over his suggested word count, I might offer to cut down on the expert quotes and some of the appendices in order to more closely meet his word count requirements.

Be up front with the publisher. Approach him or her with an acknowledgement, "My manuscript doesn't currently fit your guidelines," and a viable plan showing how you can make it conform.

However, during the book proposal stage, if your book is not complete or you're not enclosing your finished book, the word count issue might be a moot point. You won't discuss it at all, other than to type a figure on the bottom of the title page to conform with the publisher's word count requirements.

Note: I like to see the word count centered at the bottom of the page, a few line spaces below the centered contact information. Type: "Word count—50,000."

Some professionals suggest that your contact information be placed on the title page rather than in the cover letter. It could be either or both. Use twelve-point type for your contact information and the word count.

Your Title

We'll cover titles for specific book types in subsequent chapters. Here, I want to discuss some basic techniques for selecting a title. You may have the perfect title in mind from day one. For some authors, the title comes first. A title can be the inspiration for the book. And this may or may not be a good thing.

Before etching your title deeply into your soul, do plenty of research. Look at dozens of similar books and compare their titles to yours. Which of those books have spent time on a bestseller list? Which ones are published by major companies? Which ones are selling well, are getting a lot of reviews, and/or rank high at Amazon? Scrutinize titles for those successful books that share your proposed target audience and consider whether yours is up to snuff.

Every author should have a team of anywhere from three to six readers. Some authors call these *beta readers* or *pre-readers*. Sometimes these relatively subjective critics can hit on a more accurate, tantalizing, or provocative title.

Some authors use crowd-sourcing to test their titles. After all, a book title is not supposed to please the author. It is supposed to attract readers. So why not poll actual readers for their opinions? Crowd-sourcing is one way to do this. To locate a crowd-sourcing site to use for this purpose, do an Internet search using keywords, "crowd-source (or crowdsource) my book title." So how do you know when you've selected the right title for your book? For nonfiction, the title should clearly identify the book. If you opt for a cutesy title that doesn't accurately represent the book, devise an explanatory subtitle. For example, *A Thread to Hold* is rather vague. What kind of book is this? It's actually the title of a book I wrote on commission featuring the history of a local private school. An early teacher and school historian chose the title from a quote by the school's founder, Edward Yeomans (1865-1942). Because the title did not speak to the subject of the book, we added the subtitle, *The Story of Ojai Valley School*.

A Thread to Hold might work better as a title for a book on sewing or quilting, as long as there's a supporting subtitle, such as *Fun Quilting Projects for Children* or *Tips and Patterns for Community Quilting*.

For fiction, just about anything goes. It seems that short titles are popular for novels and the more intriguing, the better. I would advise, however, that the genre or type of book is clearly defined in some way—preferably in the title or subtitle. If the book is a mystery, use the word "mystery" in the title. For example, I'm writing a series of mysteries involving cats. Here's how I identify these books. I use the title, *Catnapped* and *Cat-Eye Witness* and *Undercover Cat,* etc. and then I include the series title: "A Klepto Cat Mystery." Some authors simply put "A Novel" under their title.

I suggest that you spend quite a bit of time thinking about your title and trying new ones out. But be forewarned, the publisher will most likely change your title. It's true. And if I were you, I would let him do it. Even though you may be attached to your title and even though you have done a whole lot of research to justify it, your publisher has more experience in choosing titles and he knows which ones sell the type of books he publishes. Besides, he's not emotionally attached to your book or your title like you are.

Sure, go to the effort of choosing a title, but from here on out, consider it a "working title," because it will likely be changed.

Most publishers and agents want to see your name and the book title typed at the top of each page of the proposal. You can simply copy and paste it onto each page or use the "header" function in your word processing program.

The Table of Contents for Your Proposal

Next comes your table of contents—for the book proposal, not the book itself. Prepare the table of contents after all parts of the proposal are set.

Type your working book title and subtitle on the page. Under that, type "Contents" or "Table of Contents." Then list each item in the proposal starting with page one, which is the first page after the table of contents page. Refrain from entering page numbers until you have determined the order of your book proposal. A book proposal for a situational memoir might require a different order than one for an academic book, for example. And the young adult fantasy proposal would probably take on a different shape and scope than the business book proposal. Besides, different publishers may ask for fewer or additional pieces to a proposal—so the page numbers for your proposal may change as the shape of it does.

If you need help designing this section, refer to the table of contents pages in books from your home library. Keep it simple—no fancy fonts or clever twists.

The Copyright Symbol

Where should you place the copyright symbol? Publishers agree that it should not appear anywhere on your book proposal and that includes your sample chapters. Since everything you write is automatically considered copyrighted as soon as you create it, using the symbol is unnecessary and considered by publishers and agents to be amateurish. Now if you're sending your original work to someone other than a publisher or agent—it is being displayed in a forum, for example—you might want to use the symbol © and post the date the material was created. The copyright symbol is a good reminder to those who aren't savvy about protected material that this work is not for common use.

Your Synopsis or Overview

One of the most important parts to the proposal package is the synopsis or overview. Publishers and agents want to see anywhere from one to four pages (250 to 1,000 words) describing your project. What is the book about? What is the focus/purpose? This section might go together super easily for you or it can be hair-pulling, nail-biting difficult. It might take an hour to write or weeks to fine-tune.

For those of you who are a bit overwhelmed and confused about the synopsis, let's go slowly. Start with a fresh sheet of paper. Here's where you begin numbering your pages. The first page of your synopsis is page one of the proposal. Your name and the working title of your book go top left on this page and each subsequent page of the entire proposal. Or place your name on the left and the title on the right. If you've chosen a long title, shorten it for this purpose. Rather than "Lady Godiva's Clothes and Other Fables and Fairytales," just type "Lady Godiva's Clothes," for example, or "Lady Godiva."

While some agents and publishers recommend writing the synopsis in third person (except for a memoir), I've seen authors effectively use first and second person as well as a narrative voice. What do I mean by "person"? Here's the rundown: first person, *I*; second person, *you*; third person, *they, he, she*; a narrative voice might be in first or third person. The narrative voice incorporates a storytelling aspect to your synopsis and this works for most fiction and some nonfiction.

Here are some examples. For fiction: "Michael Ivey, the local veterinarian and Savannah's new husband, is violently attacked by an enraged client and then later accused of this man's murder. The evidence quickly stacks up against Michael, until Rags, Savannah's kleptomaniac cat, starts digging up clues."

For a business or informational book, "This book is designed to teach readers . . ." or "Throughout this book, readers will finally learn how to . . ."

For a memoir, "My story begins the day I was able to see . . ."

Start your synopsis with a hook. Remember, this is the first item of any substance that the agent, acquisitions editor, or publisher will see. You definitely want him or her to read beyond this page, and they're more likely to do so if they are somehow drawn into your story or the concept of your book from the very beginning. Right out of the chute you want to shock, tantalize, or intrigue them. Perhaps you're aware of this technique in book-writing, and have incorporated a great first line in your novel or nonfiction book. Consider using it here. Make an outrageous statement. Ask a provocative question. Share an amazing, little-known fact or unusual and astonishing quote.

For Fiction

If you've used a dynamite opening line for your book, consider using it in the synopsis. Then just dive in and begin sharing your story.

You've no doubt learned over the years that, when writing fiction, you must show and not tell. When preparing a book proposal for fiction, however, you'll likely be required to tell the story in a nutshell. Use your narrative voice. Be sure to identify the genre. After your smashing lead-line, you might say, for example, "*Jungle Cat Fever* is an adventure novel featuring a fantasy excursion into the rain forest in search of a cat-eye gem that may or may not exist."

From there, share aspects of your story so it is easy to follow and so it will capture the interest of the reader—in this case the agent, editor, or publisher. If you can write a good story, you should be able to tell that story in any form—verbally or on paper, whether you're allowed 75,000 words or 500 words. While the entire novel involves every detail of the story, for a synopsis, you must simply capture the essence of it. Highlight the more important events and occurrences, describe the major conflicts, and share your dramatic or touching ending—all the while weaving enough of your story throughout for continuity and clarity. Once you consider the synopsis finished—you've encapsulated your story and have all of your innuendoes and encounters in a row—read it again. Then re-read it several more times over the course of a few weeks and make sure that you have adequately represented your story in a light that would attract and enthrall your particular audience.

Remember, you have limited space in which to tell your entire story, so use it wisely. Introduce the main characters ever so briefly, but use enough descriptive words and examples to provide a true-to-form image. Avoid bringing a lot of minor characters into the synopsis. Just mention those that help to move your story forward. Trying to insert a jumbled list of minor characters just serves to clutter your synopsis and confuse the reader.

Should you include a formal character list? Some publishers discourage it. If they want it, they will say so in their submission guidelines. If you provide a chapter-by-chapter summary as part of your proposal, the publisher will see who's who in the book and where they come into the story.

I notice that many teachers and mentors advise their students to prepare a character list for their proposals. If you decide to do so, consider making it part of the back matter, rather than allowing it to, perhaps, clutter the beautiful synopsis you have prepared. (Read more about the synopsis for fiction in chapter 11.)

For Nonfiction

Again, try to hook the agent or publisher with a startling or stunning opening. Describe your vision for the book, explain the purpose as you perceive it, and introduce your target audience. Why are you writing this book, and why should you be the author of this particular book? Yes, some of this information goes in other sections of the proposal. As you work through your proposal, you'll see some overlap of material. Consider this a good thing. Why? Because the editor or agent might not take the time to read every word in every section, and you want to provide easy access to the information that's most useful to them. Repeating it is one way to ensure this.

Include statistics, quotes, and anecdotes showing why your audience might rush out to purchase this book. What does the book include? How is it laid out? What are some of the most important and some of the most unique aspects? How will it help readers or make a difference for them?

There are numbers of types of nonfiction books and all these points might not be relevant to all of them. Pick and choose those that are pertinent to the book you're proposing. A coffee-table book on animals, for example, would be treated differently in the synopsis than a strict how-to book for easing depression in teens.

For the former, you would focus on the beauty of the book and the relevance to people who enjoy amazing animal photos and information about unusual species, for example.

In describing the book on depression, you would mention your qualifications for writing it, what you hope to accomplish with it, and how you will go about it. You'll offer statistics—how many teens suffer from depression and what difference will this book make to those who do?

Even though you'll expand on the proposed market for your book as well as enhance your bio in subsequent portions of the proposal, you should also touch on these things here as they're vital to a publisher's decision. (Read more about writing a nonfiction book proposal in chapters 5–10.)

For a Children's Book

Describe the theme and purpose of a nonfiction book for children and focus on the story for fiction. What is the age group for this book? Please do your research. I know too many people who decide to write children's books even though they have no writing experience and no background in childhood education. Children's books may look like they're easy to write. But there are formulas, standards, and rules. Do you know what vocabulary and word structure is appropriate for your target age group? What is the recommended word count, number of pages, etc?

I suggest getting involved in a children's book critique group. Join the Society for Children's Book Writers and Illustrators. Study books about writing for juveniles. And read books produced by major publishers of children's books for the age group you are targeting before ever attempting to write one or to prepare a proposal for one. Don't just pick up any attractive children's book to study. Too many authors are writing them without knowledge and credentials and paying to have them "self-published."

Read numbers of books in the age group you want to write for. Study them inside out and from top to bottom. Take into consideration the language, style, story line, and dialogue, the way the story moves along, what techniques are used to move it forward. If you aren't qualified to write a children's book, but it is in your heart to do so, stop, look, and listen. If you neglect to do it the right way, you'll never have your book accepted for publication. If you self-publish, your book may not be accepted into any school or library program. Writing for children is an art form different from any other.

If you are qualified to write for children, use the synopsis to share your story, explain any character values involved (children's books should teach a lesson), and describe your characters, give samples of the dialogue, and refer to any illustrations you might have. Some publishers do not accept sample illustrations unless they're submitted by a professional artist or illustrator. Read more about the children's and young adult book synopsis in chapters 13 and 14.

Back to Synopsis Basics

The synopsis is your opportunity to pitch the theme, object, and/or story line of your book to the publishing gatekeepers. You want the key to the gates. The more stringently you adhere to the ideas and suggestions in this book, the more likely it will happen for you.

Warning: Across the board, publishing professionals and experienced literary agents advise against using any excessive self-hype, extreme or desperate antics, or exaggerated hysterics in an attempt to sway the publisher. Certainly, share your excitement. Be enthusiastic and positive. But do not make outlandish promises you can't possibly keep. Avoid predicting millions of sales in the first month after your book is published when you have no experience in book sales whatsoever, and you haven't conducted adequate research to learn some of the book marketing ropes. In fact, don't make any claims that you cannot back up. These are giant red flags for the agent or publisher.

Prepare Chapter Summaries (Chapter Outline)

I don't usually recommend that the chapter summaries follow the synopsis in a book proposal, but it might make sense in some situations. Compile each section of your book proposal independently and then decide the best order in which to present it to each publisher. Typically, I would put the chapter summaries just before the sample chapters.

Some people refer to the chapter summaries as a chapter outline. This is where you summarize each chapter while clearly representing the material, information, activities, events, etc. of a nonfiction book and the story, emotions, conflicts, and flow of your novel.

Keep each chapter summary to around 100 to 400 words. It is not a sin to go over or under this standard. For fiction or a memoir, you should summarize the story chapter by chapter. For nonfiction, explain the content and purpose of each chapter.

Use a technique similar to that used in your synopsis. Speak to the publisher. For example, "In chapter one, we find Jacob disheveled, confused, and wandering the streets of Philadelphia on a rainy night with no coat. People notice him, but are afraid to approach as he staggers and mumbles 'She took everything. She took everything.'"

Here's an example for nonfiction: "In chapter three of my book, *Greenhouse Gardening for Green Thumb Wannabes*, we provide sketches to help readers choose the right size greenhouse for their specific needs and guide them in determining the best location for a greenhouse on their property. We also discuss the importance of regulating the inside temperature of greenhouses in various sizes."

Write in present tense—as if the book is completed. If you've quoted experts or will be including expert quotes in certain chapters, let the publisher know this. Use bullets to streamline information for a nonfiction book. Describe any planned illustrations or enhancements at the end of each chapter summary.

When I was pitching my fatherhood and fathering book to publishers, I visualized a photograph of a father and his child at the beginning of each chapter. I included this information as part of my chapter summaries.

Why do you need to summarize each chapter when the publisher or agent has seen the synopsis? The chapter summaries will provide even more information to help the publisher decide whether you actually have a handle on the premise of your nonfiction book or whether your novel flows nicely. Your chapter outline should capture the essence of your story or your nonfiction book, while fleshing it out and showing what exactly will be included. This exercise is designed to show the author and the publisher whether there really is a book in your idea. It gives the publisher a nice peek into the content of your book, and he or she will learn a little more about your way of writing.

If your book is not separated into chapters (some novels and memoirs are not), simply summarize sections of your book—breaking it down into scenes, for example.

The chapter summaries provide a welcome benefit for authors of nonfiction. You'll be pleasantly surprised at how easily your book will come together when using your chapter summaries as a guide.

Include One or More Sample Chapters

Publishers and agents often ask to see sample chapters from your novel or nonfiction book. For a children's book, typically, you would send the entire manuscript.

The most difficult thing about this request is deciding which chapter(s) to send. I generally recommend sending the first chapter, because it sets the stage for your book. If you've done it right, your beginning hooks the reader (in this case, the publisher) and the rest of the first chapter lets readers know what's to come. It sets the tone and, sometimes, the pace for your story or nonfiction book. The publisher will meet some of the characters and get a feel for the writer's methods of communication and/or storytelling. If your first chapter doesn't accomplish this, you need to do a rewrite.

If you've been asked to submit more than one chapter, choose a second one that speaks loudly to your theme or story line. For fiction, for example, you might choose a chapter that builds to the climax of the conflict, the one that has the most action or, for a romance, the most romance. You want to display chapters that clearly represent your story.

For nonfiction, additional sample chapters should include those that carry the most impact—that clearly state your main objective, and that show how well you can deliver the information and facts. Make it your most important chapter.

While we're on the topic of chapters, I'd like to touch on your titles and headings. You may or may not use chapter titles for your fiction or memoir. But most nonfiction books that are conducive to chapters include chapter titles. Before setting yours in stone, study books similar to yours. Get a feel for the type of titles others use for books on this topic.

Choose titles based on the tone of your book. If you've maintained a serious approach throughout, use chapter titles that follow suit. These titles might be curt and to the point. "Winter Crops," "Summer Crops," "Irrigation," etc. If you've adopted a more playful, light tone for your book, use titles such as, "Don't Leave Your Winter Crops Out in the Cold," "Marvelously Staunch Summer Garden Crops," "Help, I'm a Cabbage and I'm Thirsty!"

About the Author

The publisher or agent wants to know something about the author. Who are you? What is your background in the topic or genre of your book and, where it counts, what is your educational background? If you have difficulty writing this section, check out some of our sample proposals in Part Seven. Read bios on the back cover (or in the back pages) of books on the subject or genre of your book.

In chapter 2 we talked about the psychology of a book proposal from the publisher's point of view. Throughout that chapter, we stress that the publisher is interested in his bottom line. He wants to know that your book will sell—that it will make him some money. From his perspective, a major aspect of your book is you! Who are you? What makes you the right person to write this book? Who would buy a book on this topic or in this genre that you wrote?

Put yourself in the publisher's ergonomic desk chair for a moment. (Actually, this is a good place for you to hang out during the entire process of writing your book proposal.) What aspects of yourself would most likely sway him to consider your book for publication? If he has announced at his website that he needs a book for beginning quilters, and you are pitching such a book, he'll definitely be interested. If he likes what he sees in your synopsis, and your chapter outline makes sense to him, he now wants information about you.

What is your background in quilting? If you've simply read other books on the subject; as a child, watched your mother and grandmother quilt; or you plan to put together some quilt blocks your mother pieced, the publisher may be just lukewarm about your project. He would doubt that you could pull off the professional project he had in mind. If, on the other hand, you can honestly say that you have been leading a quilting club for ten years, your quilts have won numerous awards in shows, you write regularly for three quilting magazines and newsletters, and you have just started teaching a quilting class for local youth in your community, this will probably wow the publisher.

Get into the publisher's head and share with him those things that are likely to impress him and sway him to consider your book. Start with the most important information first—the fact that you have been a quilter for many years, teach quilting, and have several published books on quilting should be at the top of your list. If you've written many articles for quilting magazines, share that up front, as well.

If you're pitching a novel, the fact that you've sold a couple thousand copies of this and other novels for Kindle readers within a matter of months at Amazon is well worth mentioning. Also let the publisher or agent know if the book (or manuscript) has won any awards. The fact that you teach writing and that dozens of your stories have appeared in several literary magazines should also impress a publisher or agent.

I meet authors who don't think they have much of a bio to speak of. They're too modest, or they don't understand what the publisher wants. If this is you, bring friends and family into the mix. Ask them to list what they perceive as your assets. Make your own list of everything you've done or been involved in related to the topic of your book. You'll probably end up with a long list—much of which may not be relevant for your about-the-author section. Cross them off and then take those items that are pertinent and important and enhance them, create examples from them, and share them with the publisher.

For example, you might list *articulate*. Translate this quality into a positive by explaining how you use this skill and by suggesting how this would benefit you and your book during podcasts, radio show interviews, etc. Your teaching experience would be impressive, as this could morph into online courses or workshops all over the United States related to the topic of your nonfiction book.

Some authors have no problem coming up with attributes and they inundate publishers with mountains of relatively unimportant trivia. Here's a tip: If it relates to your credibility to write this book and/or if it speaks to your ability to market it, mention it. If it doesn't, consider leaving it out.

Some publishers and agents are even interested in the author's hobbies and how they spend their free time. Because my novels are rich with kitty cat antics, if I were approaching a publisher with one of them, I'd include the fact that I have cats and always have throughout my life. I might even share a few brief anecdotes about some of my unique experiences with cats. I'd also include in my bio the fact that I've written numerous articles for cat-related magazines and that I belong to the Cat Writers' Association. Even though I'm new to writing fiction, this would certainly add to my credibility as a writer of stories involving cats.

Along with your education, experience, and expertise in your genre or subject, be sure to include your publishing experience. Publishers will accept good projects from newbie authors, but they may be even more interested in those with publishing and book marketing experience.

They also like to know that, if this book does well, there could be more in the pipeline. So list any books in progress or titles you have planned, especially those related to the theme or genre of the one you propose. I once had a publisher reject the book I proposed, but ask to see one I listed as "in the works."

One to three paragraphs is a good goal for the about-the-author section. If you have a long list of published books or educational and/or professional accomplishments you want to share, type them on a separate sheet and include a note at the end of your bio directing the publisher to another page later in the proposal.

Elements of a Successful Book Proposal— Marketing Portion

Again, let me say that this may or may not be the way you will organize the sections of your book proposal, but it makes sense to present it this way in this book. First you had the opportunity to focus on the editorial aspects of the proposal, and now we'll discuss the marketing and promotions portion. At the end of this chapter, we'll talk about how to put it all together.

The Market/Your Target Audience

Here's your opportunity to convince the publisher that there is an audience for your book. If you've attended lectures by publishing professionals and if you've read some of the best books for authors, you've heard/read this warning: "Do not tell the publisher that this book is for everyone."

You might counter, "But everyone from every walk of life should read my inspirational or informational book. It actually does have a message important to every man, woman, and adolescent." And you may be absolutely right. This is exactly the way many new authors think about their books. They can envision a wide variety of readers gaining something of value from their fiction or nonfiction book. However, this is not a reliable measure of the book's worth or a prediction of potential sales. Neither is it realistic. Here's why: there are readers and there are nonreaders. It's true. Some people do not read books at all. Unfortunately for authors, this number is extraordinarily high. In 2007, I came across statistics collected by the Jenkins Group saying that 58 percent of adults claim they have not read a book since high school and 42 percent of college graduates never read another book. Statistics gathered by Read Faster reported in 2013 that 50 percent of adult Americans are unable to read at an eighth-grade level and that 80 percent of US families did not purchase a book during the previous year. And then there's the well-known fact that men buy few books.

Add to the mix that those people who do read do so for a variety of reasons. Some are voracious readers of fiction. Some shop for the occasional book on a topic of their interest. Some pick up a book they happen to stumble across because it looks interesting or has information they crave. And publishers know this. So you aren't going to convince them that the whole of the population of the United States and half of Asia are potential buyers for your book of daily inspirations or pruning techniques for trees in the Northwest, for example.

Your book has a target audience—those people who are interested in reading spiritual messages, who may use them for their Sunday school classes, and who buy inspirational books as gifts, for example. Your audience for the tree-pruning book might include orchardists and homeowners living in northern California, Oregon, and Washington and who are highly interested in the health of their trees.

You may have already mentioned your proposed target audience in your synopsis, and even offered statistics to back it up. It is okay to repeat some of that information here, as it is critical to your case where the publisher is concerned. He wants to know there is a market for your proposed book. Your statistics and facts regarding the scope of your audience early in the proposal just might spur the publisher to continue reading. So if you have impressive figures and material with regard to the sales potential for your book, don't save all of it for this section.

Use two to six paragraphs to explain who your target audience is. How large is it; can you prove it through statistics, facts, figures; why this book/ why now? You might also briefly remind the publisher why you are the best person to write this book.

Start by clearly identifying your target buying and reading audience. Then find out what you can about that demographic. It might be senior men who have retired young and wish they hadn't, women of all ages who are still active despite disabilities, young adults yearning to be on a reality show, or parents of multiples, for example. Spend some time studying the data that others have collected on this group. Learn more about them by visiting related websites, blogs, organization sites, forums, and so forth.

Do your own survey among those who follow a particular blog or are active at a certain forum to help determine the potential interest in your book idea. At the same time, figure out the best way to approach this audience when your book is ready to promote.

In the case of a book on teen depression, at least parts of it might be designed for the teen to read, but it is likely that the parents will be buying it. Your buying audience might also include family therapists and physicians who will recommend the book to their clients and patients.

If you're not sure who your readers are, create a list—if your book is a humorous mystery involving a dog whose best buddy is a disabled child, see what you can find out about people who read fiction involving dogs, who enjoy light mysteries, or who would potentially pick up a book featuring a disabled child whose situation is presented in a positive light.

Do not claim that your friends and relatives love your book. Avoid making up facts to support the validity of your book. In fact, be sure you cite the origins of the facts you provide in case the publisher wants to check them out. For the book on teen depression, for example, find out what percentage of teens struggle with depression. Cite the source of this information. How many commit suicide because they didn't know how to find help or their disease wasn't recognized and diagnosed?

Proof is always welcome in this section. Before sending your proposal to publishers, you might pass it around to those you perceive as your audience—in this case, family therapists, counselors, doctors, psychologists, school administrators, teens, teens' parents, and so forth. Ask for feedback, comments, and especially endorsements. (Positive testimonials from appropriate professionals could influence an agent or publisher to consider your book.)

Ask if these individuals would recommend this book, to whom, and why. If you receive a lot of negative feedback, stop and reconsider your project. Carefully scrutinize what you learn from these critics and use it to strengthen the concept or the value of your book. Do this before ever approaching an agent or publisher.

Don't Rush the Process

Take your time. I understand that you're eager to move forward with your book project. You've already spent months (or years) researching and writing it. But if your goal is success, you must make the right decisions and the best choices on your book's behalf. Just like with a good batch of wine, the best vine-ripened strawberries, or a beautiful loaf of baked bread, timing is everything.

Only when your book idea is fully matured and the proposal absolutely right should you contact an agent or publisher. Never, ever use a publisher or agent to test your book idea. Approach them only with your very best shot, because you may never have that chance again.

The Market Analysis/Your Competition

Is there room for another book on this topic? Before you even consider writing any book, you should first check to see what else is out there in this genre, or on this subject.

For nonfiction, you need to learn if there's a need for a book like the one you propose. If you want to land a publisher for your fiction and if you want to sell a lot of books, make sure you're writing in a popular genre or that there's a strong niche audience for this type of book. How? Conduct rigorous research to discover what is already published in this genre or on this topic and how these other books are doing in the marketplace.

The fact is, there are thousands and thousands of books vying for attention and only so many consumers. Remember, you are the CEO of your book. Before you thoroughly commit to your amazing book by reaching out to publishers, you need to make sure it really is such a good idea. And this means learning something about your competition.

Sometimes, through a rigorous market analysis, an author discovers that, while there are many books on quilting, for example, there is nothing featuring specific projects for quilting clubs, criteria and examples for winning quilt shows, how to start a quilting bee, community quilting projects, quilting for fundraisers, or quilting projects for teens.

The market analysis can be the first stumbling block to your successful project. If you enter a major bookstore and see dozens of books on your topic, that might be a good thing. This means it is a popular subject. But is the market too saturated to accommodate another book of this type? It's up to you to find out.

For Nonfiction

Once you have decided on a subject and a slant, start a serious study of books within the category. It might be greenhouse gardening, aviation, inspiration for people with eating disorders, thrift-store fashion statements, business management techniques for women, or how to attract wildlife into your garden, for example.

Look at books listed on Amazon and other online bookstores. Peruse books at major bookstores. Spend a couple of hours studying similar books with an open mind. Honestly, now, how many books did you find on the topic? Don't be afraid to acknowledge them. This isn't a popularity contest. It's you exercising good business sense by checking out your competition so you can make the best decisions on behalf of your book.

If you notice quite a number of books similar to yours, don't panic. This might simply mean it's a popular topic. If you've located several recently-published books that focus on the same issues as you do and in the same manner, you may want to reconsider the direction of your book.

Once you've decided on the theme for your nonfiction book and your research shows that there could be room for another book on this topic, choose four to six compatible or competing books to use in analyzing the market. Depending on the topic of your nonfiction book, you might have to review a dozen or more before settling on a handful to use in this section.

If you're not sure which of these books are most popular, check them out through Amazon.com. Amazon rates and ranks books. The number of reviews is also a reflection of the book's popularity. Ask bookstore managers how some of these competing books are selling. Do an online search and see if you can find sales figures for specific books. Contact publishers or authors directly. Some, I'm told, will relinquish this information.

For Fiction
Locate books similar to yours. Choose those that are selling well. I might say, for example, "My Klepto Cat Mystery series is reminiscent of Lillian Braun's The Cat Who series. Readers interested in The Cat in the Stacks and Cats in Trouble mysteries might also enjoy my cozy mysteries." A publisher of cozy mysteries will probably be familiar with these series and know of their popularity among cozy mystery readers. My next step would be to locate sales figures for books in some (or all) of these series.

Remember that the market analysis portion of your book proposal is designed to show the publisher that there is a market for your book. Use what you learn through the process of studying other books in your genre to make an honest case for your book project. It's all about using those books that have a similar audience to your advantage. How is your book similar to and different from other popular books in your genre/category?

If your book has two topics—sportsmanship and avoiding sports injuries, dancing and inspiration, your struggle with an eating disorder sprinkled with tips for teens, for example—compare books in both categories.

Compile Your Market Analysis

This critical part of your book proposal will consume around two pages. Choose four to six books. For each book, list: title, authors, publisher, publication date, years of each edition, ISBN (International Standard Book Number), page count, and the format (e-book, hardcover, paperback).

Include some of the more successful books designed for your target audience. Choose newer over older ones, as long as they are relatively successful. Select books published through some of the major publishing houses. If there are strong contenders within the self-publishing realm, by all means count them in. Use one or two complementary books, particularly for fiction, in order to justify your wonderful book.

What is meant by competing and what is a complementary book? First let me say that a similar nonfiction book might be considered competition, but similar books in fiction would probably complement one another. Someone wanting a book on how to row a boat or tie a tie would buy only one such book. He or she would choose from the books available on that topic. But readers of mysteries, thrillers, military stories, science fiction, or true crime would buy every book they can find in that genre.

With this in mind, your market analysis would read differently for nonfiction and fiction. For fiction, you want to show that there is a market for books like yours—that this genre is popular and people are buying these books.

For nonfiction, you want to create a reasonable balance that shows the publisher this is a valid subject (there are books on this topic and they are selling), and that your twist on the topic is viable (there is nothing quite like it and there is a strong need for a book taking this point of view).

Give a brief description of each competing or complementary book, the slant, its purpose and target audience. Then explain in a few sentences or a paragraph what makes your book different—better. Does it fill a need that the other books do not?

When I was pitching my youth-mentoring book, I discovered that the other books on this topic were aimed at mentoring in the workplace or through churches. The books all had an adult focus or were blatantly religious. My proposed book, on the other hand, was designed for parents whose children have friends who need more support, caring folks who want to help out with neighborhood children or those within their own families, as well as leaders and helpers in afterschool, church, recreation, and youth organization programs. Unlike any other book I read on this topic, mine also offered a step-by-step guide to starting a mentoring program.

Yes, I landed a publisher with my book proposal.

As I alluded to earlier, if your book is quite similar to several on the market—it's another version of a cookie-cutter weight-loss book, for example—it probably won't stand out, thus will likely be rejected. You have a couple of choices. Go ahead and publish your book through a self-publishing company and deal with the challenge of stiff competition, or change it up. Let go of your attachment to your initial idea and create something that is viable in the marketplace.

Your Author's Platform

This section is not to be confused with the about-the-author portion of your book proposal. However, there will be some overlap. You've already told the publisher why you are the best person to write this particular book. You've outlined your education, profession, achievements, accomplishments, and so forth.

Here, the publisher or agent is asking you to talk about your skills, your connections, and your aptitude related to marketing your book. What can you bring to the table that will help sell this book? How visible and accessible are you to your perceived audience both on- and off-line? How much time and energy can you devote to promoting this book?

Let's examine the concept of platform. Your platform is your following, your way of attracting readers. It's all about who knows you as an expert in your field or interest, or as the writer of good fiction. A platform might be considered a *reputation*. If your platform is lacking, the time to start shoring it up is before you publish your book. For example, if you're known only locally in your field, and you want to sell books nationwide, take steps to build a reputation on a wider scale. If this is your first novel, there are things you can do to expand your reach.

Some authors' platforms stem from personal experience—people are familiar with your escape from kidnappers or long recovery from a horseback riding accident, for example. Many of them are curious to know more about your ordeal. Certainly they can be considered members of your proposed audience.

People who are familiar with the science fiction stories you've had published in magazines and online could be considered your fans. If they like your stories, they would surely be interested in a book you wrote in this genre.

Here are examples of some of the things that might make up your author's platform for a nonfiction book:

- You have personal experience in this topic and/or a level of expertise.
- You lead or are active in a group related to the topic.
- You've written numerous articles on this topic for some prestigious magazines.
- You speak regularly on this topic to groups at churches, civic organization meetings, related conferences, and corporate events.
- You have been an active member of a Toastmasters club for five years and have achieved a level of expertise as a public speaker.
- You are the moderator for an online discussion group on the topic of your book.
- You blog regularly on this topic.
- You have a high visibility in social media.
- You produce a monthly newsletter related to this subject that goes out to 3,000 (or more) people.
- You have several e-booklets on complementary topics.
- You have a website that you update regularly and actively promote.
- You were marketing manager for a company and know something about promotion.
- You recently retired and have time to spend promoting your book.
- You're in good health and have the means to travel in order to promote the book.

For a novel, your platform might include some of the items on the list above as well as the following.

- You self-published a novel two years ago and have sold 3,000 copies. For an e-book, an impressive number of copies might be closer to 20,000.
- You went on a blog tour with your book and sales doubled during that week.
- You belong to a storytelling group and are accustomed to presenting in public.
- Your stories have been published in several magazines and ezines.
- You have a website and you blog weekly.
- You promote your blog and website and are receiving dozens of legitimate comments each week.
- You have some innovative ideas for interactive games and contests related to the theme of your book that you can run through your website and blog site.
- You regularly engage in guest blogging.
- You are on Facebook, Instagram, and Twitter and have 3,000 followers and friends.
- You are an active member of two fiction writers' organizations.

If you have trouble pulling information and facts together for this section, make a list. Add to it over several days. Ask friends to chime in with their observations—what talents and skills do they recognize in you that might translate into planks in your platform? Review your day planners for the last few years to remind you of some of your activities related to the theme of your book and marketing in general. Maybe you headed up a fundraiser that involved hundreds of people and thousands of dollars, or you launched a successful marketing program for your boss or a friend's start-up business. Perhaps you'll recall that a colleague's brother runs a chain of bookstores where you could set up signings, that you know the producer at a radio station and might be able to get a gig, and that you recently met someone with an active blog with many followers who conducts interviews with novelists.

Be thorough, creative, and absolutely truthful when compiling the aspects of your platform. Lead with your most impressive attributes, as long as they prove your case for a strong platform and demonstrate that you have exactly what it takes to represent and promote this book.

Format this section so that it is clear and clean. You can use paragraphs, a numbered list, bullets, or a mix of these options.

If you start assembling your author's platform and realize it's sadly weak, do what you should have done months ago and begin shoring it up NOW. Yes, even if this means delaying your search for a publisher. Think about it: does it make sense to rush out to find a publisher before you are qualified—before you have all of your cute little ducks in a row? Remember, a rejection is forever. Once you've closed the door on the publisher of your choice because you weren't adequately prepared, it may never be open to you again.

Instead, take the time to build a strong platform that, along with your wonderful, flawless book manuscript, is worthy of a publishing contract.

The publisher can't and won't take full responsibility for marketing your book. He expects you to partner with him in this effort. And he needs to know you can hold up your end of the partnership.

The Promotions Section

Here's another important piece to the book proposal puzzle. The publisher needs to know not only that you have the time, energy, and ability to promote this book, but also that you grasp what goes into this activity. He wants evidence that you understand marketing and that you have some ideas for promoting your book. He also wants assurance that you will follow through.

You already know who your audience is and where they are. You've figured out how to approach them and you have a handle on what skills and connections you can bring to the table. Now it's time to show the publisher how your platform translates into action.

How long should this section be? As long as it takes to make a strong case. It could run as many as fifteen or twenty pages or as few as three.

Start by noting what you have already done as it relates to your audience. This might include where you have conducted workshops, presented keynote addresses, or sold a similar book in the back of the room, for example. How many were in attendance? How many books did you sell? Let the publisher know that you'll be doing more of this in order to promote the new book. List possible venues. The more concrete information you can provide, the better—location, type of audience, number of people in attendance, etc.

Perhaps you have compiled a massive email address list and you send out a bimonthly newsletter to thousands of people on the subject of your book. Naturally, you'll use this means to promote your new book. Maybe you're widely known within your community, and plan to organize a book launch party for a hundred guests.

List impressive connections—leaders in your field, editors of related magazines, and company heads, for example—and exactly how you intend to use them for promoting your book. You'll ask for book reviews, see about having your book listed at influential websites as recommended reading, arrange for speaking engagements through major corporations, and so forth.

What if you're like most new authors and you don't have a platform of any kind or any experience in marketing? You just want to write and you'd like to publish what you write? Perhaps you've buffaloed your way through the rest of the proposal, but now you're stumped. You haven't a clue about promotion and marketing and no known skills or aptitude for this distasteful concept. You just retired as an office assistant, for heaven's sake, or you're still working part-time in a school cafeteria, pharmacy, or gift shop.

Okay, just hold your horses. Don't discourage yourself right out of the running. There may be hope. Take a look at your list of attributes and accomplishments. Note anything and everything that you do or have ever done that could contribute to a résumé. Certainly a book proposal is a résumé of sorts. Again, get your friends involved. Some of them will recall things you might not consider.

List events you were involved in, even those not related to bookselling or publishing—sales you've made, money you've raised, your volunteer experiences. What tasks were entrusted to you in the jobs you've held over the years? Have you been part of or headed up committees or organized campaigns of any kind?

Are you known locally and/or online for something? Maybe you've been active in politics, you lead an online book club, or you were a youth activities leader in your community for many years. Do you regularly follow and comment on certain blog sites related to your book's theme or genre? If you've taken steps to build a social media presence, all the better.

Basically here, in one to three pages (or more), you're going to tell the publisher how you see this book being marketed and how you can contribute to that. Avoid introducing grandiose marketing activities that you have not tested, cannot afford to do, and probably can't pull off. Examples might be: "I'll appear on *The View*, *Dr. Phil*, and/or Queen Latifah's TV shows and sell millions of copies of my book." Or "I plan to do a six-state book tour presenting workshops for 200 to 500 people at each stop and I'll sell books in the back of the room." Or "I'll get my book into the school system in every county throughout the eastern states."

The only way you can get away with making these statements is if you have an excellent connection with the appropriate gatekeeper, you're a celebrity, or you've already received an invitation to do these things. If something like this is your desire, it's best you hold off seeking a publisher until you've gathered some proof that these things are possible—even probable—in your situation.

You cannot adequately lay out a viable book marketing plan for your book and put yourself effectively in the equation if you don't know what it takes to promote a book. If the concept of book promotion is new to you, please, please study something about it. Read *Promote Your Book* and other books listed in the resource list at the back of this book. Create a viable marketing plan that makes sense based on your skills, abilities, energy level, and time element. Keep in mind that the author, whether self-published or traditionally published, is expected to promote his or her own book. Without promotion, the book will die. And with the overabundance of books currently on the market in all genres and on all topics, competition is extremely stiff. Books that succeed in the marketplace are those books that are promoted—across the board.

I had a client once who firmly believed that his book would sell itself. He had no intention of promoting it. He was all about just getting it out there. I wonder how long it took this author to come to his senses and realize what I kept trying to tell him: no one will buy a book they don't know exists. Promotion isn't so much about selling books as it is exposure. Books need exposure. The more copies you want to sell, the more exposure the book must have.

How critical is the promotions part of the book proposal? Think about it: does the publisher want to make money? Of course he does. This is the whole point of him spending time with your proposal. He wants to know that yours is a viable product—that it will fly in the marketplace and that you—the author—have what it takes to make it fly. Here are some comments from publishers in this regard:

"We expect our authors to actively promote their works at book signings, on the radio, television, and other unique events."

"Our authors are well prepared to market their books successfully."

"The true success of any book comes from the author's willingness to put themselves and their work into the marketplace."

"The marketing plan you send is very important."

These come from the publishers' pens. I recommend that you re-read this promotions section and those appearing later in this book related to the genre/topic of your project. Make notes. Let the concepts absorb into your brain. I know this is quite foreign to many of you and a little painful for some. But if you expect or desire some measure of success with your book, promotion is a reality you must digest. And the sooner the better.

Note: You might wonder why I don't provide a list of steps for you to take toward promoting your book. Why make it so complicated? Can't I just tell you how to promote your book? I wish it were that easy. The problem is, each book is different, each author is different, and you're each dealing with different audiences. The best that anyone in my position can do is to explain the concept and the reality of book promotion and offer up some possibilities, examples, and ideas you can consider and expand upon, or not. Becoming an author is similar to becoming a parent. There are few hard and fast rules. Authorship, like parenting, does not come with a clear-cut roadmap. It's up to you to study the information available and apply it in the way that works in your situation.

Gather Testimonials

For business, informational, and other specialized books, peer reviews and/or professional endorsements could help strengthen your proposal. A word or two on behalf of the book from a qualified professional might influence an editor or publisher who's considering your project. Some publishers actually ask for testimonials in their submission guidelines.

Add professional testimonials to your marketing (promotions) page. If you're concerned that they might be overlooked, however, consider creating a special page for testimonials or add them to your cover letter.

How does one go about getting testimonials? If you have friends, colleagues, or acquaintances in prestigious positions related to the theme of your book, approach them. Request permission to send them a few chapters or the entire manuscript (or portions of your book proposal) to review and ask them to write a brief testimonial that you can use on the book cover as well as in your proposal. Some busy people will suggest that you send them a few possible testimonials. This means they want you to write two or three testimonials for them to consider. If they know and admire your work, they will choose one and give you permission to use their name.

Ask a high-profile individual to write your foreword. This might grab a publisher's attention in a smashingly positive way.

For fiction, if you have the right connections, you might be able to get a few reviews or comments from well-known novelists in your genre for your front or back cover, for example. Include these in your proposal for added persuasion.

Include Sample Illustrations

Many books require illustrations. This might be children's books, coffee-table books, a craft book, some how-to books, cookbooks, travel books, and even a memoir.

If your proposed book involves photographs, sketches, or other illustrations that you want to use, definitely include some or all of them in the proposal package. Acknowledge in the cover letter and, perhaps, in the synopsis that you've enclosed/attached them. Slip them in with the back matter.

Note: Never send originals through the mail.

Publishers of children's picture books often give instructions in their submission guidelines for sending illustrations. Some publishers just want to see a sampling of illustrations and others don't want any included. When in doubt, ask.

Supply Your List of Experts

If you plan to interview experts and quote them in your nonfiction book for added credibility, by all means include your list for the publisher. If these are not well-known celebrities with household names, provide their titles and areas of expertise.

If there are five or more, include only their names and titles in the synopsis or the promotions section of your proposal, depending on which placement makes the most sense, and prepare a more detailed list with bios separate from your proposal.

Back Matter

After the last piece of your proposal—generally, your chapter summaries or sample chapters—include any additional material. This might involve your list of experts, sample illustrations, and bios of those who offered testimonials. If you have quite a number of items, create a new section for them and call it *back matter* or refer to it as the *appendix*.

Putting It All Together

Some publishers are strict about presentation. They provide explicit instructions for preparing the proposal and this makes perfect sense. If they receive 100 proposals per month, for example, it's easier on them if they know exactly what to expect when they open yours. They won't have to take time flipping through it to find the pieces they want to read first.

Publishers generally do not read handwritten proposals or manuscripts. Believe it or not, I know authors who don't and won't type. If you're one of them, hire someone to do the typing or invest in speak-and-type software.

Likewise, some publishers request that you do not send a proposal or manuscript in a box. Some discourage using staples. Some ask that authors skip the paper clips, as well. Others say, "No binding whatsoever."

My best advice to you is to follow each publisher's submission guidelines.

As far as format, most publishers like to see proposals double-spaced all except for the cover letter and contact information. I recommend single-spacing bulleted sections and other lists. Do not leave an extra space between paragraphs. Gads, I don't know where that practice came from, but it is annoying. Sure, it's okay when the paragraphs are single-spaced. But to double-space and then leave an extra line space between paragraphs doesn't make sense. Do, however, indent the first line of each paragraph. Indents will eliminate any perceived need for that extra line space.

A finished proposal is generally between thirty-five and fifty pages. Some winning proposals are as long as 100 pages and others might not reach fifteen pages, especially if the sample chapters are not included. This is okay as long as all of the pertinent information is included and the proposal isn't heavily padded with useless incidentals.

Use a header or not—but do put your name and the book title at the top of each page.

Number pages consecutively throughout the entire proposal—not by section or chapter. Start numbering on the first page after the table of contents. This is generally the synopsis.

You can prepare your proposal in any order you wish—write the section you believe is easiest. This might be the author bio (about the author)—although some authors find this to be one of the most difficult pieces to write.

Before sending out your fabulous proposal, be sure to check and double/triple check your entire proposal for organization, grammatical and punctuation errors, and typos. It happens and you know it. Read it on the computer and then print it out and read it again. You will notice things on the hardcopy that were not evident to your eye on the screen, and vice versa.

Consider your proposal and, in fact, any and all letters or emails to a publisher, editor, or agent, a professional document or communiqué. Send your best work all the time, every time.

Have several people look at your proposal before you send it. Hire an editor who is highly familiar with book proposals. Not only can they help you to make it more reader-friendly, they can guide you in strengthening the proposal. Show it to one or more experts in your field. Elicit some of your potential readers to check it over. Some of them might have ideas for additions they'd like to see in a book like yours.

Tips for Sending Your Proposal

Check each publisher's submission guidelines before preparing a proposal to send. Do they want to receive it via email, in the body of the email or as an attachment? Or do they insist that you send it through the post office? Whatever their instructions, comply.

If your proposal has been requested by a certain editor at the publishing house, note that on the outside of your snail mail package. Of course, you'll address the package to that editor. Just write "Requested" somewhere on the outside of the envelope.

(See chapter 16 for additional information about mailing/emailing your submission.)

Some publishers tell authors what to put in the subject line when sending a proposal via email: "Proposal—Chick Lit—Barbara Benson," for example, or "Book Proposal—Western Romance—Requested."

It's okay to give links for additional, supporting information in email submissions. Unless otherwise instructed by the publisher, put the entire proposal, sample chapters, etc. in one file to send. Do not send in separate files.

You've been subjected to a lot of information throughout these first four chapters. And you most likely still have questions pertaining to proposals in specific genres. The following ten chapters should respond to most of your questions related to nonfiction, fiction, and children's book proposals.

Part Two

The Nonfiction Book Proposal

It used to be that the book proposal was for the nonfiction book, period! And the author submitted it before ever putting pen to paper. The book proposal is still an excellent way to pitch a nonfiction book idea and, as far as some publishers are concerned, the only accepted way.

I've seen it happen—an author sends a completed manuscript for a nonfiction book and it is accepted, all right, but only if the author makes a lot of changes. So a book proposal sent before you write the book can save you time, agony, and energy. It's much easier to change an outline of a book than it is to do a complete rewrite.

Sell Your How-To or Self-Help Book

Some authors have trouble identifying their books as informational, how-to, narrative nonfiction, self-help, or memoir. I've had clients come to me with what they considered a how-to book. Upon closer examination, I discovered that there was no how-to element at all. Some authors try to pass a memoir off as a how-to or a self-help book because they figure readers can learn from their stories.

Certainly, a memoir can also be a how-to, but it must have the important elements of a how-to. It must be instructional—clearly show how to do something. How-to books are found on many topics—crafts/hobbies, business, inspiration, food, lifestyle, health, travel, parenting, and so forth. A true how-to book typically contains information about and a description of the topic to be taught and steps designed to teach the reader the process or activity. The how-to might focus on a skill or a new way of being or becoming. However, when the concept of the book becomes personal, as in how to become more sociable, adopt a more positive attitude, etc., it may be more aptly considered a self-help book. There are how-to books on practically every topic imaginable. The book you're reading is a how-to. One of the earliest and most well-known how-to books was Dale Carnegie's *How to Make Friends and Influence People* (1936).

Some how-to books are inspirational, spiritual, or informational. A how-to might also fit into the categories of foods and cooking, religion, gardening, parenting, psychology, pets, and so forth.

A self-help book, on the other hand, is a guide to solving personal problems and changing behaviors. Another descriptive term might be *self-improvement*. These books are often written by professionals in fields related to psychology, family counseling, medicine, or religion, for example. However, you'll find numerous books in the self-help category today written by lay people, as well. There are countless self-help books on the market by ordinary people who have found new ways to more successfully manage their relationships, their careers, their health, or their sense of joy and decide they want to share this with others.

There's nothing new in the how-to and self-help concept. There have always been teachers and mentors among us. We've always looked to others for help with personal problems. Technology has provided the canvas for even more teachers, mentors, and ordinary people to reach out and share their insights and talents. Just take a stroll through the Internet and you'll find hundreds of them. Many of these teachers and mentors are also writing books.

If you plan to write a how-to or self-help book, I urge you to put together a book proposal first. This will help you to view your idea from many angles, including a business perspective and a practical point of view. Do you actually have enough material for a book or would it be wise to start with a booklet or a series of blog posts? Is what you have to offer actually a fresh concept or a new approach to a popular issue? Would a publisher be interested in this book written by you?

So how would a book proposal for a how-to or self-help book look? Maybe the following will give you some ideas.

The Cover Letter

Follow the general instructions for the cover letter in chapter 3. Identify your book as a how-to or a self-help book and clearly and briefly describe it. While the cover letter is first to appear in your book proposal, I suggest that you hold off writing it until you've completed the bulk of your proposal—in particular, the synopsis and the market section (where you describe your audience).

You might then introduce your book this way: "I've devised an easy and fun way for new mothers of multiples to lose their baby fat while bonding with their babies. This 30,000-word guide includes twenty-two exercises mothers can do while involved with their infants and twenty-two easy-to-fix food combinations designed to burn fat."

Upon reading this, the publisher knows exactly who this book is for, the nature of the book, and basically what it will involve. If he publishes books for parents, in particular new mothers—even mothers of multiples, or unique diet books—he will most likely be interested in learning more about this project.

The next thing he wants to know is, who are you and what qualifies you to write this book? You'll expand on your qualifications later, but here, you should give a snapshot of your expertise or experience. Say, for example, "I'm an OB physician specializing in multiple births and have seen this formula work successfully for several of my patients." Or say, "I'm a personal trainer and the mother of twins. I devised this program for myself and now teach it to others."

What you don't want to do in your cover letter is confuse the publisher or tease him by concealing pertinent information. This will not tempt a busy publisher to keep reading. Instead, it might give him a reason to pass on your proposal.

The cover letter is your first opportunity to make a good first impression. Not only will the publisher scrutinize your cover letter with regard to the idea and the way you present it, he'll examine your way of writing. The author of a how-to or self-help book must be able to write instructions clearly and have a good sense of organization. If this element is obviously lacking even in your cover letter, the publisher will likely pass before reading further.

Your Fabulous Title

Think hard about your title for a how-to or self-help book. It is no easy task to attract readers these days and there's a lot of competition, so it is more important than ever to use a title that identifies a book in this category. Someone searching for a book on how to tie a tie will probably not even notice your book on this topic with a title such as, *Dressing for Business* or *Stepping Out*. They will take notice of these titles, however, *How to Tie a Tie* or *Tie Tying Tips and Tricks*.

For a book on successful online dating, avoid titles such as, *Exploring the Wild Blue Yonder* or *Catch Him If You Can* unless you use a subtitle. *Online Dating for 2015 and Beyond* might give a strong clue into the content and purpose of the book. Or use *Introduction to Online Dating* as a title or subtitle.

Check other books on this topic to make sure you don't choose a title that's already in use. I'd start at Amazon.com. At the prompt, type in your title and see what comes up. You can also do a title search through the United States Copyright office (www.copyright.gov/records) or ask a bookstore manager to look the title up for you in his database.

There's no law against choosing a title that's already in use, unless that title is trademarked. But I'd recommend that you use a title unique to your project. However, if you contract with a publisher, he is likely to change it.

The Synopsis: How Do You Know This Book Is a Good Idea?

I'm sure you have many questions. I hope this is one of them. Whether you plan to establish or strengthen your brand through your book or you hope to make some money or maybe a difference, it is important that you consider whether or not your book has a chance in the marketplace.

The research necessary to write a synopsis for your how-to or self-help book should respond to this question: Is this book a good idea? Or are you writing it only because you have knowledge in this area or it's a pet topic of yours? Some authors write the book they want, but can't find, which is becoming less and less likely these days. It seems as though there is a book on every subject imaginable.

The research necessary for the synopsis will help you determine the scope and size of your target audience. This will either validate what you thought you knew—that multiple births are on the rise (10 to 17 percent increase with fertility treatments and 36 to 45 percent increase for women who have not had fertility treatments), and that multiple birth mothers have a harder time losing their baby weight and less time to work out.

For a how-to or self-help book, facts backed up with statistics will impress a publisher or agent more than any amount of hype or theories. Sure, you'll want to explain your vision for your book—what concepts and material it will cover, how it will be laid out, and who your audience is. But when an author comes to a publisher or agent with a book designed to teach or inform, he or she had better express with clarity, authority, and evidence that the material and concept is valid. Publishers are aware that there are already multitudes of phony hocus-pocus books out there imitating books in the self-help category. They don't want to add to them.

When you look at the big picture and consider the publisher's reputation and his responsibility to his cache of readers, perhaps you'll understand how important evidence and proof is to him. And it should be to you, as well. So do your homework. Along with your great description of the proposed book, its primary purpose, and the proposed audience, you must give some indication of the need for such a book.

Note: You'll provide this evidence in more depth in the market section, but touch on it here, as well. You want the publisher to continue reading and, if you've sufficiently caught his attention with some meaningful statistics showing the need for this book, he likely will.

What Is Your Story?

Another valuable asset to the synopsis for a how-to or self-help book is *you*. What can you bring to the table as the author? What makes you credible in this field? Is the topic of your book related to your profession or is this something you experienced firsthand? Both count when it comes to these genres. Yet there are still unqualified people authoring books on subjects to which they've had little exposure. If this describes you, please start reversing this flaw now.

As part of the synopsis, explain briefly why you're the person to write a book on how to start a community garden, how to run a successful cat colony, or twelve steps toward a brighter future, for example. What gives you credibility in this area?

If you want to engage a publisher for a serious how-to or self-help book, you'd better have the credentials to support your material, ideas, and advice. Without some sort of qualification—education, training, or meaningful experience—a publisher or an agent would probably not take you seriously.

If you don't have a degree, but know someone who does, consider teaming up with a co-author for this book. A co-author with an MD or PhD, for example, might help you to get your health-related self-help or how-to book published.

Let's say you rode a horse three days in a row at a ranch one summer and you want to write a book for inexperienced riders. You learned a lot about the etiquette of riding dude ranch horses and would like to educate others on this topic. You'd be more credible to your readers if you've actually owned horses or a dude ranch. However there are ways around this stumbling block. Create a humorous memoir with a how-to element, for example. Or team up with a psychologist or horse trainer and write a book on the benefits of riding for stress control. You could include a chapter about dude ranch riding.

Don't get in over your head when writing a how-to or self-help book. Make sure you have the knowledge and tools needed to present a cogent book for your intended audience. If you don't, consider quoting experts in the field. Thousands of hopeful authors each year miss this important point and that's often because they don't write a book proposal. A book proposal can make your book idea so transparent you can easily see where it might be flawed and how to shore it up.

Yes, there are other sections in the proposal where you will share information about yourself, and that's okay. Your background in this topic will be one of the publisher's first questions and you want to respond to it as early as possible.

Once you've completed your synopsis—you believe you've adequately described your project, you've effectively introduced your audience and offered proof that they exist, and you've outlined your qualifications for writing this book—get a second opinion. Ask a professional in the field and/or a good book editor to take a look. Give them your criteria—is this material clear, concise, and complete? Do you have any questions after reading it? Does it make you want to know more about the project? Does it ramble on for too long? Ask your pre-readers to tell you what they got from reading your synopsis. Ask them, "What is this book about?"

A synopsis can make or break a book proposal. Give yours the opportunity to really shine.

The Market

The market for a straightforward self-help or how-to book is pretty easy to recognize. Finding your readers all in one area might be difficult. Why is this important? Promoting to many who are scattered throughout the states is much more cumbersome than marketing to many congregated at the same place. That's why it's so important to identify your potential readers and then follow that up by discovering where they shop, what they read, where they hang out on the Internet, what organizations they belong to, and so forth. These are the places and institutions you will approach with news of your book once it's published.

Why do you need this information now—before the book is even written? This is the sort of data that helps to validate or invalidate your book. If you can't describe a genuine audience for this book, or you discover that it would be of interest only to a narrow niche audience, you won't be able to snag a large publisher. And, truly, why would you want to publish it?

If you have a passion for the topic and you know there's at least a small group of people who could use this material, consider self-publishing a booklet and forgetting the idea of producing a book.

Presumably, your book idea has a large audience. It is your job to identify them and locate them so the publisher knows this book has a chance. If you are marketing to mothers of multiples, for example, start early locating clubs and organizations focused on multiple births. Research health-related sites for women. Start following these blogs and leave comments. Participate in online forums, subscribe to magazines focused on multiple births and healthy eating, for example. Approach specialists and professionals and leave your promo material in their offices or contact them online. Tell them about your proposed book and ask them to respond if they would recommend such a book to their patients or clients. This might include OB physicians, multiple birth specialists, massage therapists specializing in pregnant women, and so forth. These activities are great ways to test the market for your proposed book and collect valuable ammunition for the marketing section of your book proposal.

Some authors of how-to and self-help books are tempted to say their books are for everyone. They may believe that everyone should learn how to prepare for an earthquake, stay safe when traveling at night, feel more self-confident in social situations, or enjoy a more romantic relationship. This may be true, but everyone will not buy a book on the subject. There are readers who will. You need to figure out and find out who those people are. Identify the specific primary audience for your book, for the publisher's information and for your own.

There may be secondary audiences, as well. For a book on earthquake preparedness, you might target those living in earthquake-prone areas, who own their homes, live/work in large cities, are responsible for numbers of people (as in schools, hospitals, large corporations, and universities), and so forth. These people comprise your primary/target audience. Secondary audiences might include people in areas where there have been a few minor quakes recently—areas of new quaking, renters, and people with disabilities (especially if you have a chapter covering this topic). It would be fairly easy to obtain facts and figures related to these demographics.

Don't overwhelm the publisher with too many figures—in this situation, maybe simply obtain the population of a few main areas where quakes occur (California and Japan, for instance), number of homeowners in the Los Angeles area or all of Southern California, and the number of schools and offices in high-rise buildings in certain cities, perhaps.

For a book on how to meditate, rather than medicate, your way to a more joyful life, your target audience may include people who are being treated for depression, who are chronically ill with minor complaints, or who are seeking help of another kind. These people watch talk shows, seek new things to read for inspiration, and may attend church. They aren't as easy to identify, as you'll find them everywhere in cities and in the country, perhaps working and lounging at home. A major method of reaching this audience might be through targeted magazines and newsletters, doctor and psychologist referrals, social media, organizations related to depression and other mood disorders, and so forth.

Understanding your target audience early on will help you to write the right book. The exercise of identifying your readers will actually give you clues as to the direction to take with your book. So don't skimp on this task. It could make the difference between a weak attempt at a self-help or how-to book with little to offer and a dynamite, sought-after blockbuster.

Evaluate Your Competition

Before putting pen to paper and certainly before you start approaching agents or publishers, evaluate the market. What other books are out there like the one you propose?

Before we continue, let me get something straight. Some of you will say, "But there is nothing else like this book. My book is unique—one-of-a-kind." Be careful about making this claim. Say this to a publisher and he will immediately determine that either you do not understand the market and did a lousy research job, or there is a good reason why there are no books like the one you propose—because there is no audience for it.

Now let's back up. The reason for comparing your book to other similar books is to further discover if there is room for and a need for the book you propose. If your idea has been published many times over—your book has nothing new to offer a particular audience—why would you even consider writing it? If there truly is nothing published anywhere on the topic, maybe it isn't a good idea, at all. However, if this is a popular subject and you can come up with a creative new slant or a clever new approach, you might actually capture the interest of a publisher and, ultimately, millions of readers.

A dead end in the market analysis process might actually be a great new beginning for your project. So take it easy, open your mind, and be willing to learn and to change.

How will you find these competing and complementary books? Start by looking in the section at local bookstores where your book would be stocked. If you're not sure, ask the bookseller. Once your book is categorized for the self-improvement section, parenting, childbirth, gardening, relationships, etc., spend some time studying books in this section.

Isolate comparable books you find at the bookstore and at Amazon. com and find out which ones are selling. How?

- Ask bookstore managers.
- Check the Amazon ranking.
- Read the reviews on the books' Amazon pages.
- Visit the publishers' and/or authors' websites.
- Read the testimonials at the authors' websites.
- Locate the authors' Facebook pages, blog sites, and so forth.

Many authors, even those with publishers, have their own websites. Often, you'll find a media page listing promotional activities and articles relating various successes with the book—awards, sales milestones, and so forth.

If you're serious about wanting to help others with your book and you plan to write something truly worthwhile, you'll study those books that are most popular and most similar to the one you want to produce. You may passionately want to write a book teaching how to rise above negativity. But it's highly likely that you'll find several already-published books on this topic written pretty much how you planned to write yours. Move through this important evaluation process using your brain instead of your heart.

So what do you do if, indeed, there are one or more books like the one you propose? If this is a hot topic or even one that is lukewarm, and you really want to write about it, consider changing your vision for your book. If a book on online dating is selling off the charts and it covers the factors you planned to include, consider writing yours using testimonials from those who have used online dating either successfully or not so successfully. Interview people who have married after meeting online. Or create a pocket guide of tips for successful online dating, including red flags and acceptable dialogue for the first face-to-face meeting.

If you can't be objective about your project—you just don't want to change your focus, even though there are many books like yours on the market—reach out to others. A team of trusted individuals might be your ticket to a successful publishing venture.

Another way to get feedback for your book idea is to present workshops, seminars, or classes teaching the system, techniques, principles, or perspective you plan to present in your book. Encourage feedback. This is a great way to learn what works and what doesn't before you ever etch your great idea in stone. Go out and speak on the topic of your how-to or self-help book. Listen carefully to audience questions. I can't tell you how many blog posts and articles I've written based on feedback and questions from people in my audiences and workshops. Some of the ideas coming from my students and clients have actually resulted in published books.

Are you beginning to understand why it's important to study the market before getting involved? You don't want to produce another cookie-cutter copy of what's already out there—something that is directly competing with a top-selling book in a narrow niche market, for example.

So how does one prepare the market analysis? Study those books that are selling, paying particular attention to their table of contents and the way the author approaches the subject. What is similar when comparing these books to yours and what is different? If you find several books just like the one you propose, consider this: are there any chapter topics in these books that could be expanded into a viable book for this same audience?

Go to Amazon.com and GoodReads.com and read reviews for these books. Do any of the readers critique the content and/or make suggestions?

Join online forums and follow blogs on your topic to find out what people are saying—what is important to them? What do they need more of or want help understanding with regard to your topic?

Are you getting the idea? See how important the competition section of your book proposal can be? And this is why I (and other professionals) highly recommend that you write a book proposal before writing, perhaps, the wrong book.

Avoid Writing a Bulldozer Book

The how-to book will always be popular because we humans are curious and industrious. We're eager to improve our skills and learn new ones. Many how-to books come into being because the author needed or wanted specific information and couldn't find it.

First-time authors of a how-to or self-help book sometimes misrepresent the genre. Someone who is passionate about a cause or a point of view, for example, might write what I call a bulldozer book. This is a book that is intended to change minds, habits, and/or hearts. This may be a perfectly valid and useful book. What makes it a bulldozer book is the fact that the author has the wrong audience in mind. She wants to convince people to quit smoking, shame them into eating right, or entice them to go to church, for example. There may be consumers for books on all of these subjects, but it is probably the friend or family of the smoker, people who *want* to eat right, and those who are already affiliated with a church.

An author approached me once at a conference asking for advice. He said he had tried everything and just couldn't sell his self-published book. I invited him to tell me about his book, and he said, "It's scientific proof that there is no God."

I stammered a bit before asking, "Uh, who do you see as your audience for this book?"

He replied quickly and confidently, "Well, everyone!"

Yeah, he was trying to mainstream a book that probably had a nice niche audience among fellow scientists, agnostics, and others who are interested in the ongoing God-versus-science debate. He was trying to change minds—prove a point to people who probably couldn't be swayed in a million years.

I maintain that you may be able to sell your target audience a bulldozer book if you camouflage it somehow. For example, compile a book listing fascinating facts about favorite fast food hangouts. Readers who love their fast food might be interested. Then include a guide in each chapter showing how to improve your health by exchanging a fast food meal for something with more nutritional value. Compile a book of recipes for making some of the most popular fast food items. And slip in some reasons for choosing healthier ingredients or provide facts showing the actual quality of these prepared foods.

I think you get the idea. Just remember that when you give a performance in public or speak before a group, you do so with your audience in mind. Your goal is to educate, entertain, motivate, or enlighten people, right? You should look at your book in exactly the same way. If you want to write just for yourself, you have no business seeking publication. To publish a book is to share it with a large or small segment of readers and it is those readers that you must consider with every word you type.

Promotion and Platform

We have delved fairly deeply into what comprises an author's credibility for writing a particular book and why this matters. We have touched on what the author can bring to the table as far as marketing the book to his or her target audience.

The publisher wants to know that you understand the concept of book promotion and that you are equipped and prepared to promote your book. Let's start with your platform—what do you have going for you that might impress or influence your readers? Here are some ideas to consider:

- List your affiliations or involvement in organizations, businesses, professions, clubs, etc. related to the topic of your book and explain how you intend using some of them to promote your book.
- Note any of your previously published books and articles on this theme. Give titles of your other books; name the publishers and publication date. List titles of periodicals and websites where your work has appeared. (For an email submission, provide links to some of those articles.)
- Describe your website and blog site if they relate to the theme of your book. Provide links.
- Outline your education, especially where related to the topic of your book.
- List any pertinent connections: your father-in-law runs talk radio stations in three major cities, you typically travel on business several times a year and can set up presentations and signings to coincide, etc.
- Describe any highly successful promotional activities you've pursued in the past and explain how you will duplicate these in order to promote your book.

- Include the fact that you produce a monthly e-newsletter related to the field of your book that goes out to thousands of people. Naturally, you will promote your book to your subscribers.
- List some of the blog sites you frequent and explain that you have been invited to be a guest blogger at dozens of them when your book comes out.

List your most important promotional ideas and affiliations first—those that would attract, reach, or influence the highest number of potential readers.

If you aren't sure how to promote your book, you'd better take time to find out. Study books about book promotion. *Promote Your Book* (Allworth Press) comes highly recommended—not only by me (the author), but also many readers. Review the "promotions" and "platform" sections in chapter 4 of this book and follow some of the instructions. Attend workshops and presentations on book promotion. You'll likely find some being presented through your local writers' club and some of the many writers' conferences being held all over the United States.

In the meantime, I want to leave you with these thoughts: a book, in order to survive and sell more than a handful of copies, must be promoted. The more appropriately targeted and vigorous the promotion, the more successful the book will become. And the best person to promote any book is the author.

How long will you have to promote your book? Only for as long as you want it to sell. Yes, stop promoting and it will die.

Your Chapter Summaries: What Goes into a How-to or Self-Help Book?

Your chapter summaries should be revealing and telling. In 100 to 400 or so words each, describe what the chapter will cover. Include everything you'll feature and touch on in that chapter in a way that represents the tone and substance of your book. You want the publisher to understand the focus of each chapter, what it will include, what points you make in each chapter, and how these will be presented. Will there be exercises for the reader or instructions? What will he or she learn through this chapter? Here, you will outline the features in each chapter as well as the benefits— what will the reader take away from it?

Consider each chapter summary a mini-synopsis. In a how-to or self-help book, you're teaching, demonstrating, inspiring, or otherwise providing the opportunity and impetus for the reader to shift, learn, or transition. Perhaps your book is designed to help the reader change something about him/herself physically, mentally, emotionally, or spiritually.

As the author of a how-to or self-help book, you are responsible for providing ideas, encouragement, techniques, and/or tools to help readers learn something new or develop a different way of feeling or being, for example. In order to be successful in your pursuit, your instructions and explanation must be presented in a logical and clear manner. The chapter summaries provide you the opportunity to show the publisher that you can accomplish this important task and to convince him of the value and worth in your book. If he loves what he reads in this brief, five- to twelve-page section, he will ask to see more.

Your Sample Chapters

Most publishers will request one or more sample chapters. Let's say you will send two. For a book of this type, I recommend including those chapters that most represent the proposed process for whatever it is you are teaching or sharing. Choose one or two of your richest chapters—those that get to the meat of the topic and that reveal some of your teaching methods.

I often suggest that authors provide the first chapter as a sample. And this could apply to your self-help or how-to book. Typically, however, this is not the most telling chapter in a book of this type. Think about it: you're presenting a new concept or a new skill. You're asking readers to put themselves in your hands and trust your teaching methods and your level of expertise or enlightenment.

Not everyone has the aptitude for teaching or the power to persuade. And the publisher knows this. He wants to see enough of your project to convince him that your book is a potentially viable project.

(Refer to chapters 3 and 4 for additional information regarding the basic book proposal.)

How to Represent Your Business Book
Through a Book Proposal

Many businessmen and women are writing books in order to position themselves within the business community. A book is the modern-day business card. It introduces the author to the public and gives him or her credibility in the field. Write a book on an aspect of a business or industry and you soon become known as an authority, an expert, or a professional in that area.

A business book can serve to help the author establish or build on his or her brand, whether it is a product or a service. A business brand is basically how our customers, clients, and prospects see us and feel about us. Certainly one's professional standing can be enhanced by a published book in one's field.

What is a business book? It might cover an aspect of a specific business or field, explore management techniques, or expose wrongdoing in a particular industry. Some business books teach a process—how to start your own publishing company, handle an irate customer, attract more customers, do business in another country, or be more organized, for example. A business book may be informational or educational. There are also business books that spill over into other categories, such as historical, biographical, political, and so forth.

A key to the success of this proposal is clearly the author's platform. The author of a business book, while he's seeking to add to his credibility in his field, must impress the publisher with his accomplishments, achievements, and his reach or following.

Publishers of business books generally run small- to medium-size companies, and it would be unusual for them to require submissions through an agent. So head straight for the right publisher—one that typically publishes books on your book's topic or theme. You're probably familiar with other popular books within your industry. Find out who published them and contact those publishers. If you're creating a theme book—a how-to, a biography, etc.—seek a publisher who produces books, perhaps on a variety of topics, but in this style. For example, if your book focuses on how to buy and run a restaurant in a small town, you would not approach a publisher who specializes in business finance books, unless yours has a strong finance aspect. If you're pitching a customer service guide for corporate employees and business owners, a publisher of business management books or books for career-changers and job hunters might not be a match.

Your business book is probably for a niche audience. Some will be suitable to much smaller audiences than others. For example, a book featuring how to start and operate a particular business at home (party planning, bookkeeping, home cleaning, dog grooming, etc.) would not have as large an audience as would one featuring 100 businesses you can start at home, for example. A book focused on business management for the start-up or the accounting business would have a smaller target audience than a more general book on office management for women.

Before writing your book proposal, accurately determine how your book fits into the large world of business books, whether there are publishers for books like yours, how many there are, and who they are. Get a handle on the scope and size of the field and the market. The steps outlined in this chapter will help.

The Cover Letter

Probably the main thing you want to get across to a publisher is your expertise in this business and/or this topic and your unique slant. If you are trying to fit your book into a publisher's theme such as the Wiley's For Dummies series or, perhaps, business books for artists, then your cover letter should clearly confirm your understanding of this model.

Demand the publisher's attention right off the bat by offering him something within the realm of his interest—something he wants. But you'd better make it good. Conduct rigorous research to learn what he has already published and what he may be currently seeking and clearly show that you, indeed, comprehend his vision and his goals.

Think like the publisher. What are the main points he's interested in? Quite possibly that you can write, that you are embedded (well-known, active) in the business you want to write about, that your idea is new, and that you can produce a book to conform with his list. While this publisher might have a common model for his books, he still wants to produce something fresh for his readers. And it is the author's job to find that *something* that is missing from the publisher's catalog and adequately fill the void. It's not unheard of for an author to invent a whole new concept for a publishing house. All it takes is time, thought, and ingenuity. I suggest starting with the publisher's perceived customer base. Who are they? What do they read? How do they like to receive the information/material?

In the cover letter, attempt to convince the publisher that you have the expertise in the field, that you're savvy as to the publisher's products, and that you possess the skill and foresight to create something that will either fit his line perfectly or add something of value to it.

Your Business Book Title

Some authors find it just plain difficult to come up with titles for their books. I can write entire books—I have over forty-five to my credit—but it is a challenge for me to boil and pare a book topic down to a few words in order to create a good title.

Business book titles are all over the place—from clever, to spot-on, to overwhelming and outrageous. The title for a business book should explain the book. The content should be obvious at first glance. "Ah, this book is for shy entrepreneurs who need help promoting their businesses." Or "This book is a guide to purchasing the right business." Often it takes a subtitle to get the point across.

Can you imagine titles for these two books? How about *Market Your Business: For the Introverted Entrepreneur*, or *Your Career Personality: How to Choose the Right Business*.

The Business Book Synopsis

Determining which direction to go with a business book can be difficult. Presumably, you are in the business you will write about. You know what message you want to get across and what audience you want to reach. For a business book, sometimes the egg comes before the chicken or the cart before the horse, because you have an ulterior motive. You want to make points with your audience because they are quite possibly your present or future clients or customers. You want to become more well-known in your field and/or establish yourself as an expert in an area of your industry, for example. If you can combine your desire for exposure with the needs of your potential readership, this is the book you should write.

Once you have a few ideas, test them. Talk to colleagues and customers. Join in with an appropriate online discussion group. Produce an e-booklet and promote it heavily as a freebie at your company website, for example. Later, contact those who downloaded your e-booklet and ask for feedback. Did it meet or exceed their needs/expectations? What was lacking? Print your e-booklet and hand it out at conferences and business meetings. Where appropriate, develop a workshop around the theme of your proposed book and teach it a couple of times. If you are open-minded, you will learn volumes from your students.

Once you have a solid idea for your book, take time to identify its purpose. Does it match your vision for the book and your readers' perceived expectations and needs? Your reason for writing this book might be to provide more exposure for yourself among your customers/clients. But the purpose of the book should be to educate, inform, delight, inspire, or otherwise benefit the reader. This should be your goal and this is what you should communicate to the publisher.

Why this book for this audience now? Is it a topic that's been overlooked? Is this a new slant on a wildly popular theme? How many people comprise your audience? Why are you the best person to write this particular book?

Explain your vision for this book. What will the finished product look like? What will it encompass? What do you hope it will accomplish? What are some of the special and unique features? How will it benefit your readers?

Can you come up with some interesting methods of presenting the material or the technique? If you know—I mean really know—your audience, you should be able to develop a meaningful way to impart your message, and this might be the aspect that sells your book to the publisher.

The synopsis may go together easily and quickly or you might suffer and struggle with this part of your book proposal for days, weeks, months.

In the end, make sure your synopsis is succinct, crystal clear, and coherent. It must be well-organized and as easy to follow as your finished book will be. It might be a good idea to run the synopsis past a peer group. Ask each of them to tell you:

- What is the focus of this book?
- Do you perceive a need for it?
- Who do you think will read it and why?
- What are some of the unique features?
- What are the major benefits to my audience?

Who Are You?

When you write a book proposal for your business book, a major concern to a publisher is you. Why are you the person to write this book? What are your credentials or experience in this field or with regard to this concept? Presumably, if you are not well-known inside your industry and out, you can spew qualifications and qualities that give you some authority in the eyes of the publisher.

As the author of a business book, your education is important as is your training and, of course, experience. Be sure to mention awards, achievements, and accomplishments within your field. Previously published materials (articles, newsletters, and books) will surely add to your credibility.

Have you headed up any innovative programs, been a presenter at conferences on this topic, and/or developed and run workshops? Maybe you teach courses on this subject at a local college. When attempting to sell yourself as the author of a business book, everything related to your level of knowledge and expertise in this field is potentially important.

If you have a strong interest in the topic of your book, but little actual experience, you might consider involving an expert as a co-author or advisor. Or invite several experts to provide examples and quotes throughout the book. Another way to give your book credibility is to use anecdotes throughout from colleagues and company leaders. If your credentials are lacking, present what you can here in this section and then focus on the bios of any professionals who will be involved in your project.

Don't be shy. Don't put this section together so quickly that you omit significant facts.

The Market

This is your opportunity to show the publisher that you are familiar with your audience—that you know who they are, where they are, and how to approach them.

You may have outlined the potential market for this book in your synopsis. Here's your opportunity to expand on this theme. Offer more detailed specifics, all the while attempting to justify the premise of your book and its significance. Figures, statistics, and anecdotes go a long way toward swaying a publisher in your direction. If he doesn't know the market for your book, this information will be invaluable to him.

Perhaps he typically publishes books for entrepreneurs, but he knows nothing about the pet and animal market. Any figures, statistics, and anecdotes you can come up with to justify your book on how to establish and operate a successful pet-oriented business would certainly be of value to him. Without it, he doesn't have enough ammunition to evaluate the potential for this book.

Never assume that the publisher is knowledgeable in all areas of your proposed project. Even if he is familiar with the market for your book, it doesn't hurt to strut your stuff. A knowledgeable author is a refreshing breath of air for most publishers.

To recap, your job in this section is to demonstrate your familiarity with your particular audience and your ability to locate and approach them with what it takes to sell truckloads of your proposed book. And this is not done through vague promises. The publisher wants well-researched, realistic facts and figures.

What Is Your Competition?

A publisher contemplating another business book in a specific area or form certainly needs to know something about competing and complementary titles. Sure, you've already convinced him there are thousands (or millions) of potential readers. But have they already had access to this material presented in this way through other books on the market? That is the burning question. What else is out there like this book? What makes yours different—better?

Carefully study business books just like the one you propose. Hopefully, you won't find any (or many) of those. If you do, it's time to reconsider your idea. What you'll probably find are books written on themes from within the same industry (technology, restaurant ownership, home businesses, corporate management, etc.). Study them and select books that will most closely compete with yours and a few that complement yours.

Let's consider the book on how to establish and run a successful pet-oriented business. You might plan to focus the first section on types of businesses—a boarding kennel, a storefront featuring feline furnishings, a dog bakery, and a grooming salon, for example. Devote the second section to the business start-up process, the third to operating the business, and then provide a trouble-shooting section. What else is out there like this book? You might choose a few books published by major publishers focusing on pet industry businesses, a couple on general entrepreneurship, and one or two featuring complementary books. These might include popular books on specific start-up home businesses.

You must prove to the publisher that there is a need for, and room for, a book like yours. If, during this phase of the research, you find even two books just like the one you're writing, consider making some changes to your idea and your proposal. This is the whole point of this exercise. It's very possible that you'll find books like the one you want to write. There is nothing new under the sun. If you do find books just like yours, be mindful enough to damp down your emotional attachment to your project and rethink it. Is there room for another book like this? Are the other books wildly popular or barely being noticed? What information is lacking in the other books that you might be able to provide?

You'll experience greater success if you produce a book that's actually needed/wanted than if you try to compete with something that's already filling your original vision. If there's a massive audience for your book, however, and only a few competing books on the market, there may be room for your similar but carefully repurposed book.

Follow the directions for formatting your market analysis in chapter 4.

How Will You Promote Your Business Book?

The business book should be just about the easiest book for an expert or professional in the field to promote. Presumably, you would just keep on doing what you're already doing, which might include:

- Sending out a monthly newsletter to your enormous email list
- Speaking at conferences and business meetings related to the theme of your book
- Presenting podcasts and workshops
- Frequently updating your website for the convenience of your readers/customers
- Blogging regularly
- Submitting articles to appropriate industry magazines and newsletters
- Joining and participating in appropriate organizations

Describe the additional activities you'll engage in once your book is published:

- Reserving booths/space at book festivals, library expos, and industry shows
- Producing programs independently for your audience
- Contacting related company and organization leaders and asking for reviews and exposure
- Creating a book trailer for your website
- Getting involved with social media
- Continuing your membership and work with a self-improvement public speaking program such as Toastmasters

A business book will help you expand your reputation and your reputation will help sell your book.

Be Cognizant of Your Platform

Much of what we've covered throughout this chapter could fit into this section. In fact, there is some overlap from section to section, and that's okay. This is important information and needs repeating.

When fleshing out this section, simply pull in all of the most significant attributes that you believe will help to attract readers. What are your major connections and skills that will factor into opportunities for exposure, thus sales for this book?

Along with that, I'd like to see you include a list of business associates and leaders who believe in you. Ask for testimonials from colleagues and professionals who stand out in your field. You may be able to gather quite an impressive collection of endorsements for the proposal and, eventually, for the back cover or inside pages of your completed book.

Presumably you've decided to bring out a book related to your business in order to gain added credibility and visibility among your current and any potential customers/clients. You understand the concept of exposure. You may also comprehend the significance of a solid platform. The thing is, there are x number of people interested in the topic of your book. There may be dozens or hundreds of readers who would buy this book because you wrote it. They know who you are and consider you an authority. There may be thousands more who would buy it if they knew the book existed. Your job is to discover ways to become known by a wider audience—to add planks to your platform—and to get more widespread exposure for your book and for yourself.

Your Chapter Summaries

You probably have a pretty good idea of how your business book will come together. If you haven't done so already, list the main components of your perceived book in the most logical order and then list the subtopics and incidentals to be included within each section. These will, most likely, comprise your chapters. If you can't come up with at least ten chapter topics and dozens of subtopics, you may not have a book. In this case, you can either put together a booklet, a couple of articles, or rethink your book project. Maybe you can expand it by giving it another element.

Let's say you plan a book featuring business management for women and you can only come up with five or six solid chapters. If you look at what you have and still consider this a viable project with a rich and meaningful message, consider incorporating another aspect into your book. Add interviews with several women managers, include a section exploring different types of businesses and management styles for each, create some exercises for readers, or use more anecdotes demonstrating management styles that work and those that don't.

The process of developing your chapter summaries (or chapter outline) forces you to more carefully think through the scope and focus of your book. You'll find out if your original vision actually works or not. This exercise can help the author fine-tune even a rather convoluted project.

The chapter summaries section is similar to a chapter outline. Starting with chapter one, type the chapter title and then follow with a paragraph or two (100 to 400 words) describing what that chapter will contain, the main point of the chapter, its purpose, and any take-away concepts or material. Continue this process with each chapter.

Not only does this exercise help the publisher understand how this book will be put together, how it will flow, and what it is designed to accomplish, but it provides you, the author, a unique opportunity to visualize your book from start to finish. Is it the book you originally envisioned? Does it appear that it will serve the purpose you imagined? Or is it lacking? Does it need to be changed in some way? This is the moment of truth. If you are not completely satisfied with what the chapter summaries reveal, then maybe you need to rethink your project.

Which Sample Chapter(s) Should I Send?

Definitely send the chapters that best represent the theme and purpose of your book. It could be the first chapter and a chapter demonstrating your suggested exercises. Perhaps you want to include the chapter that best describes the book's concept along with the meatiest chapter. If you're not sure, turn to a few potential readers. Show them your chapter summaries (or the completed book if you have finished an early draft) and ask them which chapters are standouts. Which ones most accurately represent your proposed book?

Putting It Together

As I mentioned, a proposal for a business book may have a lot of overlap, and that's generally okay. You want to make sure the publisher knows that you have a strong background in marketing, for example, or that you've worked in the field or position featured in your book for x number of years. If this fact is repeated in more than one or two sections, that's okay, as long as you are using it to make a new point each time and that it strengthens your case for your book.

While you would review any book proposal over and over and over again, correcting errors and typos, rearranging the material, deleting overdone repeats, fine-tuning the language, and so forth, the business book proposal may require even more attention. You want to come across as the expert you are, so this must be a representation of your finest work.

While you may not be a professional writer, you should come across as such. I work with many well-schooled clients who are business whizzes, yet who could use a refresher course in writing. We all need editors. Hire a good book editor—one who knows something about the nature of a book proposal is even better. If you have never written a book proposal, run yours by an editor as well as a peer group. And then put it together in the most logical order—one that allows you to present your concept in the most favorable light.

Remember, each publisher you contact may have different requirements for submitting proposals. So take into account each set of submission guidelines as you prepare yours.

(Refer to chapters 3 and 4 for additional information regarding the basic book proposal.)

Pitch Your Cookbook through a Hot Book Proposal

While accuracy and attention to detail are important for all book proposals, a publisher of cookbooks might be even pickier. There's simply no room for error in a cookbook. If this is your first attempt at developing a cookbook, know that any representation of your project must be meticulous. From the query letter to the synopsis to the sample chapters, fastidious work is a must. Why? There are formatting issues that must be accurately addressed with a cookbook. Recipe measurements and directions have to be precise. A sloppy presentation from someone professing to be a cookbook author would not bode well to any publisher.

There are many styles of cookbooks and numerous possibilities for someone who has a knack for writing in this field. There are very simple concept cookbooks with pencil drawings, collections of family recipes formatted much like a scrapbook, specialty cookbooks featuring one type of dish, special dietary needs or age-group cookbooks, gourmet cookbooks, and everything in between. Recently, I saw a cookbook dedicated strictly to recipes calling for almond milk.

I once wrote a book featuring how to present a Hawaiian luau on the mainland. It focused on eight ways to cook a whole pig and included several recipes for luau side dishes. The recipes came from a Hawaiian/ Japanese friend. I can't say that my book was anything to write home about, aesthetically, but the theme was unique and I sold a lot of copies. I sold so many, in fact, that a Hawaiian publisher approached me with a contract. He wanted to add my little book to his line of Hawaiian books.

Cookbooks continue to sell. The market is strong and being made stronger with the huge popularity of TV reality cooking shows. Whether you have an idea for the single parent's grilling cookbook, a vegetarian cookbook, or a book featuring recipes from your native country along with a little folklore and some photographs, you might have a chance to be published.

If you are creating a book proposal, you probably already have a solid idea. So let's continue through the parts of the proposal as it relates to your specific project.

The Cookbook Cover Letter

As with any nonfiction book, your goal with the cover letter is to introduce your vision for your book clearly enough so the publisher gets the picture, and appealing enough so that he becomes interested. Make a case for your book by pointing out the current craze in home cooking due to cooking shows or the many special diets popular now. If your book features gluten-free and dairy-free recipes, you might say, "One in 133 people are allergic to gluten and 75 percent of the population is lactose intolerant." For a book on family grilling tips and recipes, locate statistics or quotes from psychologists stating the importance of family togetherness through the sharing of meals. Keep it brief and choose your words carefully. You'll have plenty of space to expand on this concept later in the proposal.

Help the publisher understand why you should write this book—why you and not someone else? Is it because you are an excellent cook, you've been creating recipes in your home kitchen for decades, you're a chef for a major restaurant, you've edited cooking magazines for ten years, you're a caterer, you participated on the TV show *Chopped* once, you teach at a culinary academy, or you're a mom (or dad) who has a reputation for creating family-friendly meals? Maybe you have contributed recipes and articles to food magazines and newsletters, or you've won contests with some of your recipes. If you've written and published other cookbooks, be sure to provide titles, dates, publishers, etc.

Add a line or two about any strong connections or abilities you can use in promoting your book—you're the director of a national organization related to the health issues covered in your book or you have an email database of 5,000 people who suffer from celiac disease or diabetes, for example. Perhaps you prepare delicious family meals for your church youth group once a month and have published a cookbook that sells to the online church community.

Your job with the cover letter is to make the publisher see dollar signs when he considers your cookbook project.

Your Delicious Title

Most cookbook covers feature beautiful photographs of appetizing meals or an image of the cook dressed in an apron or chef's hat and surrounded by food. So a succinct title that includes words such as, "cookbook," "kitchen," "chef," "culinary," "cuisine," "meals," etc. might not be necessary. If the cover photo isn't descriptive of the type of recipes inside, then consider a title that sells the idea to readers who would be interested in Indian cooking, Japanese cuisine, nondairy recipes, etc. Before becoming attached to your clever title—*Yummy to the Tummy*, or *Family Food Fights*—seek the opinion of others. Run your title by several friends and colleagues and ask them to identify the focus for your planned book.

Listen to them. They are your audience. Also spend time in a mega bookstore reading cookbook titles. If you're confused, go to Amazon.com and read more cookbook titles. At this point, you may need the assistance of your peer group (or consulting team) again.

Oh, and once you've chosen the perfect title and cover image for your cookbook, you can probably expect the publisher to change it as soon as you're issued a contract. It's typical. If you must keep your title and cover art, consider self-publishing.

The Scrumptious Synopsis

Certainly, a cookbook would be fairly easy and straightforward to describe. It's a book full of recipes. What kind of recipes? Do they have a theme? Are there sidebars explaining the origin of each recipe or alternatives (for those with gluten or dairy sensitivities, for example)? Does your book feature the recipes you've entered in contests over many years? Maybe it is filled with recipes that moms and wives prepared for their loved ones' homecomings from battle or hospital confinement. I know one mom who created a cookbook of her deceased son's favorite foods. How do you envision the recipes being laid out? Make a case for your cookbook early on.

If you've done your homework, you know how many food and recipe books there are currently on the market. The numbers vary between sources, but you can bet this is a huge market that still seems to have a large audience. You must sell the publisher on the potential in this market for your book. What is the appeal? What makes it special? Unique?

Describe your audience. How many people within your market (the United States or world-wide) are vegetarians, vegans, on gluten-free or dairy-free diets, love Salvadoran food, etc.? Cite the numbers along with some facts about the industry. Are more manufacturers catering to this demographic? Are there more stores and restaurants carrying foods and preparing meals for these special tastes? Can you convincingly tell the publisher why this book and why now?

Explain how you became involved in this topic. Why is it important or of interest to you? Why are you the right person to compile this cookbook?

Describe your method of testing the recipes. Be explicit. A little humor doesn't hurt, especially if you intend to share some laughable moments in your cookbook.

Before completing the proposal, hire a food photographer to take pictures of a few of your dishes and send copies with your proposal package. If a publisher issues you a contract, he may work with you and your photographer or he might test the recipes in-house and use his own photographer.

A beautiful thing about your audience is that if they buy one cookbook, they are apt to buy many. Cookbooks, to some consumers, are like mystery novels to avid readers of mysteries. They can't get enough.

The Delectable Market

By the time you start this section, you should know full well who your audience is. Who will be interested in this cookbook? Is it designed for children, college students, seasoned homemakers, individuals on special diets, or someone who loves to experiment with food? Is it a primer for culinary schools, budding chefs, institution and school cafeteria managers, or klutzy cooks?

Certainly you had a specific audience in mind when you first envisioned the cookbook. Now it is time to describe this audience to the publisher and provide evidence that the market is strong. Earlier in your proposal, you may have used some statistics demonstrating how many people are vegans, love Italian food, etc. Here, you should expand on that premise and those facts and then present a few anecdotes to back them up. In order to gather this information, search the Internet; check stats on Amazon.com; visit your local mega bookstore, spend some time in the cookbook section and talk to the manager; visit blog sites related to books like the one you propose and have dialogue with some of the bloggers; look up articles related to the theme of your book. Each step in your research helps you to better understand who your audience is and where they are.

If you discover that there is not a strong audience for your book, you have choices. You can seek out a small niche publisher who typically produces books like yours, you can self-publish, or you can add aspects and features that might expand the target audience for this book. If you've thoroughly researched your idea, you are well aware of what's out there, what's selling and, perhaps, what's needed. Open your mind and get creative. This could make the difference between a disappointing venture and a successful one.

You, the Cookbook Author

The publisher wants to know that you are qualified to write or compile this book. He will be interested in your qualifications as a writer, author, and within the realm of cooking and foods. This is where you will note your education and your experience in the foods industry. If your book focuses on vegetarianism, gluten-free recipes, or some other cookbook specialty, explain your background and interest in this area. Maybe you're writing an ethnic cookbook. Did you grow up cooking these recipes? Did circumstances cause you to have to learn new techniques for preparing food? Or have you been searching for books featuring a particular style of cooking and couldn't find many? Be sure to tell the publisher.

While some publishers of cookbooks produce only those from well-known chefs, others are seeking books that have a unique slant by creative authors who have something new to bring to the kitchen—at least to the bookshelf.

Have you published other cookbooks? How did they sell? Perhaps you've submitted articles to foods and cooking magazines. Describe some of the articles and give magazine titles. The publisher will also want to know if you have any additional cookbooks planned.

Yes, this is a bit of an overlap. You will be talking about yourself and your expertise in other sections of your book proposal, but that's okay. It's valuable information that could entice the publisher to consider your book from among the dozens or hundreds of proposals he sees every year. If he's a *skimmer*—he reads quickly through your proposal—he may not notice the information until he comes to this section looking for it. So make it as good as it gets.

Certainly, the author's credentials and reputation are needed in order to sell certain books. This is not always true with cookbooks. Sure, in most cases, cookbooks by popular cooking show chefs and Hollywood celebrities will sell more copies than those by unknowns like you and me. But if your topic is popular and your slant unique, you just might win a publishing contract.

How Does Your Book Measure Up?

Locating the right publisher could take some time, but it's a hugely important part of the process.

You may have to spend hours on Amazon.com, in downtown bookstores, at libraries, and poring through your own bookshelves to locate publishers for cookbooks like the one you hope to produce. This study will also help you determine if your idea is a good one. So pay attention to the cookbooks you find, their interesting features, etc., and what is missing—how your cookbook could be made better, more useful.

While all aspects of the cookbook proposal are important, you especially want to be clear as to how your cookbook will fit into an otherwise crowded market. And the publisher needs to be convinced that there's room for a book like yours.

Because there are so many cookbooks, it may take time. Search out some of the most popular books in your book's category—quick meals for busy families, sexy desserts for couples, breads from around the world, holiday cookie baking, etc. Choose five or six of those that are most similar to yours—designed for the same audience. If you can't find any books just like the one you have in mind, select something that's obviously directed toward the same audience—busy moms, young romantics, etc.

Select some published through the most well-known cookbook publishing houses, some that have won prestigious awards, perhaps, and a few that might complement yours. What do I mean by complementary books? A cookbook of holiday feast recipes might pair well with your holiday cookie cookbook. Or your book on breads from around the world might have the same audience as one on bread pudding and other old-world desserts.

List each book you will use in this section, along with publisher, publication date(s) (some cookbooks have been reissued many times over), ISBN, and number of pages. Describe the cookbook, including the illustrations (photographs, pencil drawings, etc.). If this book is popular, discuss sales figures, or number of printings, or Amazon ranking. What makes this book so popular? Is there anything missing, in your opinion? What would make it better? Is this something you plan to include in your book?

Now explain why you think your book will attract the same audience. Is there something about your book that will appeal to this particular audience? Maybe you will include tips for creating a romantic setting to go along with your romantic recipes. Perhaps you offer a few recipes the couple can make together, you show several unique ways to present your desserts, and you have a section on tantalizing sipping beverages for romantic occasions.

Now Let's Promote Your Cookbook
The last thing you may be thinking about as you collect and test recipes for your cookbook is marketing. You see books displayed in your local bookstores. You order books from among the millions on Amazon.com and other online bookstores. And you also notice people buying books at book festivals, gift shops, and specialty stores. It may have never occurred to you that someone spent time, effort, and money promoting that book. The fact is, it's in the bookstores, specialty stores, etc. because someone (either the publisher or author) took steps to make sure it is stocked there.

There may be a lot of behind-the-scenes planning and activity to bring customers to this place and to entice them to buy this book. And when you become a published cookbook author, you will be the one doing this work behind the scenes in order to make sales.

You also see cookbooks advertised on TV and hear cookbook authors being interviewed on the radio. You figure you could do that. But what you will learn and what the publisher knows is that it takes a lot of effort to arrange for these gigs. Consequently, most publishers are interested in authors who have some marketing savvy.

Here are a few ideas for promoting a cookbook. But please don't add them to the promotions section of your book proposal unless you fully understand what they entail and you fully intend to pursue them. For a crash course on the concept and execution of book promotion, read *Promote Your Book: Over 250 Proven, Low-Cost Tips and Techniques for the Enterprising Author.*

- Before the book is a book, start blogging on the topic of your cookbook. I believe that's how Ree Drummond got her start with her Pioneer Woman cooking show.
- While compiling the book, collect email addresses to add to your mailing list.
- Talk about your book wherever you go. When someone expresses an interest, ask for his or her email address and promise to notify them once the cookbook is published.
- Before approaching a publisher, hire a good book editor who is accustomed to editing cookbooks.
- Submit articles on the topic of your book to food, cooking, and/or appropriate ethnic magazines, newsletters, and websites. Let the publisher know that you will continue this practice as a way to continue building rapport with your readers and getting exposure for your book.
- Become involved with one or more organizations related to the theme of your book. Presumably the members are also your potential readers. Take every opportunity to talk about your book—place announcements in the organization newsletter, participate in the forum. Once your book is published, plan to offer it as a prize in any contests they run, ask if they will feature your book at their website, etc.
- Locate blog sites related to the theme/content of your book. Ask the bloggers to feature or review your book. Offer to be a guest blogger.
- Solicit book signings wherever your book is sold—kitchen stores, gift shops, bakeries, etc.
- See about placing an ethnic cookbook in appropriate grocery, curio, tourist stores—East Indian, for example, Salvadoran, Mexican, Asian, etc.
- Teach a workshop on an aspect of your book. Arrange for tons of publicity before and after the event.
- Create social media pages specifically to feature your book.
- Ask friends to invite people into their homes to see you give cooking demonstrations. Make it fun—and tasty. You *will* sell books.

Use your imagination to come up with more great promotional ideas. Brainstorm with colleagues. I know a woman who, years ago, wrote a cookbook for diabetics. While on a cruise, she noticed there were no diabetic desserts on the menu. She met with the chef, gave him a copy of her book, and convinced him to use one of her dessert recipes at dinner the following night. He put the item on the menu along with the title of her book. If she'd taken this idea a little further, she might have reeducated chefs from other cruise lines and maybe even had her book placed for sale in the onboard gift shop and through the cruise line's publications.

A Platform for a Cookbook Author

As we've discussed earlier in this chapter, a strong platform for a cookbook author includes being an experienced cook or chef within the area of the particular book. You probably excel in the kitchen and you want to prove this fact in your proposal. If you're a little shy about your accomplishments and skills, ask friends and family to help you list your assets. Some of your accomplishments and skills may appear not to relate to promoting a cookbook, but you might be surprised. For example, being an author often means going out and meeting your audience. So if "friendly" and "outgoing" appear on your list, that's a good thing. In fact, I'd urge you to take this concept a step further and provide some anecdotes designed to equate those descriptive terms with some potential promotional activities.

Say, for example, "I spoke at the closing ceremonies for the culinary show in New York in 2010 before 500 people."

Share how many people read your blog and something about the number and scope of the comments they leave.

Are you well known? By what segment of people? Maybe you have a brief spot on local radio each week where you talk about foods and cooking. That's a strong plank in your platform.

Perhaps if your expertise would make a difference to a publisher, you could have your recipes tested at a restaurant chain in town, on a cruise ship, or in a school district before approaching a publisher. Get on a cooking program with your dish, write articles for cooking magazines and enter their contests.

A publisher will be more apt to consider your proposal if he believes that you have what it takes to promote your cookbook. Your creative, out-of-the-box ideas will impress him. Your credentials and list of any pre-publication promotion you've done will delight him. But if you also come across as energetic, assertive, and focused on making contacts and selling books, he will have no reason not to issue you a contract.

Chapter Summaries

While some cookbooks don't have chapters, they generally have sections. In this case, you would describe the content, purpose, and special aspects of each section in your proposed cookbook. And be sure to share some of the recipes. A summary is designed to outline what each chapter covers and why. Start sentences with, "In section I of *Busy Mom; Easy Meals*, I provide a . . ." or "Section II includes recipes for . . ." or "Here, I offer ideas that the kids can help with, including . . ."

Illustrations for Your Cookbook

Illustrations are a huge part of most cookbooks. If you are working with a professional food photographer, let the publisher know this. Include copies of some of the photos. A major publisher, as well as a publisher who specializes in foods and cookbooks, may prefer to use their own photographers and even test the recipes in their own kitchens. But some smaller publishers may well consider the illustrations you suggest.

If you do not have access to a professional food photographer, engage the best photographer you know to photograph a few of your dishes and send the best photos along with your proposal with a note explaining that these are simply samples and not intended to be used in the published cookbook. Never send originals in the mail.

Part Three

The Personal Book Proposal

Personal books differ from other types of nonfiction. The style is typically narrative nonfiction and/or creative nonfiction. Because these books are inspired by any number of things, rather than researched, the author often doesn't have much (if any) writing experience. He or she generally doesn't know much about the publishing industry and isn't too interested in learning. Their motivations for writing their stories may vary. While some top-selling books in recent years were memoirs, few memoirists actually experience monetary success.

The reasons for this are obvious—most of them are devoted to producing this one book, so they see no reason to get involved with a study of the publishing industry. One-book memoirists typically slip into the industry quietly, get their books produced as easily and quickly as possible, and move on. They don't take the time or interest to learn what it takes to experience success in this field. They don't even consider it a field. The only thing some memoir writers know about publishing is that for a fee you can get your book produced and order as many copies of it as you want. They often go with the first self-publishing company they find during the briefest of Internet searches.

This memoirist pays to have her book published. She might order a dozen copies, but she's at a loss as to what comes next. Generally, this author simply gives a few copies away, places one on her coffee table, and then goes back to her former life.

So why does she write the book in the first place? What is her motivation? The author of a personal book generally has something to say or a message to share and is obsessed with getting the book out any way she can. Not all memoirists are cut from the same cloth. Some will join a memoir-writing group or a writers' club and they'll learn something about publishing and all that goes with it. Some of these more astute authors may even go to the trouble of writing a book proposal in order to get help in launching their projects. This author looks at a publishing contract as the easiest and cheapest path to publishing. She may also believe a publisher will guarantee her the success she desires.

I'm glad that you memoir writers are reading this book. You may plan a one-shot publishing project, but if you want to enjoy a measure of success, you really, truly need the information outlined throughout this book and particularly in this section.

(Refer to chapters 3 and 4 for additional information regarding the basic book proposal.)

How to Write a Book Proposal for Your Memoir

I have worked with many memoir writers. A large number of them never made it into print (or digital). Most of those who did were minimally successful. Their books were not well received. And that was mainly because their books were not well known. These authors chose not to promote their books. In most cases, this was either because they didn't want to or because they didn't understand the concept of book promotion. But there's another problem that comes into play.

For the most part, memoir writers are not the strongest writers around. Some lack writing skills, others don't understand what goes into a good story, and few of them have the desire to learn what they need to know about the business of publishing.

Yet some of the most popular books on the market today are memoirs. Some say memoirs are popular because readers like to compare their own lives with those of others. And we're nosy. We like to peek in on how others live.

I know some excellent writers who penned their memoirs and have done well in the marketplace. It seems to take a strong combination of writing and storytelling skills paired with a keen understanding of the publishing business. Having an interesting, meaningful, inspirational, exciting story doesn't hurt, either. Here's a checklist for those of you who yearn to write your memoirs. Before setting out to become the next Frank McCourt or Anne Frank, consider the following:

- Memoirs by ordinary people with ordinary stories rarely do well.
- Great—I mean great—writing can sometimes trump this fact.
- Publishing is a business and must be approached as such.

A publisher cannot make all of your dreams of success come true, unless you have a good project and you're willing to do everything you can to promote the resulting book. The main concepts I want you to take away from this chapter are these:

- If you aren't a seasoned writer and/or you've never written a book or story in the style of the book you wish to write, get help.
- Read dozens and dozens of books like the one you want to write.
- Solicit feedback from good editors and avid readers early on. Let professionals and other savvy people guide you toward a more successful experience.
- Read books on memoir writing and take workshops and classes. (See the resource list in Part Seven for suggestions.)
- Study the publishing industry so you understand the business side of producing a memoir.

I realize that some of you won't pay attention to this. You'll decide it is overkill in your situation. You simply want to tell your story and publish it, like so many before you have done. You also hope to make a little money in the process. But you have no interest in getting all that involved in the publishing industry. You just want to dip your toe in only as far as you have to and still get dream results.

I'm often asked to evaluate manuscripts for authors. And many of those are memoirs. Some are unfinished—simply a chapter or two and an outline. While some of them certainly have promise, others need a little or a lot of help.

I've sent numbers of potential memoir writers back to school by recommending they join a writers' critique group and participate for a good long time while in the process of writing their stories. Some of these authors should consider producing a book for friends and family only. You've heard people say they've known babies, children, or puppies that only a mother could love. Well, this is also true for some personal stories. Think about it: would the general public—people who don't know you—care about your story? Why? What do you have to offer them? How would your proposed book benefit readers? Put yourself in their place for a moment. Would you be inspired to read a book like the one you plan?

Is it truly that remarkable, interesting, inspirational, well written, thought provoking, and/or useful? If not, what can you do to make it so?

I wrote a memoir once. It was a situational memoir. I've lived a fairly ordinary life. No one outside of family and friends would be interested in reading a dull tome following my life's ups and downs. However, there was one year-long period when I was subjected to some extraordinary, rather otherworldly experiences that I knew would be most fascinating to a fairly wide range of seekers—people who were interested in the supernatural, hypnosis, past lives, and so forth. This story began when I was asked to write a book about a local hypnotherapist who used past-life regression with many of his clients—those wanting to quit smoking, lose weight, heal relationships, stop nightmares, etc. I spent months interviewing the hypnotherapist and his clients. I sat in on sessions with his clients and I even participated in sessions of my own. And I took copious notes.

When the hypnotherapist died suddenly, I tabled the project. Eight months later, however, when I realized how much my life had changed because of what I'd learned from him, I decided to write my own book. With permission, I included his case histories, dialogue from client sessions and my own, and the result was a situational memoir that many people found fascinating. They didn't buy it because they were interested in me; it was the subject matter—the woo-woo stuff—that enticed them to delve into this book.

I sometimes suggest to authors that they add something to their story to make it more interesting to an additional segment of readers—a historical slant (what was going on during that period in history?), a how-to or self-help section, or a focus on an aspect of your story—and weave it throughout. This might be a romance, a love/hate relationship with a friend or family member, your relationship with a special pet, or your attempt to break through the corporate glass ceiling, for example. In other words, design your story so it flows in and out of a main theme—your love affair with food, perhaps, your shyness, or the lasting effects of a rape and how it affected each phase of your life.

The Cover Letter

The pitch points for most memoir cover letters include the memoir type, the projected audience, the size of the target audience, verification of their interest in this particular memoir type, and the author's qualifications to write and market it.

A cover letter can whet the publisher's or agent's appetite for more or turn them off completely. You want them to continue reading through the book proposal, so pay attention to the details and information in this important letter. Write a juicy, tantalizing, and/or intriguing synopsis in 100 words or fewer. Carefully research your audience. If your story is similar to and as powerful as a current or past bestselling memoir, compare your memoir to that one. Say, for example, "My story is reminiscent of *Angela's Ashes* (or *The Glass Castle* or *Eat, Pray, Love*, etc.)" and then describe the audience for that book.

Be careful here. I've seen manuscripts for books that the author claimed were the next *Celestine Prophecy* or *Harry Potter* and they didn't even come close. So before you make such determinations, carefully and thoroughly study other books and then run yours by your team of critics. Every author—especially new authors—should locate or assemble a critique group or team to consult. You might find a good one through a local writers' group. Or establish one of your own by enlisting your most astute and honest friends, colleagues, neighbors, and family members to review and scrutinize your manuscript at various stages throughout the process. Your main job here is to listen to them. And one of the questions you'll be asking them is, "Do you think this book could be the next (fill in the blank)?"

Honestly, the new author isn't always the best person to judge his or her own book in this light. An author's wishful thinking can sometimes get in the way of reality. (Study the section on cover letters in chapter 3.)

Your Memoir Title

If you're like many memoirists, you have a title in mind. The title may have come long before your inspiration to finally write the story. Here's a bit of advice: do not get attached to your title. If you land a publisher, he may change that title faster than you can wink an eye. In fact, once you do the research I'm going to suggest you do, you might discover that your wonderful title isn't such a great idea. If you are attached to a title that you later discover just won't work, but you still love it, consider using it in the story someplace, as a chapter title perhaps, or use it to make a provocative statement at the end of a chapter, for example.

Your title might work just fine with a subtitle. Or it could be worked successfully and brilliantly into the back cover copy and your eventual marketing material.

If you absolutely must use your title as a title, and it is not explanatory, consider displaying a photo or other artwork on your cover that says something about the story line.

Before deciding, run your title past your team. There are a couple of ways you can handle this—give people the title and ask what type of book they think it is. Or you can explain what kind of memoir yours is, the basic story line, and the title you're considering. You will probably get a variety of responses from different people. That's okay. Listen to them all, contemplate their reasoning, and make your best decision. In most cases, if you land a publishing contract, the publisher will change the title, anyway.

I missed the boat with my own situational memoir—the story of my life-changing introduction into self-hypnosis. I published the book through my own publishing company, so I was in charge of every detail. I came up with the title *Quest for Truth* and quickly became attached to it. Colleagues advised me against this title. "It doesn't say anything," one of them said. "It doesn't speak to the reader." I listened, but I didn't learn. This was my title—the title I wanted. In order to help the rather vague title along, I devised a subtitle: *A Journey of the Soul*. But this didn't help much and I didn't sell many copies of this book. However, those who read the story absolutely loved it. Many were touched by it, intrigued by it, and even felt somehow validated by it.

I may send this book back to the drawing board—change the title, replace the cover, and start promoting it again. What would be a good title for this book? Something less ethereal and vague—I haven't a clue. But I can assure you, when I'm ready to move forward with this project, I will write a book proposal and I will assemble a team.

Your Memoir Synopsis

There are a variety of types of memoirs—the situational memoir (focusing on an event in your life), the life story memoir, the family history memoir, the celebrity memoir, and the travel memoir, for example. There are also memoirs focusing on the victim, the survivor, recovery, personal struggles, and coming of age. You'll find military memoirs, career-related memoirs, and romantic memoirs, as well as those based in spirituality and nostalgia.

I've heard of pet memoirs—some are even told from the animal's point of view.

While most memoirists write a 150- to 300-page book using chapters to divide the various events and phases of their life story, others create a series of stories. They write a dozen or so complete stories from their life and compile them, either in sequence according to timeline or randomly. These stories might each provide a lesson, generate a chuckle, or reveal an embarrassing moment or a traumatic time, for example.

Your first task in writing in this genre is to identify the type of memoir you want to write. How is your story best told? Which of your life high-lights would resonate most with the public? Do you hope to teach, inspire, challenge, help, or simply entertain readers? A good book on memoir writing might help you make this decision. (See the resource list in Part Seven.)

Next, determine your goal for your project. Do you want to make it big—earn lots of money with this book? Or are you mainly interested in making a statement? Your goal might be to get this off your chest and get closure, to share something with your family and friends, or to prove something to someone ("I am worthwhile. I did the right thing. I'm okay.").

Some people write a memoir as a form of therapy. This is especially true if there were any emotionally difficult times along the author's life path—and most life stories are peppered with conflict and unhappy challenges. Some people sit down to write their stories, not for publication, but for the opportunity to reflect and heal.

Whether you start out writing for therapy or for publication, you can count on the process of memoir-writing being somewhat therapeutic. Some level of healing is bound to take place. When I wrote my situational memoir, I experienced moments of raw emotion. It was so unexpected and, I'm guessing, somewhat healing.

Before you get very far with your project, see if you can determine your goal in writing this book and your perceived purpose. Keep in mind that there are logical and meaningful objectives in writing a memoir and some that are completely frivolous. A proposed book for publication should not be produced totally for selfish reasons. Your motivation for making it public should be rational, maybe even altruistic; certainly not self-serving. In other words, there must be something in it for a segment of readers, otherwise why would they bother to read it?

I've had authors come to me for manuscript evaluations and tell me their book is a memoir with a self-help aspect. As I'd read through it, however, I couldn't find anything indicating that it was a self-help book. The author might have written about her illness and recovery, but never once offered any take-away instructions, tips, or ideas. Obviously, she didn't understand that a self-help book must address the reader with solutions and techniques. Sure others might learn something from your story simply by reading it, but a book is not a self-help book if the author doesn't explicitly present issues and offer possible solutions.

A memoir can take many forms. You could insert letters, postcards, photographs, recipes, or poetry, for example. I've seen children's pencil drawings published in memoirs, train tickets, theater playbills, menus, and more. I once worked with a client on a biography featuring his great-grandfather, an early artist. The author told this man's story through narration and entries from the artist's journal. He also included photographs and original art.

A memoir should have a beginning, middle, and end. It should also have a point and a purpose. It is a story, after all.

If you are new to writing, before launching out with your story, consider testing it. Write a portion of your story in 1,500 or 2,000 words and submit it to a magazine, newsletter, or appropriate blog site. Keep track of the feedback your story receives through blog comments, letters to the editor, etc. Or write snippets of your story in consecutive order and post them at your own blog. Become active in social media and link to your blog in hopes of attracting visitors and feedback. Submit a few short stories related to your memoir on Amazon.com and actively promote them. Try to get them reviewed. Once you find a way to engage your potential readers, you'll learn volumes from them. One important thing you'll learn is the best way to go about telling your story—chronologically, through a narrative voice, in first person, using dialogue, through the eyes of your dog/horse/cat, or a combination of the above.

Once you have determined the best way to go with your memoir, describe it in the synopsis. Share quotes from it, where appropriate. Paint a picture of your story and outline the methods you'll use to tell it. Explain what you hope to accomplish through the telling of your story and how your story will benefit your target readers.

You mentioned your target audience in your cover letter and you will expand on them later in the proposal. Here, however, you'll want to provide a more exact identification and potential numbers. Let's say your book is a spiritual memoir involving your Spanish roots. Your research might reveal that there are 200 online book clubs that have chosen spiritual novels and memoirs to read and that numbers of them featured a specific ethnic group. Include this information in your book proposal.

Study other books similar to yours and see if you can find out how they're selling or how they rank at Amazon.com.

A concern when writing a memoir, a biography, or an autobiography is the libel issue. Often, when we write about our own life, the story involves other people and sometimes not in a good light. Some authors believe that all they have to do is change the names of those individuals and they are protected against a lawsuit. In actuality, as I understand it, if someone recognizes himself in your story or believes he recognizes himself and that others will, too, and he doesn't like what you wrote, he can sue you for defamation of character or libel.

Some authors believe that if they write the truth, even if it is unflattering, they are protected. As I understand it, someone can still accuse you of libelous action. Even if you don't feel the information is derogatory, if the subject doesn't like what you've written, he or she can file suit.

How can you protect yourself? One way is to get permission from everyone you want to include in your story.

My fervent recommendation, however, is that you hire a good intellectual property attorney before deciding the direction and scope of your story. Obviously, there are countless authors telling all kinds of stories and they seem to be getting away with it. So there's gotta be a way around it. It will behoove you to discover the best way to protect yourself and your work. One way, perhaps, is to write your story into a novel rather than a memoir. In any case, I strongly recommend that you engage an attorney before writing that book.

Your main job in writing the synopsis is to present the theme and scope of your story in a most compelling way so that the publisher can clearly understand the premise and the purpose. He is also extremely interested in your writing skill, so make sure it is the best it can be.

You, the Memoirist

The "about the author" portion of your book proposal will resemble those of most other book proposals. The publisher is interested in your writing/ publishing experience. He'll want to know if you have published before. Give details.

What is your educational background? Here's also where you'll share your achievements and accomplishments in areas that relate to this project. The publisher is interested in your aptitude, skills, and abilities within the writing/publishing realm as well as marketing and promotion. Are your achievements and experience as a public speaker of interest to the publisher? Will he be impressed by the fact that you started your own business from scratch and now employ 100 people? Will he be glad to hear that you come from a marketing background, but have recently retired, so have plenty of time to promote this book? Absolutely, yes!!! Also list your affiliations related to business, marketing, and the theme of your book.

The Market

A memoir by an unknown is a hard sell. The non-celebrity memoir is not the most popular type of book around. I'd venture to guess that memoirs fail more than any other type of book. And that's mainly because the author is typically an inexperienced writer and does not understand what it takes to promote a book.

The first step in successful publishing is to write a viable book. Next, identify your target audience: find out who they are, where they are, and figure out how to approach them. There may not be many people interested in your personal struggle with shingles, but hundreds who would read your story in order to gain some insight or tips for themselves or a loved one about this painful ailment.

There are people who want to know more about others in related fields or those pursuing similar lifestyles. They will read books about someone's struggle to recover from brain trauma, a couple's love affair, or an incredible climb up the corporate ladder, for example. There are armchair travelers who enjoy reading travel memoirs and pet lovers who will read every true story involving animals they can find. There are also a lot of readers of adventure stories—fiction and nonfiction. And if your story has a strong ethnic or hobby aspect, you have readers in that area—Italian, Brazilian,

Russian, or antique car collecting, modern-day ranching, or community gardening, for example.

The key audience for a memoir could be what you would initially consider the secondary audience—those with an interest, not in the individual, but in some aspect of the lifestyle. It may be no easy task in some cases, but it is a highly important one, to come up with some solid figures indicative of readers for your book. In the process of this exercise, which can take hours of research, you might discover a way to garner an even larger audience. Your story might focus on your family's escape from a war-torn country with a prized piece of art. During your research, you may find a whole movement interested in art of that period. This could be a viable market for your book. What if your story features your father's life as a thoroughbred horse trainer? Through research, you may locate organizations dedicated to horse racing and several forums on the sport where you could promote this book.

What does it take to sell a memoir? You must touch a chord with the reader. If he or she finds you fascinating, is curious about your life, or has an interest in a theme running through your book, perhaps he or she is a prospective customer. Just remember this: no one will buy a book they don't know exists. It takes a whole lot of exposure to sell any book—even more so to sell a memoir by an unknown.

Note: Don't forget to check out memoir clubs, organizations, and blog sites dedicated to people who like reading memoirs. How many are there? What types of books do they read? Why would they possibly be interested in your book?

Competing and Complementary Books

Here's where you find out if there is a market for your memoir. What else is out there like this book and how are they selling? If other books similar to yours are successful, perhaps yours has potential, as well.

Locate five or six books to use in making your case that there is a market for this type of travel memoir or military family legacy, etc. Select at least a few published by large companies. You might find books similar to yours among those listed at memoir book clubs, at blogs dedicated to memoir, and in local and online bookstores.

Provide the title, author, publisher, publication date, ISBN, format, page number, and price for each book. Describe each book and its similarities to your book. Provide evidence of the other book's success, and explain why you believe your book would appeal to the same audience.

Give sales figures if you can, or note the books' Amazon rankings or some other indication of their success. It's not always easy to get sales figures, but you might learn something about the popularity of a particular memoir at the publisher's or author's websites. Become a snoop. It could pay off big-time. If you discover that a similar book written by a noncelebrity has soared in popularity within a short time, this could bode well for you and your book where the publisher or agent is concerned.

How Will You Promote Your Memoir?

Again, if you are new to the concept of writing for publication, even if you have a marketing background, you may not understand the concept of book promotion. Books do not sell themselves. Producing a book does not ensure that it will sell—that someone (or a lot of someones) will scramble to buy it. Ask any published author and they will tell you that it takes a lot of time, energy, creativity, ingenuity, and sometimes money to sell books.

You might meet authors who blame their publisher, agent, cover designer, editor, minister, brother-in-law, or best friend when their book isn't selling. That's because they don't understand that promotion is up to them. It is the author's responsibility and this is true whether you produce the book yourself, hire a self-publishing company, or land a traditional publisher.

So, how will you convince the publisher that you can successfully promote your book? What are your marketing plans? This is what you will discuss in this section. You might be tempted to say that you will set up book signings at the few local bookstores that are left. You'll get reviews in newspapers countywide. You'll go out and speak when invited. No, no, no.

Publishers know that these activities are pretty much opportunities of the past. If you could say, "My sister manages the local Barnes and Noble and can arrange for signings in stores throughout the state," "My father owns the local radio station and will promote the events," and/or "I'm an advanced Toastmaster and regularly speak to groups of up to 800 throughout the country," that would be meaningful. Publishers want something as close to a guarantee as they can get when it comes to your understanding of and your aptitude, skill, and connections for promoting your book.

If you do not have these advantages and you lack an understanding of book promotion, it's time to launch a study. This should be at the top of your to-do list. Then begin a campaign to learn how other memoirists are promoting their books. Start with those in your writing group and your online forums. Locate websites for memoirists and check out their media pages. Where are they speaking, having their books reviewed, and otherwise getting publicity? Incorporate some of these ideas into your marketing plan.

Earlier in the book proposal, you identified your potential readers and determined where you can find them. Take this into consideration when outlining your marketing plan. What is the best way to approach these readers? What sites do they visit? Where do they buy their books? What influences them to buy certain books—Amazon reviews, recommendations at their favorite blog sites or websites, reviews in the newsletters they read, getting to know the author through her blog site and social media sites? This is your opportunity to use the information you gathered for the "market" section and formulate a valid and workable marketing plan to present to the publisher.

Note: Read the promotions sections in other chapters throughout this book for additional book marketing ideas.

The Memoirist's Platform

By now, the publisher knows something about you, your skills, and your marketing savvy. He knows a little about your proposed marketing plan. Here's your chance to dazzle him with your qualifications and connections that will be paramount in promoting and selling copies of your memoir.

Describe your specific skills related to marketing. List any connections you have that will give you a leg up when it comes to promoting your book. If yours is an ethnic memoir and you are the director of a large organization encompassing this culture, be sure to tell the publisher. The fact that there are, for example, 10,000 members throughout the world—5,000 active—will certainly get his attention. Maybe you have a list of 3,000 businesses owned and managed by people of this ethnic group. This would be a huge plus in the publisher's mind.

Re-read chapter 2 of this book to refresh your memory as to how the publisher thinks when it comes to choosing a project. Then, list your most impressive attributes and skills. If you don't believe that your array of skills will give the publisher enough confidence in you as the marketing agent for your book, or if you don't have any marketing sense and prefer not to learn, as is the case with many memoirists, start interviewing book publicists and marketing companies to help you develop a plan and a promise that you can present to potential publishers.

Just be warned that if you hire a publicist, you *will* be involved in promoting your book. A publicist will likely book radio and podcast interviews for you, set up speaking engagements and book signings in bookstores and specialty stores, arrange for you to be interviewed for active blog sites, and so forth. And the fees could be $3,000/month or more.

It's best that you take time out from your busy schedule or that you take steps to shed your shroud of shyness and adopt the mindset and skills needed to promote your own book.

Chapter Summaries for Your Memoir

Your memoir may or may not be broken down into chapters. If not, simply summarize the entire book by breaking it into reasonable sections. The story of your childhood could cover one section. Your troubled adolescence might be in the next. Your bout with depression as a young adult might be in the third section and your recovery in the fourth.

If this is a travel memoir, the breaks can represent countries (or cities) visited, different trips, etc.

Again, describe what goes into each section or chapter. Keep your summaries to about 100 to 400 words, longer if you are breaking your story into just three or four sections. If you absolutely need more room, of course, use it. This is not where you tell your story, it's where you summarize it. Use a technique similar to the style of writing in your book. Certainly, include interesting phrases and dialogue where appropriate. The point of the chapter outline or chapter summaries is to familiarize the publisher with the scope and flow of your book.

Your Sample Chapters

A publisher might ask to see the first twenty to fifty pages of your memoir or a couple of sample chapters. Be sure to send them only after you've self-edited as thoroughly as possible *and* you've hired a qualified editor. You may have heard that if a publisher accepts your project, he will run it by his editorial staff. Yes, he will. But this does not mean that he wants to receive an inferior, incomplete, sloppy manuscript. Many publishers say right in their submission guidelines, "Have your manuscript professionally edited before submitting."

Which sample chapters should you send? I suggest the first one, as it should provide a great introduction to your project and give a clear sampling of your writing style and the tone of the story. Begin your book with a snappy, attention-grabbing lead. Avoid like the plague a mundane first sentence such as, "This is the story of my life from age three to seventy-three. I was born the second of four boys. . . ." After reading a lead-in like this, it's likely that the publisher will not finish the first page, let alone the first paragraph.

Here's a lead-line that I heard once in a speech: A Caucasian man stood at the front of the room and announced, "I was born a black baby." It would be hard to pull that off in a book. But it sure worked during a live presentation. The audience was eager and curious to hear more.

Most memoirs are made up of several chapters that serve to move the story along—that provide background and historical information, for example. Then there are action-packed or emotionally-charged chapters. So along with your first chapter, I suggest sending the one (or two) where the story climaxes, or those with the most action, or that best represent the theme of the story.

(Refer to chapters 3 and 4 for additional information regarding the basic book proposal.)

A Proposal for Your Travel Book

A travel book, just like a memoir, comes in many shapes, styles, and formats. In fact, your travel book might actually be a travel memoir. You can tell your travel story, write a travel guide, create a picture book of a city or country, or offer advice for other travelers who want to visit certain areas—the best mode of travel, sights to see, cautions, etc. There are potential travelers who want to learn about hitchhiking or biking in a particular foreign country from someone who has done it. I know an avid desert traveler who wrote a series of books featuring little-known towns and stopovers in the deserts of California. I met an author who wrote a book about his travels to Europe with his cat.

I actually wrote a sort of travel memoir when I returned from a four-day adventure in Dubai. I edited a book on traveling in China—the good, the bad, and the ugly—and I've been working with an author on a serious hiker's guide to wilderness areas in central California. I also edited a book for a travel agent who wrote about some of her more interesting travels in parts of Italy.

If you're writing a book for avid, curious, or even armchair travelers, and you want to land a publisher, you may be required to write a book proposal. But first, you must decide on a slant. What are the possibilities? You can:

- Share your travel experiences—a memoir.
- Offer tips to others who want to travel in this area or in this way (hiking, biking, on a cruise ship, etc.).
- Write a detailed guide to the area or simply give your impressions.

- Focus your book on a specific element of the place—the churches, architecture, plant life, wildlife, people, or money-saving tips, for example.
- Compile a travel book around food—using recipes from the region or reviewing the best restaurants.
- Put together a photo gallery of the place and create a coffee-table book.
- Write about general travel—packing techniques, lost luggage issues, staying healthy while traveling, traveling with kids, pet-friendly travel, etc.
- Report on a major festival or event in a city or those in several cities throughout the United States or world.

There are as many ways to write a travel book as there are travelers. I once wrote a book proposal for a book on your travel attitude—how to develop a vacation outlook or frame of mind and truly *get away* when traveling. (Never did find a publisher for that one.)

So how does a proposal for a travel book look? Presumably like a professional document designed to sway a publisher to issue a contract. Here are some standards, ideas, and tips.

The Cover Letter

Naturally, you'll select a publisher of travel books. Just make sure you approach the right publishers. You'll notice that some specialize in guides rather than personal stories. Others might appreciate travel memoirs. Yet others focus on specific countries or even states. These are regional publishers. You'll find food-related travel books published by cookbook publishers, travel photo books published by those that specialize in coffee-table books, and you might find books featuring architecture or family travel produced by publishers other than travel book publishers. So spend some time studying the publishing possibilities for your book. Start by locating books similar to the one you propose and contact those publishers.

When introducing your book to a publisher, demonstrate in your cover letter that you know something about his list of books. You might say, "When I noticed that you published John Doe's book on bicycle travel in Egypt, I was pretty sure you'd want to see my similar book featuring family motor-biking in Scotland's rural communities."

Give a few highlights and a peek into your marketing ideas for this book. Presumably, you've spent some time studying the book you mentioned—maybe you've even communicated with the author to learn some of his techniques and ideas.

Sure, you'll cover all of this in subsequent sections of your proposal, but why not take advantage of your cover letter—your opportunity to introduce your project—to whet the publisher's appetite?

Briefly describe your experiences traveling within the region you want to write about and using the mode of travel you're focusing on, for example. If your book features African safaris, definitely include a little of your background in this area. You might say, for example, "I've been on ten African safaris since I was ten years old, and I have volumes of tips and advice for the first-timer to Africa." Or, "This was my first safari and I want to share every detail of it with those who are considering one."

Reveal your vision for the book and who your audience is. If you have a hot idea for promoting the book, mention that. For example, you might say, "I belong to a safari club, I'm on the board at the San Diego Zoo, and I'm a travel agent specializing in African travel. You can count on me to promote this book to all 4,500 of my related contacts."

Choose a Title for Your Travel Book

Your travel book title will likely include the place name. If it features a specialty type of travel or a specific focus, include this in your title, as well. *How to Do Italy on $20/Day. Amazing Architecture in the Middle East. One Family's European Cruise Ship Saga. Guide to Hostels in Europe.*

The Travel Synopsis

There are many directions to go with a travel book and millions of potential readers hungering for information, tips, and stories. The travel book arena provides a wide-open opportunity for those who can write, are highly observant and curious, can absorb what they take in and share it in an interesting manner, and are good with directions and descriptions, for example. You should be a good researcher and somewhat assertive. When you decide to write a book on your experiences or travel in a certain region, you'll need to reach out and ask questions in order to compile the whole story of a place, an event, the people, etc.

I have a friend who sometimes travels without luggage. She buys clothes from thrift stores once she arrives at her destination, and donates them back when she leaves. Now this concept might make a good story. She could write a humorous book detailing her experiences and those of others, with photographs and tips for thrift-store travel.

I met a man on a tour to the Channel Islands off the California coast who, with this trip, had fulfilled his goal of visiting all fifty-nine US national parks. Now, he could write a book from a variety of angles—his personal impressions, a description and highlights of each, his journey from start to finish, his recommendation for other travelers who wanted to accomplish this feat, and so forth. This book could feature a collection of photographs or poetry, a study of family travel to these sites, or it could focus on the personal travel goals of a dozen different people and describe how they were met.

Here's another travel book idea: I have a friend who's writing a book on fishing spots throughout the Northwest. You could write one featuring collectors' paradises for those who collect seashells, sea glass, antiques, rocks and gems, or dining, wilderness, or animal refuge experiences, for example.

Once you've established your style, your focus, and your way of organizing your book, you're ready to write the synopsis. Describe your book and its value to your proposed readers. What is the theme and the purpose? Explain why you have chosen the topic, slant, and format. Presumably part of the reason is the popularity of other books on this topic or for this audience.

Who would read a book like this? The publisher is probably savvy on this point. He knows who buys this type of travel book. So don't try to fool him by saying something stupid like, "This book is for everyone who ever visited, has wanted to visit, or has even heard of England." If your book is viable, it has an audience. You need to find out exactly who would most likely read this book and why. Who reads other books on your topic or in the vein of yours? You can get an idea from following blogs related to this topic, region, or theme (be sure to read the comments); initiating dialogue with blog visitors and other authors of similar books; and establishing your own blog early on and seeing who it attracts, for example.

Once you have completed your synopsis, ask others to read it and report their impressions back to you. Can they describe your book accurately after reading your synopsis? Do they have questions about the proposed content of your book or your audience? Listen and learn. If readers seem to have trouble understanding your intentions, your synopsis (and maybe your entire concept) needs tweaking.

Sometimes this exercise causes an ah-ha moment for the author. He suddenly realizes that his original idea is weak—he needs to consider an additional or different element to his planned book. And this is usually a good thing. You're fortunate if you become aware of a flaw in your project before it lands on the publisher's desk.

Why You as the Author?

This section should be a slam dunk. You're probably writing this book because you visited the place or experienced the event or phenomenon. You have an intimacy with the place or the people. Presumably, you have a unique perspective that you want to share with others. These are the things you would bring to the publisher's attention.

It would help if you also have some writing/publishing experience. If it's related to the book you propose, all the more impressive. For example, maybe you've written several travel articles, you're a published author of similar books, and/or you teach writing classes at a college.

You would include your education, achievements, and accomplishments here. Are you a well-educated, professional person? Do you work in the travel industry? Maybe you are an editor of a travel magazine. Do you maintain a travel blog? Put yourself in the publisher's position. What does he want to know about the author of a book before he agrees to invest in it?

The Market Section for Your Travel Book

As we discussed earlier in this chapter, your readers are those interested in the region or theme you are writing about—the history of a particular city; buildings from a certain period; specific sights—landmarks, historical, or natural; the culture; or money-saving travel tips, for example.

Clearly identify your audience and their reasons for being interested in a book on this topic. Where do they go to locate other such books and information? Are there websites and blog sites dedicated to this topic or theme? Are there statistics anywhere online showing how many people buy travel books or material on a particular country or aspect of traveling? Do an Internet search using keywords or phrases such as, "how many people travel to India," or "number of American travelers to India," or "top information center for travel material" or "hiking tips."

You have an interesting phenomenon with this topic. As mentioned earlier, there are people who travel and those who want to but can't or don't. There are avid readers and researchers among both groups of people—those who collect every tidbit of information about a place before traveling and those known as armchair travelers. Presumably, your book on hiking through Colorado, the best whitewater rafting trips in the United States, how to enjoy Europe on a budget, things to do and places to see in France, or little-known hideaways and getaways along America's back roads will attract both.

Maybe you love exquisite wines and enjoy visiting wineries, or you're a sun worshipper, climber, or animal lover. If your book focuses on wineries, beaches, mountains, or wildlife refuges, for example, your primary audience might be people who share your specific interest.

If your book has a family theme—how to travel happily and healthily with toddlers or family-friendly tours to Europe, for example—your audience will also include parents who love to travel or are contemplating a trip. Make sure to recognize any secondary audiences for your book. Also consider those folks who live in the area or who used to live there. If your book includes some history of the place, profiles of some of the businesses, and a good description of local attractions, for example, locals might buy a copy to keep and some to give as gifts.

Women typically buy more books than men, so one way to ramp up potential sales might be to give your travel book a female edge. Feature quaint shops, botanical gardens, luxury neighborhoods, and home tours one can take in this city, for example.

My book, *The Ojai Valley: An Illustrated History*, is popular with locals, visitors, former residents, descendants of pioneer families, and even genealogists and researchers. It covers the history of the valley as well as local businesses, old buildings, long-held events and organizations, and so forth. I also feature profiles of early pioneers and I introduce current tourist attractions. As you can see, there's something for everyone who has an interest or an investment in this area.

Avoid getting too carried away listing the various potential readers. In the case of my local history book, I might list as my primary audience locals, tourists and others with a tie to Ojai (descendants of pioneers, etc.). The secondary market would be history buffs, researchers, and genealogists.

In order to demonstrate how many people this might involve, I could give the population of the valley. I'd mention that I interviewed over one hundred people for this book and all of them, plus another one or two hundred pioneers and organization leaders, are mentioned within the pages. I would give the number of tourists to this town each year and illustrate the interest here in local history by mentioning the number of historical library, museum, and historical society members and donors, for example.

Note: The more people involved in your book project, the more potential sales you have right out of the chute. Presumably, everyone listed or named in the book will buy at least one copy and probably more for friends and family.

Competition

Finding competing and complementary books should be relatively easy for a travel book, even if it has a secondary theme woven throughout. Your primary theme might be travel to Europe, and your secondary one European architecture. Or it might be a book about traveling with pets. First, you'll seek out books exactly like yours. If there are several in this category—European travel and architecture, for example—perhaps you should consider tweaking your book idea.

Study the other books. Does yours include a significant difference? Maybe all of the other books focus on London, for example, and you have pinpointed a dozen amazing buildings from several different cities. In this case, choose one or two of the bestselling European travel books as well as a couple featuring the architecture.

Perhaps your book focuses on the food of the region or traveling with pets. Look for books exactly like yours. If you can't find any, choose a few that are as close to your idea as possible. This might be a book on pet-friendly hotels or a French cuisine cookbook, for example. If this is as close as you can get to your book, these are the books you would use.

But I have to warn you—make sure you are not short-changing the publisher with your interpretation and choices here. He is in the business of publishing travel books—perhaps even specific books such as travel books for pet owners. He has a pretty good idea of what's already out there. If you don't do a thorough job with your market analysis or you purposely choose not to mention a book that is very similar to yours, you could wreck your chances with this publisher.

Be professional. Remember, you are the CEO of your book. If you discover that the market is flooded with books like the one you propose, shift gears. If you can't justify approaching the publisher with a blatant clone of another book, change something about your book. Continue your research into books on this topic and discover what is missing. How could you fill a potential need?

Once you determine your book's topic, theme, slant, and purpose, choose five or six appropriate competing and complementary books to compare with yours. List the title, author, publisher, date of publication, page number, and ISBN, and describe the book in fifty words or so. Is this book popular? Can you give an idea of its popularity? Explain how this book is similar to yours and how yours is different—better.

Your job here is to convince the publisher that your book is worth producing.

How Will You Promote Your Travel Book?

There are dozens of methods to successfully promote a good travel book. If it has an audience, you should be able to find them through a number of traditional and creative means. Presumably, by the time you reach this section of your book proposal, you will have ferreted out several specific promotional avenues. Here are a few ideas:

- Contact travel agents through an email blast or a targeted mailing and introduce your book.
- Visit and participate in blogs and websites directed at travel agents and travelers. Ask them to recommend your book to their visitors and clients.
- Attend travel shows throughout the United States and hand out your promo material to agents and booth visitors.
- Secure a booth at travel shows where you can sell your book.
- Secure a booth at book festivals and events related to your book's secondary theme.
- Contact columnists for newspaper travel columns and ask for an interview or a review.

- Get a list of travel book reviewers. Send each of them your promo material and ask for a review.
- Contact editors of travel magazines about reviews and/or offer to write an article for them.
- Do a blog tour of travel-related blogs and those related to your secondary theme—parenting, pets, photography, etc. Comment at these blogs, ask to be interviewed, and/or volunteer to be a guest blogger. Some bloggers also review appropriate books.
- Get involved in travel clubs and organizations. Promote your book through whatever means they present—announcements in their newsletters, having your book featured at their websites, etc.
- Arrange a speaking schedule locally and where you'll be traveling. Sell your books in the back of the room.
- Establish your own website and blog site and offer daily or weekly perks for visitors. This might involve contests, prize giveaways, resources related to the theme of your book, and so forth. Update your website regularly so potential customers will visit often and potential readers will find you.

Your Platform

Now that you have a start on a marketing plan, it's time to consider your platform—your following, your connections, your way of attracting readers. What skills, time, and energy can you bring to the table when it comes to promoting your book? Do you have marketing experience you can use in promoting your book? Do you travel frequently? Can you set up signings and presentations while traveling? Do you know people who can get you gigs at conventions, travel and trade shows, on radio and TV, and so forth? Perhaps you're well known as a travel writer or you do a travel segment on a major television or radio station.

All of this would be extremely helpful in securing a publishing contract. If the publisher loves your book idea and is impressed and pleased by your fabulous marketing plan and platform, the next step would be to show him the money.

Describe the results of programs you've presented over the years to eager travelers, for example. Have you given lectures or workshops on this theme before? If not, do so before submitting your proposal. Then you'll have evidence of this book's potential. Think about it: saying, "I will present workshops throughout the tri-counties to people interested in traveling more conveniently, lighter, and at a lower cost," isn't as convincing as the following: "I have presented workshops to my potential audience numerous times over the last two years. We typically attract fifty to 100 attendees. I just started presenting this workshop online and have had hundreds of inquiries and 250 sign-ups so far."

Perhaps you can see how important it is to have a strong platform before you ever decide to write a book. If you don't have one, establish and build one before approaching publishers.

Chapter Summaries for Your Travel Book

This exercise is designed to show the publisher that your book is well organized and that you have captured every aspect of your topic as promised in your synopsis. If your book is broken into chapters, list each of them, insert the title of the chapter, where appropriate, and describe what each chapter will include.

Will you use photographs or other illustrations? Note your intentions at the end of each chapter summary. It's not necessary to include every detail that will go into that chapter. Just give an overview of what the chapter encompasses, the names of pertinent cities, towns, attractions, and waterways in that region, for example, how you plan to approach the information and what will be included—identification of native plants and trees, recreational activities, eateries, hostels, and so forth. Will you provide maps?

Your intent should be to familiarize the publisher with the material, information, flow, and tone of each chapter in a context that will help him to see the big picture you're attempting to paint.

Sample Chapters

Choose one or two chapters that best capture the scope of the book and your vision for it. If it is a guidebook, include a chapter that shows how you plan to present the details of guided tours and recommendations. If it is an all-inclusive travel exposé of your travel experiences, the publisher will want to know that you can express yourself well and lay out your book logically. Send him one or two chapters that demonstrate these qualities as well as your writing ability.

Maybe your focus is the architecture of a region. At least one of your sample chapters should highlight this theme clearly and expertly. When it comes to sample chapters, always lead with your best—those that most adequately express the heart of your project.

(Refer to chapters 3 and 4 for additional information regarding the basic book proposal.)

How to Best Represent
Your Inspirational/Spiritual Book

Many people today have found a way of thinking or way of life that is bringing them more peace and, perhaps, greater success, and they want to share it with the world. So they package their *secrets* to sell. The result might be a book of inspirational messages, spiritual passages, or a daily guide to happy living. Some authors create books that might be considered spiritual memoirs. Others write self-help or how-to books teaching the concept they've discovered and adopted. I've edited several such books and helped many of these authors fine-tune their book proposals.

Do you need an agent for your inspirational or spiritual book? If you work within the field or area of your book (you teach self-hypnosis or conduct workshops on an aspect of your proposed book, for example), if you are a frequent presenter at conferences nation- or worldwide, if you have done other writing on this topic, and if you are known by thousands of people (either within this field or as a celebrity), then yes. You could probably garner the attention of a major publisher and you should have an agent working on your behalf.

If, on the other hand, you have never been published, you do not consider yourself a writer, you are not involved in social media, you have no background related to the theme of your book, and you have few affiliations, you probably won't be able to attract an agent. If you hope to work with a well-respected publisher, you'll most likely have to prove yourself and your project before he'll consider it. It's possible. Others before you have successfully done so.

You may know of people who have created a brand through a company, organization, or even a concept related to spiritual self-improvement, for example, or established an empire teaching a unique thought process. Once they are established, then comes the book. A book from this author could be a major publisher's cup of tea, and the author would definitely seek agent representation.

If you're interested in the branding process, you could build your brand any number of ways. Start by establishing a blog, a website, and a social media presence. Sure, there are millions of blogs, websites, and social media pages out there, and most of them go ignored. But this doesn't have to be your experience. Do a major Internet search to find other sites related to inspirational and spiritual messages. Visit those blogs and websites and take note of the site owner's techniques and methods. Pay close attention to those sites that are most active—the bloggers post regularly and they attract a lot of visitors and comments, for example. Leave comments and ask to be a guest blogger or to be interviewed.

Spread the word at these blog sites and related websites, as well as at your Twitter, Facebook, etc. pages about your blog and your website once they're up and running. Post often, post messages that relate to your prospective book's theme, and keep your site interesting and useful to your proposed audience.

Establish workshops or start carrying your message to audiences everywhere. Advertise heavily when you have a gig. You know better than anyone else who your audience is and where you'll find them.

Locate newsletters that carry elements of your message (those that go out to your potential readers). Ask if you can submit articles. At the end of the article, of course, provide a link to your blog/website.

Once you've developed a following (it could take months or years), then you have a stronger case to use when trying to convince an agent or publisher to take on your project.

Some authors test-market their books. Once you're satisfied that you have a superior product, self-publish it and promote, promote, promote. If it does well in the marketplace, you may be able to snag the publisher of your choice.

The Cover Letter
When you're ready to send a proposal to an agent or publisher, don't hold back on your credentials. Those related to a book of this type should be

placed up front and personal. The cover letter is a great place to start listing them.

Pretty much across the board, if you do not have the right kind of qualifications to share related to the theme of your proposed book, you may be rejected time and time again. And some of the rejection might come before your proposal is read all the way through. In other words, if you are new to writing and publishing and if you are not a known guru, counselor, or speaker within the realm of your inspirational or spiritual message, you probably won't get a publishing contract. Publishers of inspirational and spiritual material can sell books by celebrities and big name spiritual teachers, for example, but those by unknowns are difficult to market. An exception would be an author who has had a near death experience, for example.

There are thousands—maybe millions—of authors launching books of a spiritual nature. While this is a fairly strong market, a new *message* book by an unknown author is a hard sell, indeed. Readers trust authors they know or have heard of. And, while the public will read books recommended by other readers and reviewers, publishers are reluctant to invest in a new author who might not know how to get his or her name out there. This is a tough market for a newbie to break into with any sort of new concept or alleged authoritative book.

Again, unless you have an absolutely great idea that will be welcomed by the masses (of course you think you do), you are well known, or your co-author is Shirley Maclaine, the Dalai Lama, or James Redfield (*Celestine Prophecy*), for example, I recommend you start working on your platform.

Presuming you have a platform, this will be the meat of your cover letter. The concept for your book is important, too—but, in this case, identifying the *who* just might prompt the agent or publisher to want to know more about the *what*.

Your Inspirational Title

Before slapping a cool title on your spiritual or inspirational book, think about your target audience. What do they want to know, to read, to hear, to learn, to understand? Certainly, you thought about this before etching your book in stone. If not, go back to the drawing board and start over. Put your audience first. Direct your information/material to a specific audience. Speak to them. And let your title speak to them, as well.

This is not to say you can't write a personal story, for example. But the point of producing a book is to have it read. So, even with a spiritual or inspirational memoir, you want your book and your title to speak to your proposed audience.

Let's say you've written a book featuring spirituality and money—in an attempt to help people look at money from a less intense perspective. This book might be called *How to Make Friends with Your Cash*. Or *Tame Your Money Rage and Enjoy Greater Riches*. Or *Love Your Money*. For a book of daily inspirations or inspirational messages for special occasions, consider *A Spiritual Counselor's Guide to a More Inspirational Life* or *Inspirational Writings from a Master Reiki Therapist*. Perhaps you aren't widely known by name, but your title might certainly carry some clout.

The Synopsis

My recommendation for a spiritual or inspirational book synopsis is very much like that of any other synopsis. Describe the focus and slant of your book, the purpose, and, where important, your reason for writing it. When the publisher or agent finishes reading your synopsis, he or she should have a clear picture of the book's content, the way it will be presented, and your proposed readership.

Don't skimp on this last section—your intended target audience. Include statistics and evidence to back up your extensive research. Too much information in this area is better than too little. So you might explain who reads books like this, why and where they buy them, hang out, learn about books in this category, and so forth.

Paint a complete picture for the publisher or agent. You don't want him moving on to the next section of the proposal with questions about the book's content and the proposed readers. You especially don't want him tossing your proposal aside because your synopsis is too complex, too brief, too skimpy, too weak, or otherwise lame.

Spiritual and inspirational topics can be difficult to explain and describe. One way to help with this dilemma is to become clear on the value of your message to readers. Explain how your book will help, enlighten, cheer, entertain, and/or delight your reader. While your topic may be a bit vague, as this theme can be, you must be crystal clear as you develop the synopsis for your book.

Is it a book of inspirational messages or is it in story form? How are the messages organized? What is the point of the story? Is it a parable? Is it your story? How is it intended to help, inspire, or enlighten your readers? What is your method of presenting it?

If you know of a book similar to the one you propose or you've written yours in the tone of a famous author, reveal this in your synopsis. Sure, you'll write a market analysis as part of your proposal, but if this information is vital, include it here, as well.

Since platform matters so much in a book of this type, repeat the most important aspects of your platform in the synopsis. This could be key in capturing the publisher's keen interest.

About the Author

Here, you will introduce yourself to the publisher or agent—who you are, what you do, the extent of your education, your pertinent accomplishments and achievements, and just about anything else that relates to the theme of your proposed book. If this book is purely a result of your personal life lessons or it came to you in a dream, for example, mention this. And then explain it in a way that may intrigue the publisher.

As mentioned earlier, a book of this type needs some credibility behind it. It might not be impossible, but much more difficult to land a publisher, even for a good book with a good premise and message, if you are not known within the field of spirituality and enlightenment. However, if you have an inspirational story to tell related to a phenomenal personal experience, perhaps this might be enough to grab a major publisher's attention.

Another way to make points with a large publisher is to partner with a co-author who is known in the field or interest of your inspirational or spiritual book.

You still have options beyond the majors, however. There are hundreds of small publishers—some that specialize in books like yours. Approach them with your proposal. Most of them prefer working with authors who do not have agent representation.

The Market

You've already mentioned your audience a couple of times. In case the publisher didn't notice, here's your opportunity to give additional details about who's likely to read this book once it's published. This might be people seeking a better way of life, a more meaningful existence, or increased enlightenment. Readers in this category might be considered seekers. Perhaps your book would attract people with mood disorders, recovering alcoholics/drug users, those being treated for depression, and so forth.

Once you clearly identify your target audience—those who would most likely read your book—find out something about them. Do they frequent counseling centers, pharmacies, psychologists' offices, religious institutions, and/or medical clinics? If you're not sure, test your idea before completing your proposal. Show your synopsis and table of contents to spiritual and life counselors, religious leaders, psychologists, healers, and AA leaders. What is their impression of your project? Would they recommend this book to their patients, clients, or followers?

While you're at it, ask for endorsements. You might get some wonderful responses and you don't want them to go to waste. Ask the minister or Reiki master if you can use their positive comment on your book cover and your promo material. Be sure to include it in your proposal, as well. If you can't influence the publisher to accept your book by your own volition, bring in the big guns. A heartfelt endorsement by the leader of a large congregation or a well-known psychologist in a major city is gold.

Competing and Complementary Spiritual Books

Choosing books to compare with yours might be tricky because there are so many books in this category and so many different slants. Your job is to locate the books typically read by your target audience. If your book fits a solid mold, this might not be such a difficult task. Your book featuring 365 inspirational messages for seniors who love cats would presumably be read by seniors (and others) who own and adore cats. A book of spiritual guidance for mid-life women suffering from depression will attract women in their forties who have some form of depression.

Search for organization websites and forums your readers would visit. Check out blogs by counselors, healers, and individuals related to the key components of your book. Often, you'll see a page featuring recommended books, or individuals will comment about the books they've read. Conduct a search using the key words in your book title or the theme of your book and locate other books on this topic.

Select five or six that most closely resemble yours—that cover the same material, have a similar format, and have the same purpose. Write a fifty- or 100-word description of each book and explain how yours is different/ better. How will your book more successfully, more completely, or more joyfully affect your readers? Think *benefits* rather than *features*. Features describe aspects of the book. Benefits are what the reader gains from reading the book.

Once you've written this section, look back at the books you've used in your comparisons. Is your book truly more useful, up-to-date, interesting, reader-friendly, fun, lively, well organized, than the others? If it is simply a cookie cutter of what's already out there, you're wise to step back, take another look at your book, and possibly shift gears a little. If this is your decision, it's best to take this step before you complete your proposal. You want to approach the publisher with your best shot the first time, because you may never get a second chance.

If your book truly does offer what your audience requires and desires, move forward with your proposal.

Promotion for Your Religious/Inspirational Book

You may have mentioned some of your promotional plans and ideas briefly in previous sections of your book proposal, but here is where you will bring it all together. You'll outline those things you've done already to promote your book or in preparation for promoting it. Explain what kind of response you've received so far. Describe what worked and why. Certainly, point out how you will use this information and experience when it comes time to promote your published book.

List promotional activities you have lined up and those you plan to engage in. Be specific—"The owner of Changing Times, a spiritual/religious store chain, has invited me to do a signing at each location once the book is published." Or tell the publisher you plan to secure a booth at a large metaphysical and holistic fair scheduled in a nearby large city. You might offer this: "I know a few authors with similar books. Together they sold forty-seven books at the event last year, and one of them was invited to appear on a local TV talk show."

Before attempting to develop this portion of your book proposal, study at least one good book on book promotion. I always suggest *Promote Your Book: Over 250 Proven, Low-Cost Tips and Techniques for the Enterprising Author* (Allworth Press). In order to write a meaningful, believable marketing plan, you really must understand what it takes to successfully promote a book. Book promotion is an ongoing commitment. You can't expect to do a promotional blast and then step back and wait for the royalty checks to start rolling in. Your books will sell only for as long as you are willing to promote them. That's why it's important to have a pre-publication marketing plan, a current plan, and a plan for the future. We've discussed some of the activities you can pursue and set up prior to publication. Now let's concentrate on the activities you can engage in once the book is published:

- Contact local bookstores and engage in a consignment agreement.
- Follow up with those people who invited you to speak before their groups or who agreed to review your book.
- Seek out additional book reviewers. Locate them through directories of reviewers, do an Internet search for reviewers of books in your book's category. Find out who has reviewed similar books and contact them. (See the resource list in this book for lists of directories of reviewers.)
- Contact all of the bloggers you've been following and ask them to review your book, or to mention it in a post, or to interview you for their blog site.
- Follow up with reviewers to make sure they post their reviews at their sites, at Amazon, GoodReads, and others.
- Contact some of the specialty religious/spiritual bookstores across the United States. Send them your promo material and ask if they would carry your book. Promise to follow up by promoting your book in that area—have the book reviewed in a local publication, send a press release or an article to the local newspaper, and then point readers in the direction of the local bookstore to buy the book.
- If appropriate, research gift shops. Visit as many of them as you can in person with your book.
- Is your book suited to religion-based school and college libraries? If so, contact the librarians.

- Prepare inspirational articles for magazines and promote your book in the bio at the bottom of the piece.
- Read the promotions sections in other chapters of this book to discover additional promotional ideas.

Because you know your audience and their book-buying habits, you should come up with many additional ideas for promoting this book. Just remember two things: go where your readers are and keep on promoting. You might be able to tell which promotional activities are working and which ones aren't. But it's possible that you will never know for sure. That's why it's important that you do your best to keep your book in front of your audience using every method available.

Your Platform

We touched on the subject of your platform earlier in this chapter, so you know a little about what it is and what it takes to develop one. Just remember that if you propose to teach or enlighten readers, you'll need credible credentials or a background in the topic that causes readers to trust you as an expert in this field.

It could be that your book features an otherworldly experience—you died on the operating table or you lived on nothing but faith at the bottom of a cliff for a week after an accident, for example. In these two cases, you are an expert because you lived your story.

How well known are you? Did your story go national? International? That would be a plus. If your story was rather shocking or intriguing, and received widespread media attention, you automatically have a very large potential audience.

Maybe you're a marketing expert. Do you have experience promoting inspirational products? Do you have amazing connections related to the theme of your book? These are the things that make up a strong platform—one that will impress a publisher.

He may also be interested in knowing that you are retiring in a few months and will have the time to spend implementing all of those promotional ideas you outlined in the marketing section of your book proposal. Or, perhaps, that you plan to tour the United States next year and intend to contact radio and TV stations in many cities to promote your book, visiting bookstores and specialty shops all along the way.

Review chapter 2 of this book to remind yourself how a publisher thinks and what elements of your platform will most affect a positive response.

Your Chapter Summaries

The chapter summaries or chapter outline should reveal the progression of your book from beginning to end and clearly demonstrate the slant and focus. Perhaps you share a spiritual message in story form, your book is a collection of inspirational quotes, or each chapter includes a different inspirational story featuring a variety of authors. Describe in 100 to 400 words exactly what will be included in each chapter. Reveal the content of each chapter so the publisher understands the flavor, tone, and flow of your book.

If your spiritual or inspirational book features a message, use the chapter summaries to illustrate how it is presented, what steps are necessary in order to apply the lessons or understand the points, and reveal the expected outcome. View your summaries or outline as a mini-rendition of the book. Make sure it has all of the elements necessary to clearly understand the premise or the promise, but don't muddy it with unnecessary clutter.

There's no need to include every quote or to repeat the chapter word-for-word. Simply explain to the publisher or agent what will go into each chapter, the purpose or meaning of it and, perhaps, copy down one or two quotes as examples, where appropriate. If you plan to interview experts, introduce them in the appropriate chapters and describe their contributions to that chapter.

(Refer to chapters 3 and 4 for additional information regarding the basic book proposal.)

Part Four

Book Proposals for Fiction

M any novelists are unaware that, if they want to be published by a major or even minor publisher, they may also need a book proposal. Most publishers of fiction that I researched require some manner of a book proposal. Often, it is what I'd call an enhanced query letter or a mini–book proposal. (Read more about this concept in chapter 16.)

Sell Your Novel through a Fab Book Proposal

Those of you new to publishing are probably surprised by the whole book proposal concept. If you've been involved in publishing for years, the news that many publishers now require one for fiction may be something you didn't expect.

It used to be that publishers requested proposals for nonfiction before the book was even written, and publishers wanted to see novel manuscripts in their entirety once they'd been professionally edited. Now, many publishers, large and small, expect to see some version of a book proposal for just about every type and genre of book. Why? There are a couple of reasons. One is the huge increase in competition. More people are writing books of all types and the number of readers is not increasing—in fact, it may be decreasing.

The other factor is the marketing issue. Publishers rely more heavily on the author to promote his or her book, no matter the category or genre.

So, when the publisher is faced with several excellent manuscripts, he typically turns to the author before determining where to invest. He wants to know more about the author than if he or she can write and more about the project than simply if it's well written.

A Cover Letter for Fiction

Your cover letter is a formality used to introduce your project. If you sent a basic one-page query letter and you've been invited to submit a more detailed proposal, this is your second chance to make a good first impression. Or, perhaps, you were asked to send the complete manuscript—professionally edited, of course.

Your cover letter should be a condensed representation of your project. Your job is to provide the information the publisher needs in order to make a snap decision (whether to continue reading or not). It must be clear and captivating. Here, you will include your book's genre, the title, a brief synopsis, projected word count, and something about you, the author.

Don't worry about writing the cover letter until you've completed the proposal. Then, pull in the most important information in the most intriguing way and condense it so it fits on one page.

Note: Follow the cover letter with a title page and table of contents for the proposal, not for the book. (See chapter 3 for more about creating your title page and table of contents.)

Here's a sample from an agent's cover letter sent to Skyhorse Publishing from Sorche Elizabeth Fairbank:

> Well, here it is, the manuscript I'm nervous, hopeful, and nearly out of my seat over sending out—I feel it could be that big and that important. *So* glad you're taking a look. Rarely does a novel come my way that makes me think *this, this one could change lives.* I hope that *The Assembler of Parts* will do exactly that. An amazing debut novel many years in the making by pediatrician and director of the Rostropovich Foundation Raoul Wientzen, *The Assembler of Parts* is about a young girl born without thumbs who is on a mission to make sense of her short life.
>
> When Jessica Mary Jackson dies and finds herself in the afterlife, boy is she pissed. It's bad enough that she's dead at age seven, but her life on earth had been no bed of roses, either. Afflicted with Hilgar's Syndrome that robbed her of thumbs, Jess is also missing a number of bones in her forearm, she's deaf, has a hole in her heart, and has only one functioning kidney. Because she's born into a blue-collar Catholic family, Jessica's view of faith is a clear lens of the story. Her understanding of God is that he is the Assembler (because, as it was explained to her, he makes all things), and he simply left out or screwed up on a few things she needed.
>
> Given her handicaps, Jess has had what most would consider a rough time of things. Yet she was loved, deeply and unabashedly. But now she has to sit through viewings of tapes of her life to figure out what it all meant. She is made to helplessly watch as her family, instead of leaning on each other and remembering

her with love and laughter, lashes out, and gets involved in a hateful malpractice case. Jess sees her parents and loved ones turn into ugly and vengeful strangers. *Why?* she asks. *What was the point of my life if only to bring first hardship, then grief, then hatred and rage?* Keep watching, the Assembler tells her.

Although not overtly a religious book, throughout the second half of the novel (told from the afterlife) we see a lot of the Assembler. But I can promise you, he's like no God you've met before. He has a sense of humor (sometimes appearing before Jess without thumbs), he delights in jokes and riddles, and, perhaps above all, he himself is a bit flawed, which is what brings me to the heart of the book—forgiveness. Although the story of Jessica's life, and then death, is a fascinating and richly worded one, it is her ability to forgive that gives the novel soul, and heart. And in addressing the axiom that we're made in His image, the book's angle of God being a little flawed himself— like us—is one that unexpectedly blossoms into a sense of relief, gratitude, and self-forgiveness for the reader. And that, I found, is what makes the book so potentially life enriching and profound. *The Assembler of Parts* is about the power of love, about the power of forgiveness, and about the grace in allowing oneself to be full with one's life, all the good and bad parts together.

I think you'll find Raoul's writing rich and carefully chosen. It is denser in style in the first twenty pages or so, as he writes lyrically of medical terms and conditions. He also does a neat thing with any word that has a time quality, as in the afterlife, time is all at once. All that said, I hope you feel the same way as I do about the reach and potential of this very special, very different novel.

Your Title

The publisher may change your carefully chosen title. But that's okay. Use your title proudly until the time comes when you have a publishing contract. Then you probably won't mind if it's changed.

Just be sure to identify your story or the type of book adequately in your title and/or a subtitle. For my cozy mystery novels, I use the title of the series as my subtitle. The first book in the series, for example, is *Catnapped*. Under the title, I follow with *A Klepto Cat Mystery*. This identifies the genre, it lets readers know there's a cat involved somehow and that the cat is some sort of thief.

As you will notice when you study other novels, titles for fiction are all over the place. Some authors choose titles from a provocative phrase in their story. Others spend weeks sifting through the story trying to come up with an appropriate title. Yet others hit on what they believe is the perfect title even before they start writing the book.

One- and two-word titles seem to be popular for fiction these days. I just saw a movie with a one-word title, *Blended*. Remember the movie *Jaws*? How about *It, Shogun, Hamlet*? Choose a one-word or several-word title. It's up to you. However, I often recommend that fiction writers assemble a team to assist with some of the trickier tasks—such as choosing a title. Bring in your most straightforward, honest friends, trusted colleagues, fellow novelists, and readers with excellent taste and good eyes. Enlist them when you need a little help along the sometimes-rocky journey toward the coveted publishing contract.

The Fiction Synopsis

You are a storyteller and you can write. You should have little trouble handling the synopsis for your amazing novel. Presumably, you have completed your manuscript. When someone asks you about your story, what do you tell them? Are you at a loss as to how to respond? Does the entire story rush to the front of your brain and become a jumble? Are you tempted to start at the beginning and tell the entire story?

It doesn't seem so difficult to write a synopsis until you are squarely faced with the task. Then you wonder, "Where do I start?" "What do I include?" "What should I leave out?" "Shall I reveal the ending?" Here's an exercise that might help. Start by writing an elevator speech—a one- or two-sentence description of your novel. Then work out from there. Some people find it easier to write the synopsis, trim it down, and then devise the elevator speech (or thirty-second commercial).

What exactly is an elevator speech? This phrase relates to how you might introduce or describe your book to someone between floors on an elevator when you have just a scant few minutes. Every author should devise one. Use it when pitching your book to publishers, when talking your book up before it's finished, and to promote your book once it's published.

Your elevator speech or two-sentence intro might say, "This is the story of three women whose friendship and values are tested when they're stranded in an air pocket under a ton of rubble after a massive earthquake."

Once you've nailed your story in a nutshell, your synopsis should be easier to write. There are a couple of ways to start it. Identify your genre early on. This can be done in the process of describing the theme and without distracting from the story. Yes, you've probably declared the genre earlier in the proposal, but it's smart to mention it here in case the publisher decides to read the synopsis first.

Make sure that you have accurately identified your genre. I consider my novels cozy mysteries involving cats. Some reviewers, however, have referred to them as "cozy mysteries on steroids," or "a revved up version of a cozy mystery." So I guess I've stepped outside the standards of this genre just a bit.

This is exactly why we have so many genres now—because authors keep drawing outside the lines. Look at the romance genre. In recent years, we've introduced adventure romance, erotic romance, torrid romance, chick-lit romance, regency romance, and category romance, to name a few. Most of these sub-genres probably emerged from the pens (and imaginations) of authors who wrote outside the box.

Here are examples of opening lines for a fiction synopsis for those who want to introduce their genre early on: "*Tumble Weeds* is a Western romance set in the Kansas prairie, during the wicked summer of 1910." Follow this with a fascinating condensed version of your story. Or how about this, "This young adult fantasy is set in a mystical garden behind the castle walls in Igoria, a mythical city . . ."

A publisher is looking for excellent writing when he views your synopsis, and a cogent story line. If you want him to continue reading beyond the first few lines and really dig into your story, continue with something amazing, tantalizing, clever, and/or alluring. You might have learned the power of the first line where novel writing is concerned. Perhaps you actually started your adventure or mystery/suspense or thriller with an attention-grabbing statement. Consider using this technique in your synopsis, as well.

C. Hope Clark wrote what I thought was a memorable first line in her first novel, *Lowcountry Bribe: A Carolina Slade Mystery* (Bell Bridge Books, 2012). She wrote, "O-positive primer wasn't quite the color I had in mind for the small office, but Lucas Sherwood hadn't given the décor a second thought when he blew out the left side of his head with a .45."

Now that's a scene-setter. It paints a picture (pardon the pun). And it is rather startling. Ms. Clark could also use this sentence to start her synopsis.

Or try this, "Emily hates everyone and everything until a stray dog shows up at the homeless shelter where she lives with her mom and baby brother." While I don't suggest copying over a lot of material from your book, using the same strong opening in the synopsis that you used in your book is quite acceptable and, in some cases, advisable.

From there, you want to share the theme and concept of your story. When you're writing fiction, you are advised to show, not tell. Well, for a synopsis, you need to tell—describe your story. What happens in your story? What happens next? Introduce your main characters. Avoid confusing the publisher or agent by bringing a lot of characters into this limited space. And most publishers aren't interested in a lengthy character list—although some appreciate having one. Follow each publisher's guidelines. If the guidelines do not mention a character list, and you decide to create one, add it at the back of the proposal. Do not put a lengthy character list in your synopsis.

Flesh out the story, sharing the highs and lows, the events that drive the story, and the conflicts that make it interesting. Put your story in a generous nutshell without dwelling on boring details and without skimping on the parts of the story that matter emotionally, visually, and intellectually.

Your synopsis might cover a page and a half to four pages. And it may be the hardest thing you've ever written. If you aren't sure you've captured your story in the synopsis or you fear your synopsis is bland, even though the story is rip-roaring exciting, get help with it. Who should you call? A seasoned editor who works with book proposals would be my first choice. But you might have friends with good eyes who could also help.

About You, the Novelist

You've introduced yourself briefly. Here's your chance to shine. The publisher wants to know, is this your first novel? Don't be shy or embarrassed if it is. Many small to medium-size publishers actually advertise that they want to work with first-time authors who have a fresh voice and new ideas.

But the seasoned novelist is generally in greater demand, especially if her books and/or stories are selling. So if you have a horn to toot, definitely do so here. This could garner you a second look.

Here are a few things you will definitely want to include—but only if they apply in your situation: you teach high school English, you've been published in five literary magazines (name them—provide links to the stories), you've written several unpublished novels over the years, some of your manuscripts have won prizes, you lead a series of online book clubs, and/or you share your fiction through your blog and get a lot of positive feedback (provide a link).

If you've done nothing more than produce the church bulletin, write newsletters for a variety of businesses, and create greeting cards using your art and messages, certainly talk about this.

Since I write mysteries featuring cats, I would also mention something about my affinity with cats and maybe introduce those in my household. I would talk about the writing I've done about cats for cat-related magazines and my membership in a cat writers' organization. In my case, I would also mention my forty-something published nonfiction books and the numerous articles I've submitted over the years. I would share the fact that I edit manuscripts for clients—both fiction and nonfiction.

As you can see, it is important to mention everything that could possibly pique the publisher's interest. If he loves your story, he wants to develop warm feelings toward you, too. Help him to do so. Make an excellent impression through the attributes and accomplishments you mention here. Don't exaggerate, but also don't hold back. Give the publisher everything he needs to justify taking your project on.

A publisher prefers working with authors who are talented and experienced, yes, but also cooperative, organized, intelligent, and flexible.

New novelists rarely approach publishers for the first time with all of the necessary qualities. Since you are reading this book, you have an advantage. You're learning what you can do to sway a publisher and part of that skill is knowing what to reveal and what to conceal. Here's a guide. Share with the publisher:

- Your education. If you didn't graduate from high school, you should probably avoid mentioning education, however.
- Any previous writing you've done, especially if it was published. Give details—where was it published, when, what is the circulation of the magazine or the reach of the blog?
- Writing awards you've earned.

- Current writing you're doing—a series of stories for a private school curriculum, for your own daily blog, etc.
- Your affiliations with writing-related or genre-related organizations. If you are an officer, give your title. As part of your duties, if you produce conferences for hundreds of people, certainly mention that.
- Accomplishments and achievements that would resonate with a publisher who dearly wants to produce your book.

Some authors find this the most difficult aspect of the proposal to compile. They aren't accustomed to tooting their own horns. They're shy and they don't want to brag. If you're having trouble fleshing out this section of your book proposal, turn to your trusted team for help and perspective. (The team I refer to might include your most straightforward friends, colleagues, fans of your writing, astute coworkers, other novelists, etc.)

The Market for Your Novel

If you are interested in writing within a certain genre, it is probably one you know something about. Chances are, you read books in this genre, know where to find them, and understand something about your fellow readers. These readers would be part of your target audience. When you talk about your audience, you are most likely describing yourself.

Your audience may very well follow the same blogs you follow, lurk in the same aisles at bookstores, frequent the most popular review sites to learn what's new in your genre, attend presentations featuring authors of this genre, and belong to book clubs and organizations related to this genre. These readers are your audience.

Explain this to the publisher. Then, do your best to find out how many people this encompasses. How large is the audience for books in your book's genre? A little Internet research should give you some idea as to how many books are published each year in this genre? Are there some bestsellers among them? How many book clubs, blogs, organizations, websites, etc., focus on the genre? How many members/visitors are involved? Perhaps you can find a statistic showing how many people are voracious readers of thrillers, spy mysteries, chick lit, etc.

For additional assistance with the market section of your fiction book proposal, review chapters 2 and 4.

The Market Analysis for Your Novel

Here you'll gather information that reveals the number of books out there that are similar to yours. There really is no competition for fiction. If a reader loves cozy mysteries, for example, and you have written a cozy mystery, she's apt to read yours as well as any others that pique her interest.

If a publisher's submission guidelines ask for a market analysis or competing titles, he wants you to compare your book to others on the market. Which books out there are most like yours and how are they selling? Choose five or six books to use in your comparison. List them by title, author, publisher, publication date, page number, and ISBN. Briefly describe each book and explain how yours is different or similar. Some mysteries, for example, feature a female detective. Some are written in first person and others in third. Some involve animals. There are even books written from the animals' point of view. Some stories take place in other countries.

Many publishers have a preference when it comes to character demographic and the story line. In the end, a publisher might deem that your story has too much romance, or not enough. Another publisher may love the level of romance in your book, but prefer books with a strong male protagonist, instead of a female-driven story like yours.

If you've done appropriate research, you know exactly what each publisher wants in a mystery or crime fiction manuscript, for example, and you'll approach the one that is right for your book. Avoid the research and you may waste a lot of your time and that of several publishers.

How Will You Promote Your Novel?

There was a time when a publisher wouldn't consider asking potential novelists this question. But more and more of them today need to know. Publishers expect their authors to be assertive promoters. Why? Competition. There are so many books being published through all sorts of companies and processes each year that, in order to succeed, books need more than a three-month promotional blast at the publishing company level.

Thus, novelists must be marketers as well as excellent and prolific writers. As the author of a novel, you need to be out there talking to people about your book, showcasing it all over the Internet, soliciting reviews, attending events and activities, and using your massive email list to keep readers apprised of any new novels being launched and reminding them to order your previous ones.

I know, I know. You'd much rather be sitting at your computer pounding out the next book in your series. And the publisher hopes you can produce more for him, as well. But if you want to succeed in this field, you really must find a way to get it all done—to actively promote published books while working on the next one. Authorship is not a hobby. In order to succeed, an author of fiction as well as nonfiction must approach authorship as a business.

So what ideas do you have for promoting your book? First you need to know something about book promotion. *Promote Your Book* has a lot of ideas for promoting a novel and it is designed to teach all authors the basics of book promotion. (See the resource list for ordering information.) Also read the next chapter, "Novel Ways to Promote Your Novel."

List the marketing tactics you are comfortable with, those you're already pursuing, and others you believe would sell this book. Do your best to wow the publisher with your marketing plan while staying true to your particular cache of skills and abilities.

I followed a trend for many novelists this past spring when I engaged in a blog tour designed to promote my Klepto Cat Mystery books. I spent some time seeking out five of the most active blogs I could find that related to cozy mysteries and/or cats. These blog hosts were also accustomed to doing blog tours.

I arranged something different with the bloggers for one day each during the week of my tour and then I began promoting the tour, as did each blog host. One of them interviewed me about my shift from nonfiction writing to novel writing. A couple of them reviewed one or two of my books. One had her cat interview my cat character, Rags. That was fun!

During the week of the tour, I sent out my newsletter to 2,000 subscribers, blogged daily, promoted the blog stops through all of my social media accounts, sent emails to remind fans and friends of the blog stops, and so forth. And what were the results? Since I'm the publisher of these books,

I have access to a daily accounting of books sold. Book sales more than doubled during the week of my blog tour.

This is definitely an activity I highly recommend, but it must be accompanied by tons and tons of promotion.

One of my favorite marketing ploys is to spy on other authors. In your case, you'll want to spy on other novelists. Visit their websites, Facebook pages, etc. To find out how they're promoting their books, view their media pages and read their blogs. How do they entice their readers? Some run contests, have games visitors can play, provide trivia related to the topic of their books, list resources for novelists or readers, and, of course, they promote their books at these sites. This is also a good way to find out who's reviewing their books.

Once you've discovered how successful novelists promote their books, borrow some of these tactics for your promotional plan and include them in your book proposal.

Define Your Platform

Where are your strengths and skills? Who do you know in the industry? If you've been reading through this entire book, you are beginning to realize what goes into this section. Whether you're pitching a novel, a children's book, or a nonfiction book, the potential publisher wants to know what you have going for you when it comes to marketing your particular book.

Do you have a marketing background, a huge email list, some important connections, a large following of readers? A yes to these questions might make a publisher take notice. He knows that your excellent writing skill alone won't sell books. Even avid readers of books in your genre won't buy it if they don't know it exists. Someone must take the initiative and start putting up smoke signals to alert the masses. A messenger must run from village to village shouting the news or stand on the street corner in a bustling city showing off the book. Don't laugh; I know of one woman who, every Saturday, would set up a crude stand on a busy street in New York and hawk her book to passersby.

So what can you bring to the table? Spell it out for the publisher. The more concrete your ideas, the better; and the more of them you have actually tried or are already pursuing, the better. You might have some great marketing ideas that you haven't tried and that you don't know for sure will work. Soft pedal where these are concerned. As I suggested earlier in the book, if you plan to produce grandiose events, consider a test run before beginning your search for a publisher.

For example, let's say that your novel is chick lit and involves a ring of women who have vowed to change something about themselves within a year's (or a month's) time. They come together to discuss their individual projects and get feedback from each other. Each is issued a hard challenge and they go their separate ways to pursue it. The story follows each of them in their adventurous pursuits.

If you are a psychologist, you might plan a workshop where women can connect with other women who have (or seem to have) the characteristic they seek and let the mentoring begin.

You would choose a catchy name for the book and the workshops—"A Woman's Magnificent Challenge," for example, or "Yes, You Can—a Woman's Way."

Preferably, you would conduct test workshops in your community, so you'd have something concrete to tell publishers in the platform portion of your proposal. If you haven't actually done a workshop, at least have one planned with all of the particulars in place—where, when, what will take place, what celebrity will be there, how many people are signed up.

Don't fabricate. Give an honest accounting.

Perhaps you're pitching a book you've already published on your own and are now seeking a traditional publisher. This occurs more and more often these days. In this case, you know something about what it takes to promote a novel and what you can contribute to the process. You may have learned, for example, that your book does well at book festivals. Give sales figures for previous festivals and a log of those you've signed up for in the future. Describe a contest you run at your website and the number of visitors you get during this period.

Talk about the blog tours you've organized and the success you've experienced.

Are you comfortable speaking in front of groups? Are you good at organizing events and activities? Perhaps you organized a successful author event at a couple of libraries in your county. Share the details and explain how you plan to capitalize on what you learned from this activity and how you can expand on it to continue promoting this book.

Even though novels are highly popular, they are a hard sell. This is no time to be shy or to hold back on anything that might possibly sway a publisher. Give it all you have. At the same time, construct a plan to hone some of your skills, make more valuable connections, and come up with some great marketing ideas. How? Take steps to become a better public speaker. Make contact with conference leaders where you could present your workshops. Continue studying the publishing industry and, in particular, book promotion.

Chapter Summaries for Your Novel

Novels don't always have chapters. If yours does, simply tell/describe your story chapter by chapter, trying to stay within 400 to 500 words. If your novel doesn't have chapters, use natural breaks when relating your story. Again, tell the story rather than copying it down. Summarize it. This would mean skimming over long scenes and dialogue—just explain what happened and what happens next. You can copy over small portions of the story for emphasis or an emotional impact and to show your style. You want the flavor of the story to shine through.

Make sure the publisher can follow the gist of your story, understand the story line, and learn a little something about your characters without being overwhelmed, thus confused.

(Refer to chapters 3 and 4 for additional information regarding the basic book proposal.)

Novel Ways to Promote Your Novel

For most authors of fiction, the very idea of promotion is distasteful. It's not uncommon for novelists to break out in hives or develop a nervous twitch when faced with the reality of marketing their books.

By now, you know that you must promote your book and you scurry to find your comfort zone. You'll make sure your book is on Amazon.com, of course, put up a website, start blogging, and solicit reviews through traditional literary magazines and review sites. You'll locate blog sites on the theme of your book and ask for reviews and interviews. You'll volunteer to be a guest blogger at appropriate sites.

Those of you with more nerve will try to arrange book signings and maybe attend a few local flea markets and other community events. And mostly, you'll be met with disappointment.

But there is so much more that you can do to draw attention to your novel—to let readers know that it exists. Here are a few ideas that you may not have thought of (and they don't even require that you develop the persona of a hard-selling hawker).

First, let me say that you may not want to give up on doing book signings. Sure, signings are not typically as well attended as they once were, but there are things you can do to bring in a crowd when you're signing or giving a presentation. I can sum it up in one word: exposure.

You need to get word out about your event—send an announcement/invitation to your massive email list. How do you acquire this massive email list? Start collecting email addresses from everyone you meet, those who visit your booth at book festivals, those who attend your presentations, people who sign up for your free offerings at your website, and so forth. Post notices about the event at all of your social media sites, your website, and blog site. Ask colleagues, friends, etc., to pass your invitation along. Create posters and post them at community kiosks, the library, bookstores, and in the window of the establishment where you'll be signing. Send press releases to local newspapers as well as newsletters for local writers' groups, book clubs, churches, your clubs and other affiliations, and so forth. Create a classy postcard or bookmark with the time, place, date, etc. and hand it out and leave them everywhere you go. Plan a drawing—have some nice prizes donated and list them on your promo material. Or simply give away free books, book lights, or something else to the first fifty guests. Amazon gift certificates are always welcome.

I realize that most authors don't sell many books at book signings. Heck, they can't even attract more than a handful of people. But this isn't true across the board. I know authors who sell as many as 300 books at signings. How do they do it? I just gave you the key above.

Here are eight additional ideas for promoting your novel.

1. **Promote to organizations and sites related to a topic or theme** that's even loosely woven throughout your book. For example, let's say that your novel features a bird that makes occasional appearances in a few chapters. This might be a crow that appears just before the wicked woman is sighted, a hawk that, when spotted, gives the main character courage, or a canary that lives with the protagonist and drives him crazy. Contact birding organizations, bird rescue and rehab websites, sites for bird fanciers, bird experts, sites dedicated to specific bird types (canaries, wild birds, parakeets, exotic birds, for example) and other authors who are promoting books related to birds.

   Of course, the same concept works for any subject: cats, dogs, horses, an amputee, a diabetic, a transvestite, twins, homelessness, the nightclub scene, Hollywood, competition swimming, golf, car racing, carnivals, regions (New Hampshire, Chicago, British Columbia, Seattle, Kansas City), the college scene, gambling, the corporate world . . .

   What do you do once you find these organizations or sites? After carefully studying the site, email the operator or director personally and make some solid suggestions for how your book would fit into their scheme of things. Ask for a book review. Offer to contribute articles to the site. Request inclusion on their resource list or recommended reading page. Offer your book as a prize in an upcoming contest. Suggest and head up a contest that would help to promote your book and raise money for the organization, perhaps.

2. **Participate in appropriate forums.** Many dedicated sites have forums and message boards where like-minded people communicate, network and share. Locate some of them through a Google search. Look for message boards and forums when you visit various sites. Using the bird theme, rather than just diving in and saying, "Buy my new novel, there's a bird in chapter three," adopt a strategy. Bring an interesting story or some new information or facts to the forum. Say, for example, "I was surprised to find that Ventura is among the top three California counties when it comes to wild bird species. Is there any way to find out what species are involved in this count? I'm particularly interested in this subject because I've just published a novel wherein I feature an unusual species of wild bird." Then sign your name and add the title of your novel and ordering information.

Maybe your book is set in a small town in Montana. Find regional sites and get involved in Montana, Idaho, and Wyoming-related message boards. Write, for example, "Is anyone familiar with Darby, Montana? I'm the author of a brand new suspense novel set in this historic town. Read excerpts at (your website address)." And then include ordering information. Offer up some interesting trivia. Ask what others know about this place. Your main objective in participating in targeted message boards and forums is to make friends, build a rapport, and get exposure for your novel.

3. **Solicit reviews in magazines** that have an element related to an obvious or an obscure aspect of your novel. You have probably contacted magazines and newsletters that typically review novels, but have you thought of approaching publications related to a lesser, but interesting aspect of your novel? Maybe your story includes a main character with Multiple Sclerosis. Seek out magazines and newsletters focusing on MS and those with an overcoming-disabilities aspect. Perhaps yours is an ethnic novel. Solicit reviews in appropriate ethnic publications. Of course, if it has that bird in it, go after magazines that bird lovers read. And don't forget to take advantage of any regional aspect. There are a growing number of regional magazines these days. I located fifteen

magazines for Ohio in just a few minutes time and about the same number for Texas.

How do you find specifically focused publications? Do a Google search. Use *Literary Market Place* and *Writer's Market* and thumb through *Gale Directory of Publications and Broadcast Media*. (All of these volumes are available in the reference section at your local library as well as online, usually for a fee.)

4. **Contact online and local bookstores that specialize** in a topic or theme presented in your novel. I located ten bookstores specializing in bird or pet books in three minutes through a Google search. There are also bookstores dedicated to books on cooking and foods, cats, mysteries, crime, fantasy/horror/science fiction, nature, economics, and spiritual/ religion. Once you've found several, approach them with your book and request a consignment agreement.

5. **Approach specialty stores**. You might convince some pet store owners to carry your novel that includes birds, a cat, or a seeing-eye dog, for example. If your book has a women's fashion element, consider designing a point-of-purchase display for willing managers of small clothing stores. If your book does well locally, you can use your success to entice stores in other cities to carry it. Maybe one of your characters thrives on daily espressos or there are a lot of scenes occurring in a coffee house. You know the next step—solicit space for your novel in Starbucks and the many copycat coffee shops sprouting up everywhere throughout the United States. Sometimes a non-bookstore can be convinced to carry a book when the author offers to set up a point-of-purchase display.

6. **Take advantage of your memberships and status**. Are you a college graduate? Send news of your book to your college alumni magazine. The editors are always hungry for information about successful alumni. If you don't belong to Sam's Club, Costco, or other such membership-oriented stores, sign up today! These mega-stores love to feature special members achieving interesting things in their widely circulated publications. Most organizations have newsletters with

a section that features member announcements and activities. Take advantage of this perk.

7. **Build promotion into your novel**. If you are only in the idea stage of writing your novel, you are in luck because I'm going to give you a key to promotional success. Write a nonfiction hook into your story. How? Involve the American Diabetes Association, the American Heart Association, or the National Mental Health Association by developing a character with diabetes, a heart condition, or a mental illness, for example. Give a character a Harley, a tattoo, or send him cruising on the Princess Line. Make sure that you have permission to use the name of the company or organization in your story. And, with the right angle and approach, you might be able to get them to participate in promoting your book. At the least, they might give you a positive endorsement.

8. **Tap into what's hot**—something that's in the news or an emerging trend, for example. Involve your characters in a life-threatening storm. Write a story set during an extreme heat spell. More and more people are developing enjoyable and satisfying online relationships—women are creating friendships and some couples are even getting married. Is this an intriguing trend you could incorporate into your book that might entice readers to purchase your novel?

As you can see, whatever the topic or thread of a topic that you've woven through your book, you can find organizations, publications, and/or websites to support it. Tap into these resources to broaden the audience for your fantastic, soon-to-be successful novel.

Part Five

A Book Proposal for Your Children's Book

The prospect of writing a book proposal for a children's book might seem odd to some. But when you consider that a book proposal is a business plan and a formal pitch package, it doesn't seem so unusual. A publisher of children's books is also running a business and wants to know that your book is a viable product.

Yes, Your Children's Book
May Require a Book Proposal

Children's books, while cute and fun, are also big business. Publishers of children's books use the same high standards in the selection process as other publishers—it must be well written, relevant to the target audience, and marketable. A publisher will scrutinize the author based on her platform and her ability to promote the book. The author must also accurately determine the age level for the book and write it within this criterion.

What items of enticement should you send to a children's book publisher? It depends on the type of book, the age of your audience, and a publisher's requirements. While some request the complete manuscript, several others I researched ask for a synopsis; author bio, including publishing history; information about competing books; and sample chapters. Some publishers want to see your illustrations, but others won't look at them unless you are a professional illustrator or you've hired one. Most want to know something about the author—what qualifies you to write a children's book or one for a particular age group?

Here's a rundown of a proper proposal for a children's book, should a publisher request it or various parts of it.

The Cover Letter for a Children's Book
Your cover letter might accompany the complete manuscript or specific parts of the book proposal. Please study chapters 1 through 4 of this book to gain an understanding of the basic book proposal and some of the variations. You'll also find information about the all-important publishers' submission guidelines. Some publishers state in their submission guidelines exactly what material and information to include in your cover letter.

Basically, they want to know whether this is an exclusive or a simultaneous submission. In other words, have you sent the manuscript or proposal out to other publishers? Are there other publishers considering your submission?

Naturally, you will include the title of your book and a brief description. What age group is it for? How do you see it being distributed—through grade schools, religious sites, bookstores, etc.? Please think outside the box. What is your vision for this project? Some authors link their children's books to a charity organization and the organization helps to promote it. Sometimes the organization will also publish the book.

The publisher wants to know something about you. What are your qualifications to write this book? Are you a teacher, a child psychologist, an author of other children's books, or an expert on the topic of the book, for example? What is your educational and writing background?

If the cover letter is for a book proposal, you would just touch on these things. If your letter accompanies the manuscript only, then expand on your bio and marketing plan.

Your Book's Title

It's probably easier to come up with a title for a children's book than any other type of book. Just look at the titles for books that have done well over the years. Some are so silly—*Conkle and the Statchabelly Jellyfish*. Others are spot-on descriptive—*Sally Loses Her Doll* or *This Is the Way We Brush Our Teeth*.

As I suggest for any book, before settling on a title, see what else is out there. Check titles for books similar to the one you suggest. Test it with kids you know and their teachers/parents. If you're fortunate enough to land a publisher, he will probably change the title, anyway.

Synopsis or Overview for a Children's Book

There is a wide range of children's books for a wide variety of age groups, so it's important to clearly identify your intended readership. A pure sign of an amateur is to say, "This book is for all children of any age." Don't make this mistake. Study the range of children's books in your book's category and topic. Look at the recommended age group for each book, which is generally printed on the book cover.

You'll find that there are guidelines for writing children's books for different age groups. They include number of pages, vocabulary used, number of words per page, number and use of illustrations, and so forth. Before writing a children's book, be clear about the guidelines and standards. See recommended books in the resources section of this book. Read numbers of books in the age range you want to write for and in the style and or topic you want to cover.

For nonfiction, describe the book you have in mind or that you have written and its purpose for a particular age group. You might want to teach hygiene to preschoolers, help seven- to eight-year-olds appreciate the bugs and other critters they see around their homes, show middle school students how to manage their feelings in a healthy way, and so forth.

Perhaps you hope to teach a character value through an action-packed adventure story. Describe the story, introduce your characters, and explain the method you use to make the all-important point.

You might also explain the nature of your book by comparing it to similar books by known authors. Say, for example, this book is reminiscent of the Hardy Boys Adventures or Lewis Carroll's literary books for children.

About You, the Author

Even though writing for children might seem like child's play, the children's book industry is huge.

A children's book publisher often judges a book by the qualifications of the author. He wants to know that you are qualified to write this book. What is your background in writing or working with children? What is your experience in this topic and/or in publishing? Some credibility in the area of childhood development could prove most helpful in swaying a publisher. So be sure to tell him if you are an elementary school teacher, Sunday school teacher, preschool teacher, child psychologist, graduate with a degree in childhood education, or if you've written and published other popular children's books or stories.

Maybe you are a scientist interested in the ocean and you're pitching a picture book featuring whales from around the world. Perhaps you're a great cook and you work with handicapped children who want to know more about food preparation. Your book on cooking for the younger set would be a good match for your skills and experience.

Describe your educational background, achievements, accomplishments, and pertinent experience. What can you say about yourself that would make a business-savvy publisher want to publish your children's book?

Describe the Market for Your Children's Book

Does the market come before the idea or does the idea come before the market? In other words, do you plan the book to meet the needs/desires of a specific group of children, or should you write the book and then search for interested readers?

Different authors seem to approach the task of writing a children's book using a variety of methods. Here are the basic ones:

- The author is aware of a need and sets out to fill it through a book on the topic.
- The author is an expert or is highly interested in a subject and decides to write a book for children on that topic.
- The author is aware that kids love high adventure books (fantasy, etc.) and sets out to write one geared toward a specific age group.

Some authors today decide to write a children's book because it looks easy. They believe this would be a good way to break into the publishing business. They aren't aware of the strict guidelines for children's books and often miss the mark. These authors typically self-publish because their books don't qualify under any traditional publishing standards.

If you aren't sure who your readers are, study the market for your particular book per the suggestions outlined in the "Synopsis or Overview for a Children's Book." Don't leave this area blank and expect the publisher to tell you who your audience is. You are the CEO of your book. If you've done your homework prior to writing your book, you already know that you're writing for students in kindergarten to first grade, preschoolers, middle school kids, or girls ages eight through ten, for example. Maybe you've written your book for children who have lost a family member to a violent act, or for adopted or foster children.

Now you must find out how many potential readers this comprises. Use your research skills to find statistics for how many children are in foster care. How many are adopted in the United States each year? How many students will enter kindergarten and first grade next year? Perhaps you can start with some local statistics—what percentage of students in local schools are in the welfare system?

If you have already written your book without identifying your audience, it may not be too late. However, once you start your research, you might determine that you've written the wrong book—that you don't actually have a significant number of readers for the book you wrote. I've seen a few children's book authors shift gears at this point. They suddenly realize that they are targeting the wrong audience with their idea. Or they discover that there's a group of children not being served by books on this topic and they decide to revise their book for a different audience.

There's a lot to learn about the children's book market. If you come into it a relative newbie, it is important that you conduct thorough research so that the book you add to the market is worthwhile, the message is right for the age group, the vocabulary is appropriate, and the story is fitting and proper.

Once you think you know where your book fits in, always, always test it with same-age kids at the library, in the classroom, or in the neighborhood.

Ask educators and parents with children in that age group to review it for content and age appropriateness. Your findings belong in this section of your book proposal. Not only does the publisher expect the information you share with him to be reasonable, he wants to see facts and figures confirming your claims.

In this section, you may be required to show fancy footwork you used in determining your target audience. This is where statistics come in. Can you tell the publisher how many copies of a similar book sold? (Use impressive examples.) Can you provide the number of kids in the eight to ten age bracket who went to camp last year, who are involved in organized sports, who own cell phones or an iPod, who have divorced parents, who have a pet, or who are being raised by their grandparents, for example? These are important figures if they reflect your book's proposed audience.

What Are Some of the Competing Titles?

If your book is fiction, locate other books similar to the one you propose— in particular, those that are selling well and those published by major publishers. Make the point that your similar adventure story could possibly delight as many children over the years as X, Y, and Z books have.

For nonfiction, choose books on your topic. Select those that are selling well and some from major children's book publishers. Explain to the publisher what the other authors have attempted to achieve through their books, and how well you believe they did so. Talk about what is good about these books and what may be missing. Does your book fill needs that are not being met by the other books?

Let's say that your book features how to care for a backyard horse. You notice that there are few books in this category for children, but most of them are missing elements you've included, such as a list of age-appropriate responsibilities for kids with horses and fun activities for horse and rider. This may be a great selling point for your book. So be sure to play it up.

Don't hurry through the market analysis portion of your book proposal. Carefully and thoughtfully select books from the myriad of children's books on the market that most closely compare with yours. Scrutinize them to accurately determine what your book can offer that the others can't or point out how similar your book is when comparing it to the most popular books, for example.

In other words, don't just go through the motions here; use this opportunity to sell the publisher on your great project.

Fill Out the Promotions Section of Your Book Proposal

Yes, it's only a little children's book—maybe even a picture book for preschoolers. But if you want to sell copies, you'll have to do your part to promote it. You need to introduce it to the children in your demographic, their parents, their teachers, and so forth. And this is something you must start thinking about now because the publisher wants to know that you understand the concept of book marketing, that you are equipped to promote this book, and just how you plan to do it. What can you bring to the picnic that will provide exposure for your book? How will you get this book into the hands and the minds of your young audience?

First, you must understand how children acquire books. It's been my experience and observation that if they see it and it has an aspect that interests them, they want it. So it's a rather simple concept to promote to children—just put the book before them.

You've seen the paradigm with television. What toys do stores run out of most often at Christmastime? What items are always reported to have been the top sellers during the holidays? Those that have been advertised during family shows on TV. The kids see the item and immediately want it. So getting a gig on TV could certainly sell books.

Since the cost of advertising on TV is prohibitive for most of us, let's take that concept into another dimension. Okay, so the key is to get the book in front of children. Where do children congregate? At school, church, fairs, and community family and children's events. Do a reading at a bookstore or library. Get permission to bring your appropriate book into the classroom. It's not always easy to get an invitation into the school system. A connection would come in handy. And so would a really meaningful book. That's why I urge authors of children's books to include in their fiction or nonfiction a positive take on a character value. This might be honesty, responsibility, caring, selflessness, respect, etc. Educators and parents love to see their children reading books they can trust with some of the values they're trying to teach.

In fact, if your book has a character value, you might be able to get it in the Character Counts program (www.charactercounts.org).

An interactive website is a real attraction for children. Once they're familiar with your main character or the premise or story of your book through reading it or through visiting your site and playing the games, etc., they are hooked. Now is the time to come out with another book in the series. And this is a great marketing tactic to share with the publisher. Let him know that there are definitely more books in the pipeline.

Add something to your book. Dangle a plastic superhero ring from a piece of grosgrain ribbon to create a bookmark as an added impetus for kids to want this book. Notice, I didn't say "buy" this book. Generally, it is the parents, teachers, or school librarians who acquire the books, but the children themselves can be instrumental in encouraging the adult to make the purchase.

With this in mind, consider presenting a two-pronged marketing plan. Create a plan designed to reach the children and one directed toward the adults who would be making the purchase.

Your Platform

One of the most valuable planks on the platform for a children's book author is storytelling skills. If you don't have them naturally and you've never had lessons, join a storytelling group and participate. Toastmasters is another great self-improvement program where you'll receive an enormous amount of public speaking and storytelling training.

Join up early on and practice every chance you get. Borrow children from the neighborhood and read to them. Read to your cats and dogs. There's nothing quite as annoying as listening to someone with a gravelly, monotone voice reading out loud. Even if the story is interesting to a child, he will not sit still long for this reader. A skilled reader, however, can make even a mundane catalog entry or computer textbook sound exciting to a child.

For more about honing your public speaking skills and developing your reading voice, read *Talk Up Your Book*. (See the resource list.)

If you have storytelling skills and/or you're an educator or school administrator, for example, you might have a leg up when it comes to getting speaking gigs in schools. Develop an entertaining presentation for your age group and you may be able to take it into the schools where you're known. After you've been invited into one school district, it will be easier to elicit an invitation to others throughout the county, state, and beyond.

Tell the publisher if you have an affiliation with local libraries, a youth organization, or the Sunday school program at your church.

List any skills you have that would be useful in promoting a book. What are your previous marketing experiences?

Here again, you want to put yourself in the publisher's chair. You know that he is looking for a good, salable book, but he also wants an author who can successfully promote it. Your job is to present yourself in a light that will make the publisher want to say "YES" to your project.

Chapter Summaries

Some children's books are too brief to be broken into chapters. In this case, simply summarize or outline the entire book.

This section may even be eliminated for some children's books as the Synopsis/Overview would take the place of the chapter summaries. Many publishers of children's books want the manuscript along with some of the information that would ordinarily go into a book proposal. As for any request from any publisher, you will send the information and material he asks for either via his submission guidelines or his letter of request.

(Refer to chapters 3 and 4 for additional information regarding the basic book proposal.)

The Young Adult Book Proposal

The young adult book category has been popular for several years and continues to expand. While it seems like a fairly new genre, it is actually just coming of age. The first distinction between children's books and books for adolescents was made in 1802 when the division was called "books for young persons" and encompassed youths in the fourteen- to twenty-one-year-old bracket. But librarians didn't create a young adult section in libraries until the 1970s and '80s.

Now young adult (or YA) is more of a category than a genre because it includes genres of its own. In fact, more genres are added each year. Probably the most popular genres in the YA category are fantasy and romance; however, young people enjoy good adventure and mystery books, as well. Recent additions are graphic novels and Christian fiction. There's also young adult nonfiction.

So what does the young adult category encompass? YA fiction features young adult or adolescent lead characters and explores themes that are important to young adults—adolescent relationships, peer pressure, heroes in action . . . and the heroes in these books can take some unusual/other-worldly forms.

Young adult stories typically cover issues that young adults can identify with and very often involve conflict and tension and/or humor. Adolescents, like their adult counterparts, appreciate and are drawn to stories with memorable characters and authentic dialogue.

Amidst the young adult book craze, which tends to attract readers in middle school on up into the early twenties, there's a new category emerging. They're calling it new adult fiction. This category of books, created for eighteen- to thirty-year-old readers, is designed to bridge the gap between young adult and adult genres. While young adult books certainly contain a heightened measure of tension—with very adult issues coming into play—new adult fiction will take these a step or two further for this more mature audience.

If you want to write in the YA or NAF (new adult fiction) categories, read many popular books for these age groups. Study the language, vocabulary, the characters, the way other authors handle sensitive issues, the level of conflict and tension, and notice some of the topics that are covered. This is not an invitation to copy other authors. That would not be cool. However, it's important that you understand what's acceptable for this segment of readers before attempting to write in this category.

The Cover Letter for Your YA Book

The key is to choose a publisher of young adult books and to approach him with a good representation of one. Introduce your book by title and genre, explain the plot or purpose, and describe what you believe is the take-away value for the reader.

Most young adult books are designed to leave something with the reader. There's a lesson in the message, and it often provides an escape. The reader walks away feeling better about herself. Often, she can relate to the main character. Perhaps the story made her laugh and lightened her mood. If this is the case with your young adult novel or nonfiction manuscript, explain how you will accomplish this.

Also in the cover letter, you'll reveal something about yourself—the author. Have you written for a young adult audience before? Describe the type of writing you've done and for whom. Do you work with young people? Are you a parent, librarian, teacher, grandparent? Perhaps this is your first book and you wrote it because you've been involved in or observed a sensitive situation involving drugs, bullying, divorce, teen sex, or rape, for example. You want to alert, educate, and/or help young adults.

Provide a hint as to your connections and skills related to promoting this book. Get some additional tips and ideas for this cover letter from the "cover letter" section in chapter 13.

Your YA Title

When studying titles for books in this category, you'll find they are all over the place. It appears that anything goes—from the descriptive to the bizarre. Many of today's most popular novels have one- and two-word titles. If you use this technique, consider adding a subtitle that identifies the genre—*Hot Stuff: A Teenage Love Story*, for example, or *Cruel: A Fantasy*. Your book cover design will also help to identify your book as mystery, science fiction, fantasy, etc.

A nonfiction book should have a title or subtitle that is descriptive so anyone seeing the book, even briefly, knows exactly what topic it covers—blind dates, cupcake-baking, skin care, horseback riding, texting shortcuts, etc.

Spend some time studying titles and the books they're attached to and then give it your best shot. The publisher will probably change it, anyway.

The Synopsis for Your Young Adult Book

The standard for a young adult novel or nonfiction book synopsis would be quite similar to that for any novel or nonfiction book. Just make sure you appropriately capture the meat and the essence of your story, for a novel. Describe the story—tell what happened and what happens next, and do so in a charming, succinct way. For nonfiction, explain the purpose of the book—what is involved and how you expect it to affect (help, teach, change) the reader. Again, what do you see as the take-away value for your young adult audience?

Does your book address a certain segment of young adult or adolescent readers? If your nonfiction book covers first dates, you would target a younger group than you would for a story of a rapist on a college campus, for example.

Your synopsis should run anywhere from one to four or five pages. Here, you should not repeat the story or recite your nonfiction book verbatim. You're simply expected to describe your story or explain each chapter/phase/section of your nonfiction book, what it involves, what it is designed to accomplish and how it is set up to do so. In other words, make your long story short.

For fiction, write pretty much in the style of your story. If your book is light and humorous, adopt this style for your synopsis. If there's a lot of suspense and tension in your story, express this in your description of it. Insert a little dialogue for impact here and there.

Avoid asking questions such as, "Where will Marci and Frank's relationship take them?" or "How will the young adventurers slither out of this mess?" Answer the questions, instead.

As I suggested in chapter 11, practice describing your story or your nonfiction book in a few well-chosen sentences. Put it in a nutshell. If you can capture the essence of your story in a scant few sentences, you should be able to write a condensed version of your book for the publisher. Before sending it off, however, have your team of interested readers go over it for accuracy and readability as well as clarity. Can your pre-readers accurately describe your story after reading your synopsis? Do they have questions you really should have answered within these pages?

Your synopsis might go together easily or you might rewrite it numerous times. Just be sure that, when you send it, you are absolutely certain that it is the best representation of your project that it can possibly be.

Why Are You the Author?

The author who addresses young adults and adolescents must either be of this generation or know something about them. Here, you will explain why you are qualified to write this book. What is your experience with this age group and/or with the subject matter of your book? Be explicit and thorough. Remember, your project is being compared with many dozens or hundreds of other book proposals, so you want to provide anything you can truthfully offer that puts you in the lead.

If you aren't sure how to respond to this section, begin an "All About Me" file. List your education, accomplishments, achievements, skills, and experiences. What is your background in writing/publishing? Do you work, live with, teach, counsel, or write for adolescents or young adults? What is your history with the genre or theme of your proposed book? I've written numerous books on publishing and book promotion for adults, so it followed that I might have something to offer in a book for young writers. I'm also a mother, grandmother, and great-grandmother. I've been a youth mentor, a writing workshop leader for a group of home-schooled students, and, years ago, a Girl Scout and 4-H leader. These would be some of the qualifications I'd list in my about-the-author section for a book of this type.

Again, let me remind you to keep the publisher's POV (point of view) in focus at all times. Give him what he needs in order to choose your project above all the others.

The Market for Your YA Book

The young adult market is solid and widespread. Publishers of these books understand the nature and scope of the market. However, since YA is a category now with its own genres, you might find it necessary to describe your proposed audience, especially for a nonfiction book. It is up to you to explain who your potential readers are and where they are. Is this a large audience? Demonstrate the size and scope by gathering some statistics—how many college students are attacked and raped each year on campus? How many teens experience divorce in their family in their lifetime? How many are being treated for depression? How many commit suicide, are bullied, etc? If your book focuses on a specific topic such as one of these, it is your job to identify your potential readers, tell how many there are, describe where they can be found, and explain why they would read this book.

A book proposal is a pitch to convince a publisher of the viability of your book project. If you can't prove there is a large and strong audience for this book, he will move on to the next project. Sure, your story line is important to the publisher, as is the theme and purpose of your book. But if it lacks an interested audience or if you can't accurately identify it, he will pass.

If you're not sure who your audience is and where they are, it's time to shift into serious research mode. Spy on other authors who have books like yours. Visit their websites. What segment of people do they address? Check out their media pages. What groups do they speak to? What activities are they involved in? Where do they go to interact with their readers? How do they attract young readers to their sites?

Visit sites dedicated to books in this category/genre/theme and see if you can get a sense about the audience—how large it is, where they buy books and so forth. Spying is an excellent way to learn more about your audience.

Your Competition

Since most YA fiction genres have a large and healthy stable of readers, your job is more along the lines of pointing out successful books in this category and showing how yours is similar. Compare yours to the most popular fantasies, mysteries, romance, adventure stories, etc., keying in on the fact that if millions of readers loved the competing book, they will enjoy yours, as well.

Compare your book with those that rank high on Amazon. If you can do so legitimately, try to convince the publisher that your book has some of the same appeal to this particular audience.

If you have difficulty locating books similar to your nonfiction book for adolescents and young adults, bring in a few appropriate adult books for your comparison. This is a good way to demonstrate the need for a book on this topic for this age group. As you would do for any nonfiction book, describe the competing book and explain how yours is different—in particular, how yours offers more benefits to your audience. (For additional tips and techniques, review the competition section in chapter 4.)

The Promotions Section

Yes, Virginia, you will be required to promote even your amazing young adult novel (or nonfiction book). If you don't do something to put it into the minds and hands of your readers, it will just sit in the publisher's warehouse. Sure, he has some means to get word out to the readers, especially if he is a strong publisher of young adult books. He knows his audience and where some of them are. However, he will count on you to take it from there. So be prepared.

Locate reviewers in this category—in particular those that have reviewed similar books for Amazon and GoodReads.

Find blog sites and websites designed for the young adult reader.

Do you have a connection to a local school district or university library system? This could be the beginning of a strong distribution opportunity. Can you get an invitation to speak to a class or for the entire student body?

What about magazines for this age group? Do the editors review books? What are the criteria to get a book reviewed in these publications?

What other impressive contacts do you have?

Do all of this research before completing your book proposal because you want to give the publisher a list of your leads based on reality. You want to be able to say, "I've been invited to be guest blogger at this list of blog sites. These thirty-five reviewers have agreed to review the book. I have a dozen school and college librarians interested in acquiring this book for their libraries and, as a longtime member of the local school board, I've started the process of becoming an assembly speaker at three local high schools."

Compile an organized, complete marketing plan as part of your book proposal, and you should be able to impress any publisher of YA materials. The more concrete the planned promotional activities, the more interested a publisher will be. Can you see how much more professional and appealing this approach is than if you said, "I plan to contact librarians and I'll try to get the book reviewed and I'll research blog sites . . ." Publishers want action, not promises. You must demonstrate action, not blow in the wind with promises.

Your Author Platform

The publisher expects you to promote your book, so he needs to know how well equipped you are. What can you offer by way of your skills, aptitude, and understanding of promotion? If you've followed my directions for the promotions section, you have an excellent start in the task of proving yourself capable. Here, however, you might want to elaborate on some of your qualities as they relate to the area of promotion.

Maybe you are a teacher or a youth leader. You run a successful business or you're a retired corporate marketing manager. The terms *retired* or *part-time employee* look good here as they imply that you have the time to promote the book. Share the fact that you are a youth leader at church or a local recreation center in order to play up your connection to young people—that you know them and are around them. Preferably you test-marketed your book with these youths.

Maybe you have a background in social work with young people as a probation officer or a youth camp director. Or perhaps you're a foster parent, a health-care professional, or a counselor who works with young people.

Whatever your personal story, if it relates to your qualifications, interest, and aptitude for identifying and/or communicating with young adults, you'll want to share it with the publisher.

Chapter Summaries

The chapter summaries or chapter outline for a young adult novel or nonfiction book would not differ much from those for adult novels and nonfiction books. Read the chapter summaries sections in these chapters. The difference would be the targeted audience. You want to make sure that your story comes across or the information is presented so that it is appropriate for this younger audience. The point of the story or the purpose of the nonfiction book must be evident in your carefully developed chapter summaries.

Describe what each chapter contains and includes. When you read through your completed chapter outline (or chapter summaries), the entire story or the complete theme of your book should be evident and clear.

Note: As writers, we often become so close to our material or story that we see what we expect to see and not necessarily what's typed on the page. There are two ways to get around this obstacle. Set your work aside, wait a few days and then take a fresh look before sending it off to the publisher. Or bring in your support team to look over your outline. Ask them, "Does it make sense?" "Is the flow of the story or information logical/clear?" "What is your first impression upon reading this?" Ask them to repeat your story or the point of the nonfiction book back to you.

(Refer to chapters 3 and 4 for additional information regarding the basic book proposal.)

Part Six

It's Time to Submit Your Amazing Proposal

While there are several options for authors who wish to be published, those of you reading this book are probably attached to the idea of landing a publisher either through an agent or on your own.

Some of you don't know that there are other options or what they are. You might come from the old school—author writes book, author engages an agent, agent reels in a big publisher, and everyone lives happily (and richly) ever after.

Or perhaps you picked up this book in order to learn more about exercising your authority and control over your project. If this describes you, high-five and a fist bump.

So what are your publishing options? Here's the rundown:

- A **traditional royalty publisher** assumes the expenses involved in publishing a book and gives the author a percentage of each book sold. Depending on the policies of the publishing house, royalties are figured on either the retail or the wholesale price and generally range between five and eighteen percent.
- **Subsidy** or **vanity** and **co-publishers** produce your book for a fee. This publishing model has changed in recent years. Under the original premise, the vanity or subsidy publisher was hired to produce books for authors who didn't want to establish their own publishing companies. With the advent of the digital age, a new model of subsidy publishing

began to take shape. And today, there's a blurred distinction between the old vanity press and the modern-day all-inclusive pay-to-publish services.

- **Pay-to-publish services** (formerly known as fee-based POD publishers or self-publishing companies) charge anywhere from a few hundred to many thousands of dollars to produce your book. They print the number of copies you need as you request them and charge accordingly. They also offer various promotional packages and advantages for additional fees. These companies are extremely popular right now, but they are also the brunt of numerous complaints. I maintain that this is due mostly to the authors' lack of industry savvy and unreasonable expectations. Too many authors emerge from their writing rooms and step right into a pay-to-publish company den without taking the time to learn something about the hugely competitive business they are entering. They want to trust the company representative because the alternative (to actually study the publishing industry) is too time-consuming. They are in a hurry to get their books out and they blindly dive in and often find themselves in very deep water.

- **Self-publishing** means that you establish a company through which to produce your book and you arrange for and pay for all of the necessary components—copyright, ISBN, barcode, cover design, and so forth. You audition printing companies and hire one for your project. You also promote, distribute, and ship your books, or hire a distributor.

You are reading this book because you have your heart and mind set on being traditionally published. So let's continue learning about the publishing industry.

Who's Who in the Publishing Chain?

This can be a puzzler for the new author. You might wonder, *Which editor should I address? Or should I address the publisher directly? Do I need an agent? What does an agent do? Maybe I should try to get a publisher on my own before contacting an agent.*

Here's the deal: some publishers will not give you the time of day (nor will they even look at your manuscript or proposal package) if you approach them without agent representation. Most, however, will work directly with authors. And some *prefer* that you come to them on your own—no agent involved. We had a long discussion about submission guidelines in chapter 1. A publisher that requires you contact them through an agent will generally state this in their submission guidelines. If you're looking up publishers in an online or print directory, often there are symbols indicating which publishers require that their authors have agent representation and which do not.

A literary agent represents authors and their projects to publishing houses. They're also known as an author's agent. With the huge increase in authors, there are more people hanging out their agent shingle than ever before—possibly being outnumbered only by manuscript editors.

An experienced agent knows a good project when she sees it. She understands how to make a promising book idea shine. She has connections within the publishing industry and knows who publishes what and what certain publishers want at any given time. She might be considered an insider and she can help you get your foot in the door.

The publisher owns or runs the publishing house. He is responsible for printing and distributing printed and digital material. There are publishers of newspapers, periodicals, calendars, software, etc., as well as books. As far as the author is concerned, the publisher is the gatekeeper. He generally has the last word when it comes to which projects will be published and which will be rejected.

While some publishers operate a one-man show—they act as acquisitions editor, manuscript editor, art director, publicist, and so forth—most publishers hire a staff. The staff member you would be interacting with initially is an editor—often known as an acquisitions editor.

The acquisitions editor is in charge of choosing manuscripts for his or her publishing company. Basically, the acquisitions editor's job is to evaluate proposal packages and/or manuscripts and campaign for acceptance of the most promising projects before the editorial board or the publisher, depending on the size of the publishing house.

Who do you contact first? This depends on the scope of your project and your publisher of choice. If your book is suited to a mass market and you have the connections and following to get the attention of a major publisher, you might start your search at the top. In this case, you would need an agent.

If you are new to publishing and you believe your book would fit nicely into a strong publishing niche, you will most likely approach small to medium-size houses. In this situation, you probably do not need an agent. Most publishers do not require an agent.

If you're not sure, take time to contact a few appropriate agents—those who represent books in your genre or topic. Show them your proposal and ask them about your chances with a major publisher. Take your proposal (or your idea) to writers you trust or turn it over to a publishing professional for his or her opinion.

Sometimes we get so involved in our story or nonfiction book that we lose sight of the big picture. All we can see is the monumental amount of work we've put into it, the sacrifices we've made to get to this point, and our fervent hopes and dreams attached to our project. No one can see clearly through rose-colored glasses.

If you are new to the process and concept of publishing, first and foremost, study the industry. Start by reading *Publish Your Book*. Next, get peer and professional feedback on the concept of your book and the proposal or manuscript before making any publishing decisions.

How to Locate and Approach a Literary Agent

A literary agent acts as a representative on behalf of authors with promising book projects. He or she shows your proposal and/or manuscript around to the publishers they know and are accustomed to working with. He may work with you to make your proposal more attractive to publishers. Working with an agent to prepare a stronger pitch or to shift your book's focus can be grueling, but it can be worth your time and effort. What are the rewards? Not only will you learn volumes, this could result in landing a larger publisher and a richer contract.

Agents reject authors, too. In fact, statistics show that agents turn down as many as ninety-five percent of submissions. If you are fortunate enough to get a good agent, he or she can become a great support system and provide valuable educational opportunities for you.

If a publisher issues a contract, the agent may negotiate for a larger advance and higher royalties. After all, this is how the agent gets paid—through a percentage of the advance and royalties you collect.

An agent can often get your money sooner than if you work with a publisher on your own. They have methods the nonprofessional doesn't.

Choose the Right Agent

There are probably more agents today than at any other time in the history of publishing, because there are more authors vying for an opportunity to make it big with a book. If you've been around the publishing scene for a while and you've spent time researching your options and your responsibilities, you've heard some nightmare stories involving agents. Believe them. Some of them are probably true. While some stories are biased because of author ignorance, others are absolutely factual. There are individuals posing as literary agents or authors' agents without enough experience in the field. And there are some who have jumped on what they consider a lucrative bandwagon with the sole purpose of scamming authors.

I'm told that this practice is on the decline, however, because more authors are taking charge of their own books and are not seeking agent help. When a scam becomes less profitable, it all but goes away.

If you'd like more insight into publishing scams and scammers, visit the Science Fiction & Fantasy Writers of America's "Writer Beware" pages. Here's a link to the current list of purported scam agencies. You'll notice that one of them has changed their name over twenty times. This is one red flag for authors seeking an agent. You'll find others at this site:

http://www.sfwa.org/other-resources/for-authors/writer-beware/thumbs-down-agency/

I actually had what could be considered a bad-seed agent once. After she got a few bucks from me, she flat disappeared. Naw, I didn't pay her much, just enough to make copies of my proposal. But she must have been hiding from someone because she suddenly stopped replying to my letters and phone calls. When I realized she wasn't a real agent or at least one I could work with, I asked her to please let me know which publishers she had approached, so I wouldn't be following in her footsteps. That would not be professional. I never received even that information from her.

This is not an isolated case. The more agents or editors or publishers or publicists who come on the scene in times of abundance in any industry, the more bad apples you'll find in the bunch. How does one weed those out? Here are some tips:

- Approach an agent who was recommended by someone you know.
- Accept recommendations from trusted professionals.
- Look to see who other authors thank in their acknowledgments pages of their similar successful books—they often thank their literary agent.
- Always trust the Association of Author's Representatives. The agents listed there have been screened (aaronline.org).
- When you decide on one or two possible agents, ask for client recommendations.

- Do an Internet search for red flags. Type in the agent or agency name and "complaint" or "warning," and see what comes up. If there are a couple of complaints, it could be sour grapes. Sometimes the author is at fault. Someone who neglects to study the publishing industry may not understand how an agent works and might misinterpret an aspect of their working relationship. What you're looking for are many complaints of similar types about this particular agent or agency. Heed those red flag warnings!

The Association of Author's Representatives (A.A.R.) lists 400 agents, and all of them have been screened. They adhere to the organization's "Canon of Ethics." You can read the "Canon" at the site: www.aaronline.org/canon.

There are other agent listings and directories available, as well. (See the resource list in Part Seven of this book.)

You may feel as though you're at the mercy of an agent and that it doesn't matter much which one you ultimately choose. Wrong! Don't approach agencies so aggressively that you pay little attention to their requirements. Agents have guidelines and so should you—the author. Agents also specialize; they come in different sizes, shapes, and personalities. It will be to your advantage to shop for an agent as carefully as they shop for the perfect client.

Once you have a finished book proposal and/or a complete manuscript (for fiction or a children's book), it may be time to seek an agent, but only if you have your sights set on a publisher who requires their authors to have representation.

Study each agency's list of books represented and their current requirements. When you are serious about a handful of them—they match all of your criteria and you match theirs—check them out independently.

Meet Agents Face-to-Face

Have you ever attended a writers' conference? Many of them today organize the most wonderful feature for authors—editor and agent meetings. Yes, you can meet face-to-face with an agent or an acquisitions editor.

First, find out if the conference you plan to attend offers this service. What will it cost you? Study their list of editors and agents who will be available, and conduct research to learn more about those who seem to match your needs.

When you've isolated appropriate agents/editors whom you'd like to meet, sign up for a consultation. The conference organizers may allow a scant ten minutes with the agent or editor, or a full thirty minutes.

Your job now is to prepare yourself to pitch your project in the most professional manner in the most succinct way. Practice, practice, practice. Ask someone to fire questions at you so you are prepared to respond if the agent or editor asks, "Who is your audience?" "Tell me about your marketing plan." "How will you market this in your hometown?" etc.

Always, always prepare some small but meaty item to leave with the agent or editor. I suggest a postcard-size or even bookmark-size piece of promo for your book. Sure, your book may not be published yet; it doesn't even have a cover design. I've seen authors rise above this obstacle and create a cover using a provocative or otherwise memorable photograph representing the theme of their books. There's no reason why you can't do this, too. Blast the working title across the top of the handout, give a thumbnail sketch of the proposed book's content, and make sure your contact information is on the handout. There are many sites where you can have quality promotional materials created at reasonable prices.

Here are some things to avoid when meeting an acquisitions editor or agent in person:

- Don't try to give them a bunch of stuff to read, unless they ask for a sample from your book or pleasantly agree to accept it. Keep it simple, small, and attractive.
- Don't ramble. Stay focused on the editor's/agent's questions. Remember to think like the agent or the publisher's representative. They aren't as interested in hearing about your hurdles and disappointments in finding a publisher as they are in how your project can benefit their company.
- Don't discount what they tell you or, heaven forbid, argue with them. What doesn't make sense to you now might resonate deeply with you in the future.
- Avoid saying, "Yeah, I already tried that," or "That won't work." Instead, listen and take notes. If it's something you've tried, ask questions. "How do you suggest I go about that?" (Maybe there's an angle you missed.) "What else would you recommend?"

Do respect the representative's time and expertise. It just might be the secret to your future success.

How to Work with an Agent

Before ever contacting a literary agent, locate his or her submission guidelines and follow them. You'll find their individual submission guidelines at their websites. If you don't have a website address, simply do a search using the agent's or agency's name. If they have a website, you should find it quite easily.

To refresh your memory about submission guidelines, review chapter 1. Submit exactly what he or she asks for in the method, form, style, and order they request.

Once you've been contacted, establish an understanding from the beginning. What is the process? When should you expect to hear from the agent? How often? What can you do to help? Will you get a list of publishers he has approached with your project? What are your responsibilities as a client?

You'll notice that while some agents prefer email submissions, other want to receive material through the mail. Some of those who request email submissions refuse to open attachments. Everything goes in the body of the email, except, in some cases, illustrations. Most ask that you use something specific in the subject line for queries and proposals. So look for this information in their submission guidelines to be sure your submission will be opened.

Most agents whose sites I visited adhere to a standard response time of sixty days. They claim that if you don't hear from them within that two-month period, you can assume it is a "pass."

What do agents want to see? Pretty much the same thing a publisher would request—a query letter with a pitch and something about the author. Some request a book proposal and even provide a link showing how to write one. You should disclose when you are sending multiple queries/proposals (proposals to more than one agent at a time). If you are auditioning agents, do not also send your material to publishers on your own.

Provide all of your contact information, including your phone number. While agents want the option of calling you, they don't encourage authors to call them—at least not during the submission stage. Why would they call you? If they are highly interested and want to sign you before you sign with someone else, or if they have a question that isn't covered in your presentation, perhaps.

You might wonder, "What if I get shot down by every agent and realize I need to revise my proposal? Can I send my revised proposal to the same agent again?" Some agents invite you to resubmit heavily-revised material after a period of six months.

Why would an agent say no? It's not always because they don't like the author, the proposal stinks, or they're in a bad mood. As one agent puts it, rejection (or as they like to call it, "a pass") occurs often because the agency has something similar in the works, the idea is no longer trendy or viable, they know a publisher who is coming out with a book like this, the agent doesn't love it, or it just isn't right for them. In some cases, timing is everything. A perfectly viable project can be rejected simply because you sent it to the wrong person at the wrong time. As one agent says, "This is a highly subjective business," indicating that while he may not be captivated by your proposal, another agent might love it.

Your demeanor and attitude can carry you in one direction or the other. Agents, like publishers, prefer working with authors who are polite, professional, and well-mannered. And isn't that exactly the kind of agent you'd like to work with? I think most authors would also choose an agent who is communicative—who responds within a reasonable amount of time to submissions and questions.

Why wouldn't an author be pleasant? Oh my, I've seen my share of insolent authors. I was on the listening end of a crazed, belligerent author once who thought I'd misled him with regard to booth space at a book festival I was involved with. He was way off base with his accusations and threats. His wife overheard his rant and made him call back and apologize.

I've had authors tell me about some of the heated conversations and over-the-top tactics they've used in trying to coerce and bully a publisher or agent into issuing them a contract. If you are upset about a response (or lack of) from an agent or a publisher, stop and think. Where is this coming from—your feelings of inadequacy? It's darn hard having agent after agent and publisher after publisher reject the project you've poured your heart and soul into. But does it make sense to blame the professional? If you alienate the gatekeepers, how are you ever going to get a foot in the door?

Believe it or not, a rejection may be a perfect opportunity for you to learn—to take a step back and evaluate your project from a different angle. Maybe you have been blind to the fact that your story is flawed. Perhaps you do need to hire a good book editor, take a story-writing course, or shore up your platform before pitching your how-to book. Maybe all twenty-five agents and fourteen publishers you've contacted aren't wrong.

I used to write articles fairly regularly for *The Toastmaster Magazine*. At a regional Toastmaster event once, a man came up to me and said, "I wrote an article for *The Toastmaster* and I've sent it to them twice, but they keep rejecting it. Can you help me get it published?"

I asked him to send his article to me. I looked it over and replied that this magazine publishes how-to articles and that his was an essay. I suggested that he make some changes so that it is more useful to the reader and appropriate for the magazine.

A few months later, I saw this man again at an event and he said, "I'm still trying to get the editors to publish my article. You saw it, isn't it a good article—can you help me get it published?"

I asked, "Now did you make the changes I suggested?"

He said, "Oh no. I don't want to do that. I want them to publish it just the way it is. It's a good article, don't you think?"

Again, I told him, "But this is not the type of article they publish. If you want to break into this particular magazine, you have to submit what they traditionally publish, which is the how-to."

If your project has been rejected numerous times, it could be a reflection on the validity of the submission. But maybe not. Yours might be one of thousands that are worth publishing and that could be successful, but that didn't quite make the cut in an agency or a publishing house.

There are reported to be over a thousand literary agents eager for good projects. But there are many times that many authors seeking representation. And even if you land an agent, this does not guarantee that you will be published. While an agent has a greater chance of getting you a publishing contract, there's always the chance that he'll fail.

If you plan to approach agents, do not submit your material to publishers. And especially do not make any submissions to publishers once you're working with an agent.

When you are fortunate enough to land an agent, this doesn't necessarily mean you are off the hook. Don't relax and go back to writing quite yet. First, contact other agents you might have approached and let them know you are working with an agency. Be prepared to produce various information and materials at the agent's request.

What can you expect from the agent? She will contact those publishers most likely to publish something like yours, offer an argument for accepting it, negotiate a contract should one be placed on the table and for this, once the project is accepted by a publisher, she generally gets fifteen percent of your royalties and advance.

How to Land a Publisher for Your Amazing Book

If your book doesn't require or warrant a major publisher, there are many hundreds of small to medium-size publishers eager to work with savvy authors who have potentially successful projects. In this case, you do not need agent representation.

Before starting your search for the right publisher, however, you must understand enough about the industry, your options, and your responsibilities to form realistic expectations for your book's level of success. Study the publishing industry. Read *Publish Your Book: Proven Strategies and Resources for the Enterprising Author*. And enter into your quest for publication with the information and education you need.

Like agents, many publishers specialize. It's well worth your while to study numbers of publishers who typically publish books like yours before deciding which ones to approach. Visit the websites of those that publish books similar to yours (the same topic, theme, or genre). Study their lists of published books. If yours seems to be a match, check out their submission guidelines first, paying attention to their current requests. Some publishers keep their websites so current that you can go there and find out what they're accepting on any given day. Their needs can change. So if you've printed out a publisher's submission guidelines several months or even a few weeks before contacting the publisher, always go back and check the website and guidelines again before submitting anything.

A publisher who publishes young adult mysteries might suddenly become inundated with them and decide to cross this off his list of desired books for the season. He might launch a new line of children's adventure stories. If you keep abreast of your potential publishers' wish lists and dead lists, you will save yourself a lot of time and possibly score big-time.

Check the number of books a publisher produces each year against the number of submissions they receive. This information is often noted in their listing in *Writer's Market* and other publisher directories. (See the resource list.) You might have a better chance of breaking in if the publisher produces twenty-five books per year and only receives 200 submissions than trying to infiltrate those that receive 800 submissions per year and publish only ten to fifteen titles.

If you are a new author, also consider publishers that advertise for first-time authors. Some even give the percentage of first-time authors they work with each year—ten percent, twenty-five-percent, etc. Some publishers say they are actively seeking first-time authors.

Some authors approach the largest publishers in the industry first. They start at the top and, if necessary, work their way down hoping to find a publisher along the way. Others sabotage their chances of landing a publisher because they're in such a hurry. They give themselves a month to find a publisher or they vow to approach a certain number of publishers before taking the easy way out and signing with a pay-to-publish company.

Let me remind you that you should put as much (or more) energy and time into publishing as you did into writing the book, and patience is going to be part of your job. Publishing isn't a game, although it can certainly be a gamble. Publishers are up against the same challenges the self-publishing author is faced with—a huge boost in competition and, in some areas, a decrease in readers. So publishers are more cautious than ever about the investments they make. In this publishing climate, it isn't only the project that must be pristine and solid; the author's level of skills, energy, time, and cooperative nature must all come into play before a publishing staff can make a decision.

As you can see, it is critical that you lead with your best shot. Make sure that your proposal is as good as it gets before contacting any publisher. It doesn't matter if you start big or small—approach the majors or some of the minor publishing houses. Just make sure you are completely prepared with your best effort.

What About the Acquisitions Editor?

You may have noticed that, so far, I haven't said much about the acquisitions editor. I've focused on publishers and literary agents. Certainly, many of you know that you're going to address your proposal package to an editor at the publishing house. Often, it is the acquisitions editor. In some publishing houses, a promising proposal is then handed around to a team of editors and marketing managers before a decision is made. This is one reason why it can take so long to receive a response to your proposal. Sometimes waiting is a good thing. It may mean that your proposal is being seriously considered.

Okay, so you will likely communicate first (and throughout the submission process) with an editor from the publishing company. In fact, you may never hear from the publisher at all, except to see his or her name on the contract. Your relationship with the editor may end at that point and you'll start working with a publicity agent or publicist from the company.

If it's a smaller company, you might deal with the publisher from the beginning right on through the issuing of the contract. It depends on the size and policies of the company.

For the sake of simplicity, I will continue to refer to the publisher in a general manner as the gatekeeper, policy-maker, and decision-maker at a publishing company, rather than using *editor* or switching back and forth between the two.

Where Do You Find Publishers?

You will hear and read professionals advising authors to study the publishing industry before getting involved. As you know by now, I'm on that bandwagon, as well. The more you understand about the industry, the more well equipped you'll be to make good decisions on behalf of your project.

One valuable technique you'll learn is how to locate appropriate publishers. Here's a list of possibilities:

- Through recommendations by authors you meet at writers' group meetings
- At writers' conferences

- By checking books like yours to see who published them. Be sure to check those in your home library.
- By joining authors' organizations and participating in forums and meetings—networking
- By subscribing to industry newsletters and reading/studying them. *Publisher's Weekly* has a free daily e-mag version you can subscribe to. This e-mag does a pretty good job of keeping authors updated as to the publishing scene. (See the resource list in this book for more.)
- By meeting publishers at large book festivals. Often, they are there with their books hoping to recruit readers and possibly the occasional author who will make them some big money.

You'll notice that in every article and book you read and lecture you attend, the professional stresses approaching the right publisher. One of the biggest complaints for practically every publisher is that way too many people send the wrong project to them.

Publishers make it pretty clear—some are blatantly (almost rudely) clear—as to the type of books and subject matter they do and do not publish. Yet, still-arrogant (or uninformed) authors continue to submit a novel to a publisher of business books, a children's book to a cookbook publisher, and so forth. It sounds absurd, but it's a fact of a publisher's and an agent's life.

In chapter 1, we discussed submission guidelines, including tips for locating those that are difficult to find. Here's another tip for locating the sometimes-vanishing submission guidelines. Do an Internet search using keywords, "XYZ Publishing" + "submission guidelines," or "submission guidelines," + "mystery," "romance," "thriller," "cozy mystery," "young adult fantasy," etc.

There's no excuse for ignorance when it comes to a publisher's requirements. If you can find contact information for that publisher, you surely can find out what type of books they publish.

I've known authors who have trouble deciphering between genres and styles/types of books. They can't even understand the difference between true crime and mystery fiction. They figure that if a publisher published a biography set in the 1920s featuring a mass murderer, why wouldn't he be interested in a historical fiction story of a serial killer?

If you aren't clear on genres and you've adopted a scattershot method of approaching publishers, get help. Ask the most successful author in your writer's group to mentor you or pay a professional to guide you through this confusing process.

Remember, publishing is a business and must be approached as such. If you have never been in business and you've never had the opportunity to establish a persona of professionalism, you might need some coaching to prepare you for this somewhat foreign journey.

Use a Professional Approach

Often, a publisher wants to see a query letter first. Have you ever written a query letter? Do you know what it is? I've written thousands of them. I used to write articles for magazines and the procedure of introduction for an article idea was through a query letter. Those of you who have been involved in the publishing industry for any length of time probably know that a query letter is a one-page introduction to your project. Publishers typically want to see a query letter in which you introduce yourself and your project. A query letter is an invitation for the publisher to request additional information—generally a book proposal or the complete manuscript. If the publisher isn't interested in the topic presented or the way it's presented, he sends a rejection slip saying, "No thanks," "Not right for us," or something of this nature.

That's how it used to be. And this is still the process in many publishing houses. However, you've probably heard about or have even experienced the tremendous and ongoing changes within the publishing industry over the last dozen or so years. Old procedures and practices are being updated. We're gaining publishers and losing bookstores. There are new services that were never considered in this industry before. And the query letter is among those things that have recently changed.

That one-page query letter, in many cases, is now expected to be a several-page sales pitch for your book. I call it a mini–book proposal, as it includes a synopsis, marketing plan, market analysis and, in some cases, even sample chapters.

So, when you read in the submission guidelines that you should send a query letter first, or you're personally invited to do so, take a moment to find out what that particular publisher's or editor's expectations are. Do they want the original one-page intro into your project or are they expecting the mini–book proposal?

Here are sample query letter guidelines I found at a variety of publisher's sites:

- "Send query via email only. Include author's name, address, email, synopsis, length, your qualifications, market, and audience, other books you've published, and your ability to promote the proposed book."
- "Send a query letter with the opening of the book (ten pages), synopsis, and biographical info/author."
- "Send a one-page, single-spaced letter describing why, what, who, and the hook."
- "Send a letter describing the subject, your audience, your competition, and how your book will improve the topic or fill a special niche, author's relevant experiences and writing accomplishments."
- "Submit a short query letter (no more than fifteen–twenty double-spaced pages); sample of your work; a cover letter; SASE or, if you would like your manuscript returned, a self-addressed envelope and a check to cover return postage."
- "Each query must include: Cover letter with total word count, brief synopsis, and information about yourself (publishing credits, writing memberships, etc.), marketing strategy and first three chapters of your manuscript."

Whatever approach the particular publisher requests, do it right. Make a professional, clean presentation. Represent your project as if it is already successful. If you've done the right thing on its behalf from the very beginning, it's probably headed for success.

Publishers' Tips for Sending Your Package

Should you send your submission via email, as an attachment, or through the post office? Generally, the submission guidelines will include instructions. Some indicate what to put in the subject line of an email or they suggest whether or not you should enclose a return envelope when sending via the post office.

Sometimes these instructions are missing from a publisher's submission guidelines, and you aren't sure what to put in the subject line for an email submission. Where instructions are lacking, identify an email submission with something like: "True Crime Book Proposal," "Book Proposal—Requested—Young Adult Adventure," "Children's Picture Book Proposal—Sally Crayne." Use common sense. If your name is meaningful to the recipient of an email, use it in the subject line. If the proposal or manuscript has been requested, indicate this in the subject line. For a proposal that has been requested and that is submitted via the post office, write "requested material" on the front of the package.

Address the package or email to the right person. Most publishers' websites and submission guidelines indicate the name of the contact person. Use it. If there is no contact person listed, visit the staff pages and locate the right editor. This might be the acquisitions editor, the editor of books in this genre, or the managing editor, for example. At smaller publishing houses, very often you deal directly with the publisher. At any rate, do your best to find a name and use it in your correspondence.

You'll discover that some publishers do not let out the names of their staff. You're asked to submit to "Acquisitions Editor," or "Editor." It's awkward. What's even more awkward is when editor Jane Robbins is no longer working there and no one has bothered to update the website and the submission guidelines. It happens. I've even had my submissions returned with a note saying, "Jane Robbins no longer works here." Why they didn't pass it along to another editor, I'll never know.

What to Expect from the Publisher

Many publishers today do not return rejected manuscripts and they do not respond to rejected manuscripts, proposals, or letters. They're more likely to respond if the proposal or manuscript is requested, however. This means that they received a query letter from you and asked you to send the proposal or the manuscript. In this case, they may give your material more respect and actually respond to it.

Whether requested or not, if you don't receive a response after an appropriate length of time, check on your submission. What is an appropriate length of time to wait for a response? You'll sometimes find this information in the publisher's submission guidelines. If not, check *Writer's Market*. If the publisher is listed in this directory, his response time might appear in the listing.

If this, too, is a dead end, consider waiting four to six weeks for a response to your query letter and two months for a book proposal or manuscript.

Some publishers still practice the courtesy of returning your material if you have enclosed a self-addressed-stamped envelope; others refuse to, even then. Some will return your self-addressed-stamped postcard letting you know they received the package.

One publisher says, "You'll get a response in anywhere from five minutes to six weeks."

Another claims they will not look at submissions that do not follow their guidelines.

What About Previously Published Books?

This is a good topic because there are a growing number of self-published books and digital books being published by traditional publishers. Previously published books with impressive sales and good potential are of great interest to publishers. Some of them even seek out these sometimes-unknown treasures.

Perhaps you have a previously published book that's doing well, and you'd like to snag a publisher in order to reach new markets. Certainly this is a viable plan, if you own the rights to the book. First, check the publisher's submission guidelines to see if he or she mentions accepting previously published works. If so, move ahead following the publisher's guidelines. If not, send a one-page query letter describing your project and asking for permission to submit a proposal.

You may have an advantage over those pitching new, untried, untested books. You've come to know your audience intimately. You've learned some sales techniques that have already worked with this book. You have sales figures to prove its worth. A publisher should be highly interested in your project.

Some authors of already published books are timid about approaching an agent or a publisher. They fear they've already exhausted their potential market. Really? If you've crunched the numbers, you may have discovered that, sure, you've sold a lot of copies, but this number might only represent a fraction of the current and future market.

I write books for authors and I've sold a whole lot of them. I've personally presented programs and workshops to thousands of authors throughout the United States over the years and hundreds of my articles have appeared in dozens of author publications of all sizes. Yet, everywhere I go, I meet authors and professionals who have never heard of me or my work. Yes, there is still a large and growing market for my books. And the beauty is that there are also thousands of authors who are familiar with me and my work; thus, publishers are interested in any new books in this field that I might come up with.

What are the chances of landing a publishing contract for a previously-published book? I don't have the figures, but I can tell you that it has happened to me five times!

Here is an excerpt from author Diana Zimmerman's pitch for the young adult fantasy she had previously self-published. Scholastic Books issued her a contract based on this pitch.

- *Kandide and the Secret of the Mists* is the first book in Diana S. Zimmerman's *Calabiyau Chronicles Trilogy*, and is in its fourth printing.
- *Kandide and the Secret of the Mists* has a fan base of over 62,000 sold books, and over 12,000 opt-in email fans.
- *Kandide*'s average sale at author appearances/signings is over 125 books.
- *Kandide* has broken sales records, and sold out at virtually every Barnes & Noble where Diana has appeared, including sales of 256 books at a B&N in Phoenix, and over 325 books at a B&N in Mesa, AZ—with three-hour lines.
- *Kandide and the Lady's Revenge,* Book Two, is completed; Book Three, *Kandide: The Flame Is Fleeting* is currently being story edited; and Book Four is in outline form.
- *Kandide* is revving up for a major merchandise pitch, with perfume, clothing, print, calendars, and toys.
- *Kandide* reached #4 on the Amazon.com Best Seller List for "Fantasy Fiction."
- *Kandide* is on the Accelerated Reader list—9 points.
- *Kandide* (and its author Diana S. Zimmerman) have appeared at over 500 bookstores, festivals, libraries, book clubs, and schools nationwide—with more being added all the time.
- *Kandide* (and Diana) have appeared in front of more than 45,000 school kids.

- *Kandide's Attack of the Garglans* game reached #1 on Viral Charts, with over 1 million plays.
- *Kandide* has received hundreds of rave reviews, and is loved by kids and adults—boys and girls.
- *Kandide* is praised by teachers, school principals, and librarians, and is used in schools to address critical peer pressure and bullying issues, as well as increase interest in reading and art.
- *Kandide* is endorsed by the nationwide anti-bullying organization *S.A.V.E.* (Students Against Violence Everywhere).
- *Kandide* took honors in the Next Generation Indie Book Awards in an unprecedented three categories: Children's/Juvenile Fiction, Young Adult Fiction, and Science Fiction/Fantasy.

Keep Track of It All

Whether you send a query letter or a full-blown book proposal via email, or through the post office, it is up to the author to keep good records.

Are you feeling more and more like a CEO? There's a lot of responsibility for the author. That's right! Remember, writing is a craft, but once you decide to publish your little ditty or your professional book, you've entered into a fiercely competitive, serious business.

It doesn't matter how you manage your submissions log, just devise some means of tracking all submissions. When did you send it, what was it—query, book proposal, full manuscript? If you don't think dates are important, just wait until something is lost in the mail or in the midst of the muddle in a publishing house.

Note whether your submission is exclusive or simultaneous and if you gave the publisher or agent a deadline date (when the exclusivity option ends). Did you send illustrations? Was there a return envelope or return postcard enclosed? What was the response? Who will you send it to next? Good recordkeeping is good business.

It's not as easy to keep track of submissions as it once was. The fact is that many publishers today do not issue rejection letters. They don't communicate with an author unless there's a question, he wants to see more, or he issues a contract. This is why it is important to keep track of each publisher's estimated response time. If you don't hear from the publisher within that time frame, plus a week or two, contact him and ask for an update on your submission. He may respond or he may not. It's frustrating, for sure, and there comes a time when you have to move on.

But here's another scenario—one that has served me nicely in the past. When I contact a publisher or acquisitions editor to inquire about my project, they might say, "We didn't receive that submission. We have looked everywhere and it is not here—please resend."

Now you might consider this a big fat waste of time. But here's the reality of the situation. It's actually a gift. You've been invited to resubmit the project. (See why you never, ever send originals?) This time the editor or publisher is watching for it and will probably make it a priority. You've opened up a dialogue with the publishing house representative. Chances are, he will contact you once they've taken a look at the project. If you don't hear from anyone after a few weeks, feel free to email them again. The submission still might be rejected, but at least you know it was given a good chance.

Tips for Surviving the Dreaded Rejection

Rejection is part of the publishing game. If you participate to any degree in this industry and for any length of time, you will experience rejection—unless you wish to call it something else.

The fact is, rejection isn't the most descriptive word one can use. A rejection letter does not mean that you have been rejected; you shouldn't take it personally. A "no thank you" may mean that your idea doesn't fit the company's publishing plans for that year. Maybe they've recently accepted a similar book or they've met their quota of projects for the season. It could also mean that your project just doesn't measure up to this publisher's expectations or standards.

While most rejection letters are generic, you might occasionally receive a few words of encouragement from a publisher. Or you may get an explanation as to why the manuscript was rejected. Consider this an opportunity to learn. Relish it. Embrace it. Maybe make different decisions the next time you send out your proposal.

What if you get the silent treatment—no acceptance, no rejection—nothing? Authors report this happening more and more often. Understaffed publishing companies receive more submissions than they can handle and many of them have eliminated the courtesy of responding to each one. The silent treatment seriously irks most authors.

It's aggravating to think that while you wait patiently for favorable words about your carefully prepared proposal, it's being taken out the backdoor of the publishing house with the rest of the trash. And this is a good argument *for* simultaneous submissions.

Simultaneous submissions means that you are free to send your proposal or manuscript to more than one publisher at the same time. Some publishers frown on simultaneous submissions. They don't want to get into a bidding war with another publisher who also wants your book. While a bidding war between major publishers is a dream scenario for an author, publishers would rather not find themselves in this position. But wouldn't you like having two (or more) publishers fighting for the right to publish your amazing book and bidding against each other to win your favor and your signature on a six-figure contract? It can happen and it does happen, but rarely.

Many publishers still request that submissions be exclusive. Others don't much care. Generally, you can send out as many query letters as you wish—but that was before the query letter became, in some cases, a mini-book proposal. Most publishers are okay with simultaneous book proposals. But many either require exclusivity when it comes to accepting your manuscript submission or they want to know at the time of submission if your manuscript is currently with any other publishers.

Here's where receiving a rejection letter can be useful. At least you know the status of your project where that publisher is concerned, and you can move on. If you receive some advice from the publisher in the letter, you can consider acting on it. Perhaps your proposal is weak—you need to shore up your platform or you're approaching the wrong publishers for your book.

Even if you are rejected by every publisher on your list, you still may have plenty of options. First, seek a professional evaluation of your proposal and/or manuscript. If you are advised to get some impressive endorsements or build on your platform, for example, take the time to do so, then continue your search for a publisher.

Consider going the self-publishing or pay-to-publish route. If your book proposal is solid, and if you've followed the guidelines in this book, it should be easy enough for you to manage all of the details of publishing and marketing yourself. Thousands of authors do so each year.

If a publishing contract is important to you, produce your book yourself. Work hard at promoting it, build a reputation and impressive sales, and you should be able to capture the interest of a publisher, just like Diana Zimmerman did with her YA fantasy, *Kandide*.

That's the way of the business these days. Sometimes a new, unknown author must come into her own on her own before being noticed by the publisher of her choice. Rejection is not necessarily a closed door to your publishing success.

On this upbeat note, I leave you to pursue your publishing journey. Use some of the resources listed in the next section and be sure to study the actual book proposals I've collected as samples for your information. You'll notice that they don't all fall exactly within the parameters I've outlined in this book. The one thing they have in common, though, is the author's obvious understanding of the publishing industry and the author's responsibility, as all of the books represented by these proposals have been accepted by traditional publishers.

Part Seven

Resources for Authors

Books for Authors

Publish Your Book: Proven Strategies and Resources for the Enterprising Author, by Patricia Fry (Allworth Press)

Promote Your Book: Over 250 Proven, Low-Cost Tips and Techniques for the Enterprising Author, by Patricia Fry (Allworth Press)

Talk Up Your Book: How to Sell Your Book Through Public Speaking, Interviews, Signings, Festivals, Conferences and More, by Patricia Fry (Allworth Press)

Writing Picture Books: A Hands-On Guide from Story to Creation to Publication by Ann Whitford Paul (Writer's Digest Books)

The Business of Writing for Children, by Aaron Shepard (Shepard Publications)

Writing the Memoir: From Truth to Art, by Judith Barrington (The Eighth Mountain Press)

7 Easy Steps to Memoir Writing, by Mary Ann Benedetto (Writer's Presence)

The Writer's Legal Guide, by Tad Crawford and Kay Murray (Allworth Press)

Business and Legal Forms for Authors and Self-Publishers by Tad Crawford (Allworth Press)

Author Periodicals
Publisher's Weekly
www.publishersweekly.com

Publishing Basics
www.publishingbasics.com

Book Marketing Matters
www.bookmarketing.com

SPAWNews
www.spawn.org

Directories of Publishers
Writer's Market (print and digital)
www.writersmarket.com

Literary Market Place
www.literarymarketplace.com

Directories of Authors' Agents
www.aaronline.org
snipurl.com/safest (article about locating agents)
www.agentquery.com (searchable—over 900 agents)
www.guidetoliteraryagents.com/blog

Directories of Writer's Conferences
www.shawguides.com
www.newpages.com/writing-conferences
client.writersrelief.com/writers-classifieds/writing-conferences.aspx

Tips for finding conferences in your area
Search the Internet using keywords, "writers conference" + "your city/state"

Directories of Blog Sites
www.bloggernity.com
blogs.botw.org
www.blogtopsites.com

Directories of Book Reviewers
www.bookrevieweryellowpages.com/book-reviewer-list.html
bookreviewdirectory.wordpress.com/fiction-book-reviewers

Book Clubs
www.bookmovement.com
profnet.prnewswire.com (connects reporters to sources)

Intellectual Property Attorneys
www.calawyersforthearts.org (California)
www.law-arts.org (free legal services)

Miscellaneous Resources
www.librarything.com (for book promotion)
www.shewrites.com (community for women writers)
www.scribd.com (largest social publishing site)
crowdfundingforauthors.com (raise funds for your project)

SAMPLE BOOK PROPOSALS

Following, you will see samples representing a lifestyle how-to, a children's fiction, a memoir, a young reader's nonfiction, and a contemporary mystery suspense novel. You'll notice that each of these proposals has a different tone, order, and emphasis. This will give you an idea of how creative one can become and still land a publisher.

A Lifestyle How-to

There's a lot to love about this proposal. I'm particularly fascinated by the tone Ms. Levy uses throughout, replicating the wit and humor she'll use in the completed book. Any acquisitions editor will know right away that this book features a fun approach to a wildly popular topic. In today's hectic world, we welcome humor, even in the face of something as frustrating as dieting. Ms. Levy's funny and fun approach is most refreshing, and the fact that she was able to carry that over into her proposal is a huge plus. Not only that, her synopsis (overview) is clear and concise and her chapter summaries are spot-on as far as content, appeal, and word count.

She has also let the publisher know that she will "pepper" the book with photos, illustrations, sidebars, and other asides. The editorial staff can visualize this book without being inundated with a lot of unnecessary (at this point) materials. One thing missing is the market analysis—where Levy would compare this book to others on the market. However, it appears that she covers this issue, as well as the question of her proposed readership, quite adequately in her overview section.

The fact that Ms. Levy has a platform and knows how to present it would get any appropriate publisher's attention. Add to that her creativity in approaching the task of marketing and you can see why this proposal might be a slam dunk. I mean, what publisher of books on this topic wouldn't be interested in this unique twist on such a popular issue, authored by someone with a built-in following?

Sure enough, this proposal did win over the editorial team at one publishing company as the book is scheduled for publication by Skyhorse Publishing in spring of 2015. And Ms. Levy gets to keep the original title.

Calorie Accounting
The Bankable Diet for Fatties Who Won't Do Crunches but Will Crunch Numbers

by Mandy Levy / www.xxxxxx.com

Overview

Calorie Accounting is a fun and funny, visual and vibrant, cool and creative approach to a real-world, real-girl (or real-guy, I suppose) diet plan that <u>actually works</u>. As most of us know (and piss off, you lifetime skinnies who don't), typically, there's nothing less fun than dieting and nothing less funny than being fat and ugly and not fitting into anything you own and hating yourself... so let's cut the crap and face this thing head-on, like any strong, modern woman should: with jokes and self-deprecation! And sincere, unfaltering effort. And patience. And pictures. And puns.

With an Amy Sedaris-esque whip-smart/smart-ass character voice and a colorful, stylized, vintage aesthetic, *Calorie Accounting* will be the best time anyone's ever had losing weight. I, a nobody, but an EveryMandy, will become the reader's sarcastic best friend: I know how it feels, I've been there, I've done that, I'm just like you. I am not a *Today Show* nutritionist, I am not a doctor, I am not even Dr. Oz. I'm just a girl who's been on one diet or another since I'm 16 years old, and finally, I've found the one that works for me. So let's go to brunch and bitch about it. I'll tell you all my secrets, and you can get skinny too!

Calorie Accounting is an extended metaphor for achieving and maintaining guaranteed weight loss through our trusted mathematical system of checks and balances, ins and outs, deposits and withdrawals. It's black and white arithmetic that any dummy can calculate, but the difference between this and your Econ 101 seminar is that *Calorie Accounting* is fun and hilarious and taught by the coolest professor on campus! (Think Sedaris-meets-Amy Poehler-meets Tina Fey-meets-Lena Dunham-meets Prince. (Just kidding; no part of me is really like Prince at all, though he does have a lovely figure; I just wanted you to understand how wonderful the conglomerate of my essence can truly be for your readers.))

This is a diet book, sure, but not one you'll want to hide under your bed, collecting dust and shame in a dull, dated pile with *Atkins* and *The Zone*. No no. *Calorie Accounting* is an art and entertainment piece as much as it's a weight-loss guide, and it's as good-looking as you're bound to be when you're done with it—You'll want to display this beauty loud and proud on your coffee table, right next to *Bossypants* or *I Like You.* It's the fun and funny way for the fun and funny gal to take a breath, admit she's fatter than she wants to be, have a laugh, and do this thing.

Marketing and Publicity
Calorie Accounting is a lifestyle how-to for any regular gal, a lot like me: 24–40; probably has a decent, steady job; probably thinks she's funnier and more creative and more interesting than her decent, steady job allows; keeps a hectic social calendar; probably drinks a lot, maybe too much; might be single, might be married, likely doesn't have kids yet—still pretty selfish and self-obsessed; stylish; quirky; might have blond hair, brown hair, maybe pink hair; likes money, likes to shop, likes to look good in what she buys; maybe in a little bit of a funk, a little bit of a quarter- or third-life crisis, trying to find a good way out, make some positive changes, i.e. get skinny. Let's just all admit that being thin makes everything better. It does.

It's the kind of book that's going to pop on whatever shelf you place it, but I see it hanging out most aptly amidst the fashionable and funny titles and sundries at *Urban Outfitters, Anthropologie,* and *Madewell,* in addition to the smaller lifestyle & décor shops like *Sterling Place* and *Table Top,* with the coffee-table books. And obviously in the diet/self-help (and BESTSELLER) sections at Barnes & Noble. Duh. Oh—and it'll be huge in Japan. But more than just a hardcover, *Calorie Accounting* will be a movement, a community, a consciousness. There will be a big-time web presence (I do own calorieaccounting.com, thank god) with a blog, products, recipes, forums, and more.

My "personal brand" has been growing steadily as an Emmy-winning writer (Google me!), host, and comedian here in NYC, and I'll be able to reach a good cross-section of the intended audience via my social network and connections with *Upright Citizens Brigade, The Moth, Entertainment Weekly,* VH1, Bravo, and my own devoted following with my successful local "drinking games": Slurring Bee and Wino Bingo. And in Cincinnati, Ohio, if it pleases you, I'm something of a small-town socialite. Just sayin'.

Chapter Outline
Peppered with colorful photography, illustrations, sidebars and asides, the basic backbone of *Calorie Accounting* will be laid out as follows:

- Introduction
- Calorieconomics 101
- Budgeting Your Bulge Away
- Getting Your Calories' Worth, Or, The Jew in All of Us
- Moving Your Moneymaker
- Your Money's No Good Here
- Embezzlement
- When All's Accounted For
- Recipes/Glossary

Introduction:
After a disclaimer (put that thick skin to good use and don't get offended), a dedication (to all the people who lied to me and said I wasn't fat when I clearly was), a foreword (Hi Reader! I'm your friend!), and a Four Word (Let's Get Skinny, Bitches!), I pose a valid question in my proper Introduction: Well who the hell are you? And it's worth asking. Because after all, who am I? And why should anyone care about what I have to say about diet and weight loss? I'll give a brief tell-all of how a life-long superiority complex eventually made my waistline grow as big as my head, and how a rollercoaster of frustrating failures—healthy and not so healthy—in trying to whittle away the fat left me super depressed, hopeless, and unrecognizable to myself... which is scary. But a new chapter in my life gave me the kick in the pants I needed to develop a fresh approach, and it turns out that it's the easiest thing I've ever done. It's *Calorie Accounting*, I feel like I've hit the jackpot, and I want to share my riches with the world.

Calorieconomics 101
We dive right in. There is a simple equation (I call it "The Equation of Equations of Equations") upon which the entire world of *Calorie Accounting* is based. We'll go over the equation in detail, maybe twice for dummies, plug in your particulars, and via a budget and financing plan we'll find the unique numbers (calories in and calories out;

BMR (basal metabolic rate)) you're going to work with in order to lose the weight you want to lose. We'll look at "Calories as Currency," taking into account that old adage "A calorie saved is a calorie earned," and gather together our tools of the trade: ledger, calculator, camera, scale, pedometer, tape measure.

Budgeting Your Bulge Away

Budgeting is the most basic component in responsible money management. You look at what you have, you look at what you need, you look at what you want, and you find a way to ration it all out in a system customized specially for you. Same thing in *Calorie Accounting*. Establish a dream and finance its reality, either penny by penny or calorie by calorie. Here I'll lay out a step-by-step plan to get started (*Your Starting Balance* (weight now); *The Goal Mine* (what you want to/should weigh in the end); *What Price Skinny?* (how many calories is that goal going to cost you); and *The Payment Plan* (how you'll get there)). This—and knowing yourself—is all you'll ever need.

Getting Your Calories' Worth, Or, The Jew in All of Us

(I'm allowed to go there because I'm a half-Jew and my last name's Levy and that's like Smith in the Jewish phone book. And I had a bat-mitzvah on a boat for my 30th birthday party.) Here's where we look to the Jews for inspiration, who are famously good with money because they're tight as hell and always looking for a deal. What foods can we stuff down our collective gullet at the lowest caloric expense? We'll talk about penny-pinching and waist-cinching, calories on clearance, Loehmanns (RIP), Designer Imposter foods, evil foods that trick you, and a sampling of my own favorite go-to snacks that deliver the most bang(in' bod) for their (caloric) buck.

Moving Your Moneymaker

Exercise! Now that we've got a handle on calories-in, and how best to be clever and thrifty and get a deal based on your budget, we'll get on the treadmill and talk about calories-out! No healthy, maintainable weight-loss solution is a reality without regular exercise, so here are my pointers for burning calories, misery-free. The Gym is The Bank, and it's where you go to get your pocket change, so you can live a free and fruitful life and throw bushels of grape tomatoes down your maw guilt-free. If you hate running, walk. And get a pedometer too. Every step is one in the right direction.

Your Money's No Good Here

A budget is still a budget. Not everything's a reality and within your reach. You're still fat, so can you really afford the fried-cheese cheeseburger at Bennigan's, even if it's just the one time? Your money's no good in a situation like this, so don't put yourself out of business. This section is all about living life IRL (or In Real Life, for squares). We'll talk about ideas and tips for going out to restaurants, bars, and any other place where you're not confined to the safety and comfort of your own couch and pre-measured-pre-calculated kale chips. After all, the readers of this book would never want to give up their social lives—here's how they can keep their calendars full, and keep their caloric checkbooks balanced at the same time.

Embezzlement

What happens when we screw up? When we steal from our own savings accounts and put ourselves in the red? When we lie, telling ourselves we'll just have one piece of cheesecake, and then cheat, eating the whole rest of the cheesecake, a la mode? *Embezzlement* is a setback in *Calorie Accounting*, but if you catch yourself red-handed soon enough, you'll limit the time you have to do for the crime. Just don't do anything stupid, don't do anything dangerous, don't binge, don't give into get-thin-quick schemes. You'll put yourself in debt and you don't want to be there. This chapter is about talking it through. Being honest. Being real. Being healthy. Get to the gym and start over. Everything's going to be okay.

When All's Accounted For

We wrap up the *Calorie Accounting* adventure with SUCCESS. Sweet, sweet success. Losing weight is absolutely a bipolar, manic-depressive experience, and you should feel so insanely proud of yourself for making it to your goal, once you have. But here's where I urge readers not to give into "The Hammertime Effect"—making a fortune and blowing it all, almost instantaneously. Please, don't toast your achievements with entire pizzas and 12-packs of Bud Light Lime-a-rita. At least not immediately, and at the very least not continuously. Knowing your numbers and knowing yourself will be instrumental in keeping *Calorie Accounting* a part of your day-to-day forever, and you'll be able to maintain your healthy weight as long as you stick to the plan and the mindset. It's a delicate thing. Could be fleeting. Just like money. Stay smart, stay accountable, stay awesome, stay you, and you'll maintain the wealth of health for years to come.

Recipes/Glossary
This is self-explanatory, right?

About the Author
I'm a girl. I'm a girl who obsesses over her body, her hair, her face, her age, her love life, pop culture, fashion, movies, music, Benedict Cumberbatch, and cheese. I'm a girl who faces problems with funny, because I'm far too flawed of a person to take myself seriously. I'm a girl with a lot of stories and a lot of lives, with a lot of wonderful friends and the best family in the world, a pretty nice job, an amazing boyfriend, a really cute apartment, success, opportunity, an Emmy, a little bit of small-time fame/recognition/ dare-I-say-adoration, and yet, nothing feels like anything unless I'm the best version of myself… which means thin. My right size. Maybe that's screwed up, I don't know. But it's the truth, and it's my mission here to be honest. I think there are a lot of girls who are just like me, with big dreams and big ideas but their big thighs have gotten in the way. Diet books are ridiculous. Dietitians are ridiculous. Personal trainers are the sons of Satan. All my life it's seemed like in order to get fit and healthy, you have to leave your sense of humor at the door. Like in yoga class… how are people not laughing hysterically over the whole-hearted ohms and namastes?? The point is, the world is too heavy, and so are we. Time to lighten up.

Calorie Accounting is more or less my real-time diary of the successful diet plan I designed and lived and documented when I moved to New York 3 years ago. I lost 35 pounds and have kept it off, and feel it's my duty to share my stories, my struggles, and my successes with anyone who wants to listen. My vision is a fun and colorful one, but honest and earnest all the same. I've been an actress, a musician, a professional audience member, a greeting card writer, a poet, a parodist, a constipation commercial voice-over artist, a podcast star, a stand-up comedian, a storyteller, and a hostess with the mostest, but through it all, I'm just a girl. Just a girl who wants to look good and feel great.

Children's Fiction

Leanne Shirtliffe has created a very strong proposal for her children's fiction book, with her platform as the shining star. You'll notice that she has filled three pages—single-spaced—with her extremely detailed marketing plan. I especially like the way she broke the marketing potion into tidy sections for easy and quick reference. But there's enough meat to her entries in case the editor or publisher wishes to study each one more carefully. The marketing aspect of this proposal would impress any publisher. And the "about the author" section encompasses nearly a thousand words on her behalf. She has a real handle on the art of representation when it comes to selling herself.

She has done an excellent job of analyzing other books similar to hers, both making a case for the topic of her children's book and demonstrating a market for it. The original proposal included a lot of photographs to accompany the information—personal and professional photos, book covers of the books in her competition section and so forth. We removed the photos and other illustrations in order to facilitate the space and formatting required for this book.

Ms. Shirtliffe's book was published in 2014 by Sky Pony Press. Here's another one that was allowed to keep the original title.

The Change Your Name Store
by Leanne Shirtliffe

Table of Contents

Overview

Having recently decided that she no longer likes her name, Wilma Lee Wu sets out to find the Change Your Name Store. Once there, the feisty girl is bedazzled by Ms. Zena McFouz, the outrageous owner who encourages Wilma to try on new names in the magical change room. Each time Wilma tries on a new name, she is transported to the country from which the name originates. Will Wilma find a new name? Will she discover her true identity and where she belongs?

The Change Your Name Store is a whimsical, rhyming picture book written in 650 words. It will entertain children aged five to eight, especially those who are intrigued by their own name or who want go on imaginary adventures to new countries.

The Change Your Name Store offers readers many takeaways, including the following: there are many beautiful names from around the world; many children go through a stage where they wish they had another name; exploring other cultures and countries is a fun adventure; and it's possible to grow into your own name.

The story leaves plenty of room for the illustrator, who will be able to bring alive not only the inside of the actual Change Your Name Store but also each country Wilma visits.

In addition to the text, there is substantial possibility for the end pages, such as:

- A map of the countries visited
- A brief explanation of naming traditions in different cultures
- A place for children to explore the meaning of their name

The themes of identity, belonging, and multiculturalism (as well as teacher-created lesson plans and activity sheets available on the author's website) will make *The Change Your Name Store* a hit in primary classrooms, among home-schoolers, and with kids and parents in our increasingly global society.

About the Author

Leanne Shirtliffe, also known as Ironic Mom, is a published writer, mother, award-winning blogger, and award-winning teacher.

Leanne is the author of *Don't Lick the Minivan: And Other Things I Never Thought I'd Say to my Kids* (Skyhorse, May 2013), a humor book that has received advance praise from Jenny Lawson (The Bloggess), Jill Smokler (Scary Mommy), Kristyn Pomranz (Nickelodeon), Stefanie Wilder-Taylor, Elizabeth Doyle, Terry Fallis, Kathy Buckworth, and others.

Leanne is a contracted writer for Nickelodeon's humor site, NickMom.com (which according to Alexa.com is ranked in the top 5000 most popular websites in the US). In 2011, Nickelodeon editorial staff sought Leanne out to be one of the flagship writers for their new brand, NickMom.com, which aims to become the top humor site in the world for moms.

Leanne Shirtliffe lives by the motto, "If you can't laugh at yourself, laugh at your kids." She's the mother of seven-year-old twins who provide more entertainment than Cirque du Soleil on speed; to escape, she teaches and finds that dealing with 97 teens is easier than being trapped in a house with her own spawn. Leanne's blog, IronicMom.com, has been called the most laugh-out-loud blog in Canada. She also writes a humor column for the *Calgary Herald,* is the co-editor of StuffKidsWrite.com, and is working on her first humor book. Follow her hilarious musings on Twitter and Facebook.

An editor with the *Huffington Post* also sought out Leanne and asked her to blog for them. She has written humorous pieces for them, including "Top 13 Horror Movies for Parents" and "You Know You're Canadian When: the 2012 Version."

Leanne's blog, IronicMom.com, was declared the Best Humour Blog by the Canadian Weblog Awards, a juried competition. IronicMom.com garners 8,000–13,000 hits per month and has been featured on high-traffic sites such as the *Christian Science Monitor, ProBlogger,* WordPress's home page, *Canadian Family,* CBC, the *Calgary Herald*, and *Sweet Mama.*

In September's print and online editions, *Reader's Digest* published that Leanne Shirtliffe was one of Canada's Top 10 Mommy Bloggers. They recognized her as "the blogger most likely to make you snort coffee out of your nose."

She is extremely active in social media and has a large network of bloggers and tweeps she interacts with, giving her an amplified audience well into the hundreds of thousands.

StuffKidsWrite.com ("Like Stuff Adults Write. But Funnier."), a website Leanne co-edits, has over 4500 subscribers and continues to grow quickly. The website's content has been featured on BuzzFeed, the Huffington Post, Babble, and NickMom.

Leanne was profiled in the *Queen's University Alumni Review* magazine (circulation 106,000), and she was also a WordPress featured blogger twice, garnering her site nearly 5000 hits in a single day (see screenshots below). IronicMom.com was recognized as one of the top five new blogs by the *Canadian Weblog Awards* (2010) and as the top parenting blog in Calgary (a city of over 1 million people) and as the Most Laugh-Out-Loud Funny blog by *Sweet Mama*, a popular Canadian website.

Leanne is viewed as a parenting expert with a sense of humor and has been interviewed for numerous articles by the *Globe and Mail* (Canada's *New York Times)*. She has also written for national publications, including a humor essay, "So Much for My Kid Commandments," which was developed into a podcast. Leanne's article, "Seven Worst Christmas Toys for Kids," appeared as the lead story of the online business section of the *Christian Science Monitor* (website ranked in the Top 500) on December 6, 2011. That story reached more than 230,000 page views, a rare achievement according to the Monitor's business editor. She has an open invite to submit story ideas to the *Christian Science Monitor*.

Leanne wrote a humor column for the *Calgary Herald* (circulation 800,000) for two years. In addition, select posts from her blog appeared in the magazine *Multiplicity*, a monthly periodical published by the Calgary Twins, Triplets and More Association. Each holiday season, Leanne offers a humorous critique of the worst toys for Christmas. She has done lengthy segments on CBC's *The Calgary Eyeopener*, the city's number-one morning radio show, as well as segments on CBC-TV and Global TV (see photos below) and on sixteen CBC radio stations across the country.

Much of Leanne's material comes from the mayhem of raising eight-year-old twins. How she obtained such a family is a story in itself: She left Canada for the Persian Gulf as a single woman, found a husband in Bahrain, and birthed her children in Bangkok. While in Thailand, Leanne wrote articles for BAMBI, Bangkok Mothers and Babies International. Two of her humor articles include "Pregnant or Tourist: Is There a Difference?" and "You're Not That Fat: Bizarre Comments Made To Pregnant Women."

Adept at public speaking, Leanne frequently emcees major events, including her school's awards gala and corporate events. She has also presented humor-writing workshops and taught children's writing workshops for the English Language Arts Council of the Alberta Teaching Association. She loves an audience and a microphone, unless she has to sing. She has worked with a humor coach and taken stand-up comedy workshops. Leanne is also under contract to teach online writing courses, including "Introduction to Picture Books" and "How To Be Funny. Er."

Leanne has more than 6500 like-minded followers on Twitter and she can be found listed under categories such as "fonts of hilarity," "mad mommies," "sanity cocktail," "necessary evils," "people who make me laugh," and "cool like polar bear toes."

She is an active member of the Calgary Critique Group and the Alberta Writers' Guild, and she regularly attends the Surrey International Writers' Conference.

Learn more about Leanne Shirtliffe at (she lists several social media sites).

Competitive Analysis

Many children's books in the marketplace explore identity, frequently touching on themes of bullying, family differences, and self-esteem. There are some picture books, however, that approach a child's quest for identity with a multicultural angle and/or an imaginary journey. Here is an overview of six of those titles:

I Could Be, You Could Be by Karen Owen and Barroux (Paperback, 40 pages, $6.99, Barefoot Books, 2012 (Reprint Edition)). This adventure story looks at what kids would like to imagine themselves to be today: a dragon, an alien, an Arab pony. Like *The Change Your Name Store*, it deals with identity and imagination, but *The Change Your Name Store* explores countries of the world in catchy, rhyme-filled fun.

The Name Game by Donna M. Jackson and Ted Stearn (Hardcover, 40 pages, $16.99, Viking Juvenile, 2009). This nonfiction mini-almanac offers facts about the names of people, pets and companies, and it touches on a few cultures, including Blackfoot, Icelandic, and Chinese. As fiction, *The Change Your Name Store* includes similar facts in the end pages, but they are contextualized since the cultures discussed are mentioned in the story.

The Name Jar by Yangsook Choi (Paperback, 40 pages, $6.99, Dragonfly Books, 2003 (Reprint edition)). This book tells the story of a recent Korean immigrant who gets teased about her name, an occurrence that prompts her to select a new one from a name jar. *The Change Your Name Store* explores a similar theme of identity, but covers more than one culture. As a rhyming, whimsical narrative, *The Change Your Name Store* also invites all children to reflect on their own name.

My Name is Sangoel by Karen Lynn Williams, Khadra Mohammed, and Catherine Stock (Hardcover, 32 pages, $17.00, Eerdmans Books for Young Readers, 2009). This non-rhyming book is about a Sudanese refugee recently arrived in America, who—since no one can pronounce his name—draws pictures on his shirt as a mnemonic, prompting other children to do the same with their own names. Wilma Lee Wu, the protagonist of *The Change Your Name Store,* is a Western child who magically visits many cultures, allowing readers to journey with her outside of North America.

My Name is Yoon by Helen Recorvits and Gabi Swiatkowska (Hardcover, 32 pages, $16.99, Farrar, Straus and Giroux, 2003). This book tells the story of a recent Korean immigrant who does not like how her name looks in English; as a result, she tries new names as she learns English, names such as cat, bird and cupcake. In *The Change Your Name Store*, Wilma Lee Wu was born in America, but still dislikes her name. In fun rhyme, she explores other "unusual" names before falling in love with her own moniker.

The Seven Seas by Ellen Jackson, Bill Slavin, and Esperana Melo (Hardcover, 36 pages, $16.00, Eerdmans Books for Young Readers, 2010). This adventure tale, told in humorous rhyme, tells the story of a school-aged child who daydreams when the teacher begins talking about the Seven Seas. Although the child goes on imaginary journeys to

Marrakesh, Peru, and Istanbul, these places are used simply as rhyming words; in *The Change Your Name Store*, there are basic facts about every country discussed within the rhyming narrative and a stronger multicultural theme.

Marketing and Publicity
Primary Market
Potential readers of this book include children aged five and up as well as their parents. This book will especially appeal to children in more multicultural, urban areas and to parents who have knowledge of the world around them.

Secondary Markets
The special appeal of *The Change Your Name Store* is that it will fit extremely well with social studies and language arts units around identity.
  Other markets can be found in the following places:

- **Parent-Teacher Events:** The author has taught at private schools in three different countries; consequently, she has access to thousands of influential parents through school and alumni newsletters.
- **Family Exhibition Shows:** Thousands of parents attend annual trade shows in major North American cities, such as the Calgary Baby Show.
- **Blogs:** The online parenting community is massive. Posts on networked blogs, cross-posts, and a blog tour have the potential to increase sales substantially. The author is extremely active on social media and has a strong network eager to promote the book. (More detailed information is available in the Online Marketing section.)
- **Expatriate Communities:** Given that many of the book's early essays are set overseas, the expatriate community is another possible market. There are many associations and newsletters that can be pursued for sales potential. The author has strong connections in ten countries (Australia, Singapore, Spain, Thailand, Bahrain, United Arab Emirates, Switzerland, Portugal, Mexico, and New Zealand) that are willing to promote her book among expatriates or local populations.
- **Baby Boutiques:** The recent explosion of upscale baby clothing and furniture retailers is a strong possibility for parents with disposable income.

Promotion Plan
To promote the book, the author will do the following:

Press Kit
- contact Nickelodeon, for whom the author is a contracted writer, about reviewing the book on their ParentsConnect blog. The legal department at Nickelodeon already approved a blurb for Leanne's previous book, Don't Lick the Minivan (Skyhorse, May 2013);
- contact *Today's Parent*, a magazine that boasts a readership of 1.6 million. The author is well acquainted with the magazine's managing editor, who has already requested a review copy of Leanne's soon-to-be-published humor book;
- send press releases to major parenting magazines including *Parents*; *Parenting*; *Parent & Child*; *Twins*; *Brain, Child*; and *Canadian Family* (on whose blog the author has guest-posted multiple times);
- send press releases to school libraries;
- contact 100 metropolitan newspapers to raise interest in reviews. She will begin with regional media and network affiliates, including the *Calgary Herald* (circulation 800,000), for whom she penned a humor column; the *Globe and Mail* (Canada's National Newspaper), for whom she has written and been interviewed as a parenting expert; and the *Christian Science Monitor*, for whom she has written.
- send press releases to expatriate organization newsletters and newspapers, including Bangkok Mothers and Babies International (with whom she was a member and a published writer) and the New International School of Thailand (where she taught). Thailand's two English-language newspapers, *The Bangkok Post* and *The Nation*, have a combined circulation of more than 100,000;
- contact twenty-five publications throughout Alberta;
- promote her book through organizations of which she is a member, including the Queen's Alumni Association (whose magazine, circulation 106,000, has already featured her blog) and the Alberta Writer's Guild;
- be profiled in her school's newsletter.

Media Engagements
- contact local and national general consumer television shows such as *Breakfast Television* and *Canada AM*. The author is also acquainted with Canadian network level news anchor Dawna Friesen, and with Ali Velshi, CNN's Chief Business Correspondent;
- contact fifty local, regional, and national radio shows to appear as a guest, including NPR and CBC Radio (Canada's NPR); the author has appeared previously on CBC Radio and CBC-TV;
- contact parenting and books-related radio programs including CBC's *The Next Chapter* as well as popular Blog Talk Radio programs (the author has an open invitation to appear on *Real Life with Susan and Friend*s which boasts more than 20,000 listeners).

North American Appearances
- arrange speaking engagements, book signings, and tweet-ups along the route at bookstores, summer fairs, coffee shops, and pubs. Get local bloggers and tweeps to promote;
- contact the hundreds of teachers she knows;
- apply to speak at the national convention of the National Council of Teachers of English (NCTE), an annual event in a large US city that draws over 5000 people. The topic will be either "teaching humor writing" or "teacher as writer," presentations the author has given to rave reviews at other conferences.

Regional Appearances
- contact bookstores to set up signings in three provinces;
- arrange book signings at several local bookstores;
- attend local author events to promote her book;
- contact writers' conferences about speaking opportunities;
- use her connections with a large, wealthy, influential parent community in Calgary to promote her book (the author teaches at the top university-prep school in Alberta);
- arrange visits to local schools;
- sell her book at the bi-annual sale for the Twins, Triplets, and More Association of Calgary (which has an attendance of more than 1000 people per sale).

Online Marketing

- create and coordinate an online street launch team of fifty influential bloggers on social media, who will commit to the following:
  - reviewing the book at Amazon, GoodReads, Barnes and Noble, and Chapters-Indigo,
  - promote it on their social networks,
  - help develop marketing ideas;
- develop a full set of teacher-tested lesson plans to use with *The Change Your Name Store* on her website;
- use her **network of Nickelodeon's NickMom writers**, many of whom are professional comedians and published writers (*Comedy Central, The Onion, McSweeneys, HuffPo*), to promote the book (the author already manages a Twitter list of those writers);
- include a link to the book's website on her **Nickelodeon bio** page (http://www.nickmom.com/blog/author/shirtliffel/);
- use her blog, IronicMom.com, to offer readers an opportunity to purchase her book;
- use the influence of Kristen Lamb, American social media maven, to promote the book to her thousands of followers;
- use her writing group's blog, wordbitches.com, to promote the book;
- use the blog she co-edits, StuffKidsWrite.com ("Like Stuff Adults Write. But Funnier"), to promote the book;
- send copies to **high-traffic parenting blogs** (which will reach tens of thousands of target readers) including Theta Mom, Motherlode, Mommy Wants Vodka, Free Range Kids, MommyShorts, Mom 101, Notes From the Trenches, Dooce, Woulda Coulda Shoulda, Girls Gone Child, Redneck Mommy, Scary Mommy, The Bloggess, Her Bad Mother, Rachel Held Evans, and Finslippy;
- arrange a **multi-week intensive blog tour** that will include fifty appearances at different blogs in five weeks, including the blogs of Kristen Lamb (warriorwriters.wordpress.com), bestselling romance author Elizabeth Boyle (elizabethboyle.com/blog), and Lenore Skenazy's popular blog (freerangekids.wordpress.com); together this will reach a combined audience well into the tens of thousands;
- use Twitter and Facebook to promote the book effectively.

General Promotion

- block out a launch window dedicated to promoting the book, its publication, and sales;
- line up speaking engagements with regional parenting groups, such as Twins, Triplets and More Association of Calgary (TTMAC), of which she is a member and a newsletter contributor;
- mention her book in her bylines for local and national publications, including pieces she writes for the *Huffington Post*;
- be a highly effective spokesperson for the project, as a teacher with more than seventeen years in the classroom and substantial public speaking experience;
- work with her agent and publisher to develop an effective promotion plan.

Potential Cross-Platform Development

- Develop an **app**, where children can enter a virtual Change Your Name Store, click on a name, and be taken on an educational trip to that country. They could "friend" some of these imaginary characters and go on adventures with them. They could also search for the meaning of their names, and play games (e.g. word scrambles) with their names.
- Develop a series featuring Wilma Lee Wu:
  - Wilma Lee Wu volunteers in the Change Your Name store, assisting Ms. McFouz and going on adventures with other children unhappy with their names;
  - Wilma Lee Wu takes a trip to other countries to explore their cultures. She gets into trouble wherever she goes, but always manages to land on her feet.

<u>Manuscript</u>

The Change Your Name Store

A smart feisty girl named Wilma Lee Wu
Liked climbing tall trees and chasing frogs too.
She loved puzzles and trains, even reading a book,
Tormenting her brother and attempting to cook.

But one tiny item she longed to throw out:
"My name! It's so boring, so blah," she would pout.
Determined to fix the one thing she deplored
She set out in search of the Change Your Name store.

She trudged and she trudged with a map as her guide,
Up and down streets that were busy and wide.
Her feet now both tired, her hair a real mess,
At last Wilma spotted the proper address.

"Hello," Wilma said, to Ms. Zena McFouz,
"Can you help me select a new name I can use?"
"Of course," she responded, "there's many right here.
Though before we begin there's a rule to make clear.

"With names that you like, you must take them inside,
Try them on gently, then go for a ride.
And there you'll discover what's in every name
And which one fits you," Ms. McFouz did proclaim.

So Wilma looked up at the names on the wall,
Till she saw a fine name in the tiniest scrawl.
"Babette Bijou?" Ms. McFouz said amazed.
"A French name, a great choice," she quickly appraised.

Soon Wilma felt odd and could not even move.
Before she could shout, she stood at the Louvre.
A beret on her head and a café-au-lait,
She felt rather stared at, like art on display.

And when she returned, she said with a start,
"Oh no, that's not me. I can't play that part.
This name is better, it's this one, you see:
Salima bint Sami al Sala, that's me."

She stood in the shop, but did not remain,
For landing on sand, she arrived in Bahrain.
"I love it," thought Wilma, as she studied the place
Then rivers of sweat streamed off her round face.

And when she returned, she said with a start,
"Oh no, that's not me. I can't play that part.
This name is better, it's this one, you see:
Dominga Delfino, I love it, that's me."

Without time to add that special word, please,
She found herself on a big hill in Belize.
The beauty amazed her, the friendliness, too.
But she opted to leave when a hurricane blew.

And when she returned, she said with a start,
"Oh no, that's not me. I can't play that part.
This name is better, it's this one, you see:
Nuru N'zinga, I love it, that's me."

She soon was in Kenya, the night sky all dark,
But a sign was lit up that read National Park.
With creatures around her, she saw their big eyes,
She wondered if choosing a new name was wise.

Now back in the store, she sat on a chair.
"There're no names I like," she said in despair,
"Not Nuru, Salima, Dominga, Babette,
I do not like one," said Wilma, upset.

Then Zena McFouz brought her special name drawer,
And Wilma continued her search for one more.
"This name, it's mine, it's this one, you see:
Wilma Lee Wu, I love it, that's me!"

She thanked Ms. McFouz as she grabbed her name card.
She ran all the way and arrived in her yard.
She rushed up the sidewalk and through the front door,
Leaped over her brother, who played on the floor.

Her dad sat there reading, her mom on her phone.
"Guess what?" Wilma asked in an excited tone.
"I found it, my name!" she said, a real trooper.
And finally her parents looked up from their stupor.

"What is it? Do tell us," they urged and they cried.
They waited and wondered, *What did she decide?*
At last Wilma exhaled and shouted with glee,
"I'm Wilma, I'm Wil-girl, I'm Wilm-sy, I'm me!"

A Memoir

I like the way Cami Ostman has organized her memoir proposal. It is rich in just the sort of information a publisher wants to see. This memoir has a purpose and a focus and it is made clear from the beginning.

In her overview, Ms. Ostman does a masterful job of drawing the publisher into her story. She uses the technique we discussed within the chapters of this book—grab the reader with your opening statement. And she uses clever means to hold his attention throughout the overview (which she manages to keep brief) and on throughout the proposal.

Notice that she follows the overview with the chapter summaries. It works in this proposal. Immediately, the publisher is treated to an outline of the unique story she's pitching. The chapter titles are intriguing and these may entice the publisher to actually read the summaries.

The summaries are a little long, but they carry a lot of weight. They describe the events and activities as well as their emotional impact for the author—an important technique for a memoir proposal. Her method for explaining her target audience is clever and probably effective. You'll notice that she labels this section: "People who will love this book."

This book was published by Seal Press in 2010. They changed the title and revised the subtitle just a bit. It is now *Second Wind: One Woman's Midlife Quest to Run Seven Marathons on Seven Continents*

In the Long Run
One Woman's Midlife Quest to Run a Marathon on Every Continent

Proposal Table of Contents
Overview
Table of Contents
Chapter-by-Chapter Summaries
Author Biography
Target Audience
Marketing Strategies
Competitive Titles
Length and Delivery

Overview

Sometimes a personal crisis can open the door to a new life. For me, in the midst of a divorce and paralyzing self-doubt, with anxiety making it impossible to get air into my lungs, I had to find a way to breathe. So one morning, I went out into the elements and I took a slow run. It was exactly what I needed: As it turns out, you have to breathe when you run.

In the Long Run: One Woman's Midlife Quest to Run a Marathon on Every Continent is the story of a woman creeping into midlife who is an unlikely athlete and an unlikely hero. The book begins with my divorce and the messy grief I was muddling through when an old friend challenged me to go for a run. That first run gave me the gift of breath and some clarity of thought, so I kept it up. The reader comes with me while I run my way out of sadness and the patriarchal rules around "being a woman" that had held me captive, and into authenticity and self-love.

In the Long Run tells of a true vision quest, the one I willingly submitted to as I put myself on every continent of the world for seven 26.2-mile grunts and a chance to change my life. Up hills, through flash floods, past dead kangaroos, and into realistic love for self and others, the reader will follow me into some of the most exotic places in the world and some of the darkest and most enlightened places in the psyche.

There are fifteen chapters in this book. Preceding the chapters that chronicle the seven marathons on the seven continents are the chapters that describe the preparations for each of those races and the self-learnings that each particular training period drilled into me. The last chapter is the summary of the gifts this long journey has given me (and the reader) and some thoughts about how readers might integrate the lessons I've learned into their own lives.

In the Long Run is a memoir, but it is also a model of how anyone can take on a midlife vision quest of her own, with or without the running. Readers of this book will be inspired to take chances, to tell the truth in their lives and to listen to their inner voices in a new way.

Table of Contents

Introduction
Chapter 1. Beginning the Race: The Starting (Over) Line
Chapter 2. Europe: The Prague Push, May 2003
Chapter 3. Together and Alone: My Own Vision Quest,
        September 2003–June 2007
Chapter 4. Australia: The Mudgee Nudge, August 2007
Chapter 5. Back of the Pack: Finding Community
Chapter 6. North America: The Whidbey Island Grind,
        April 2008
Chapter 7. Powerful and Vulnerable: Tales From a
        Sub-Continental Race
Chapter 8. Asia: The Tateyama Trek, January 2009
Chapter 9. Getting Ready for the Long Haul
Chapter 10. Africa: Killer Kilimanjaro, June 2009
Chapter 11. A Brief Reprieve
Chapter 12. South America: Sao Paulo Celebration, June 2009
Chapter 13. Resting and Recuperating: Preparing for Antarctica
Chapter 14. Antarctica: South Pole Shout Out, March 2010
Chapter 15. Reflections: How to Prepare a Midlife Vision Quest

Chapter-by-Chapter Summaries
Author's Note:
All chapters through Chapter 7 reflect events that have already occurred. Chapters 8 through 15 have yet to be written because I am still in the process of completing preparations for participation in those marathons.

Although it is impossible to know what each race will bring in terms of insights and lessons, it is certain that every marathon brings ample opportunity for self-reflection, as well as plenty of struggles to overcome and learn from. Please note that I have plans to complete three races in 2009 and one (Antarctica) in Spring 2010. Chapters will be completed in a timely manner after the running of each race.

Introduction

I didn't become a committed runner until I was ready to run away from my eleven-year marriage and from the rigid rules of my religion. I'd been "born again" when I was thirteen years old. My family was in shambles at the time. My parents had divorced a couple of years earlier, and my mother had quickly remarried. I got a new baby brother just before I started junior high. I needed some attention and some structure. In walked God and a literalistic view of the Bible with a big load of rules. I took to the rules, as do many people who come out of chaos looking for security, and they gave me a foundation to stand on for many years.

Twenty years, an unhappy marriage, and a master's degree later, however, I was ready to leave the patriarchal structure that had taught me that obedience was more important than happiness. Unfortunately, I didn't have anything to replace it with.

That's where running would come in. My friend, Bill, first challenged me to take up running, and then invited me to train for a marathon in Prague. I accepted the invitation not knowing that soon enough I would find myself embracing a vision quest that would take me to all seven continents to run a marathon on each, and that the Marathon would teach me everything from how to embrace the chaos I'd always been afraid of to how to be alone—among other lessons. This is the story of seven marathons on seven continents, how the marathon is a metaphor for life, and how it has given me the information I've needed for a long-term vision of how to live my life.

Chapter 1. Beginning the Race: The Starting (Over) Line

I started my new life floundering and afraid. I'd lost my church, my home, my marriage, at least a dozen friends, and all the foundations that had held my life together. I didn't know how I would rebuild, who my new community would be, or what I would spend my life doing. The roles available to women in my old paradigm were limited, so I had some new ground to cover as I inched my way into a new life.

A dinner with my old friend, Bill, put a bug in my ear to take a run one afternoon. He claimed it would help me manage the psychic pain I was in. As I ran, I found it hard to be patient with myself, but it was also oddly meditative. It forced me to focus on my body and breath and my moment-to-moment experience rather than reliving my mistakes or dwelling in the fear I had for my future.

I began to wonder if maybe I didn't need to figure out and measure how I'd gotten myself into this mess, or how I was going to redeem myself. Maybe I needed to live in the now, to accept what life offered right this instant instead of trying to force it into a box the size and shape of a church or a theology, as I had been doing. Being outside in the elements, vulnerable and alone, I ran and breathed and let my tortured heart rest a little. And then, later in the week, I did it again.

Over time, Bill cheered me on and ran with me some weekends. We started to spend more time together and became more than friends. For months I just ran a few miles a few times a week and let myself heal. And then on a beautiful August day, while hiking in the Cascade Mountains, Bill popped a question I wasn't ready for: Would I run a marathon with him next May—in Prague?

Since I was in charge of myself now, I could pick up and go to Prague with this man if I wanted to, but I couldn't run a marathon on free will alone. I would have to train hard for that part. I had to think over Bill's proposal. But in the end, I decided to do it. My life needed something to organize around. It would turn out to be the beginning of the most significant relationship in my life: the relationship between my aching soul and the truths about self that the Marathon insists we learn.

Chapter 2. Europe: The Prague Push, May 2003

As it turned out, training for a marathon had just enough of the devotion and misery in it I had experienced in religion that I felt right at home, even as I was stretched by the physical requirements of the task. Through the hours and hours of training, I began to discover that there was more value in the simple act of engaging in the journey than in whether or not I had a successful run. Unlike with the religious focus on sin and perfection, running was always about the moment, about picking up one leg and then the other, and about remembering to breathe. This was new and revolutionary for me. In the past, every choice in life was about heaven and hell, about the future rather than the present. I was changing.

And there were opportunities to take these lessons one step further once we got to Prague. Traveling and all of its challenges, combined with the rigors of the marathon and spending three straight weeks with Bill, would give me a chance to decide to throw perfectionism, a very old and entrenched nemesis, to the wind and see that the world wouldn't fall apart if I made a mistake.

Finally, I was ready to do my first marathon ever. (For Bill, it was a first, too: his first international marathon in the country where his ancestors came from.) The morning of the race, Bill and I tragically mistook the starting time and found ourselves at the starting line fifteen minutes late. Devastated and unable to communicate with the race organizers because of the language barrier, we had to make a number of difficult decisions about how to proceed in the face of having completely screwed up the intended experience. We chose to "complete" a modified version of the race (we actually cheated by cutting into a horde of runners two miles into their race), and in the process I had the epiphany that although life is as likely to be a shitty mess as it is to be happily organized and successful, it's just as valuable either way. One thing was for sure, it wouldn't ever be perfect—and neither would I. All those years I'd spent trying to perfectly please God and all the people in my life could be put to rest. Chaos happens. Big deal! What freedom!

The run was hard. I had trained to walk every four minutes, but since all of our plans were thrown out the window, instead I ran straight through until I was in excruciating pain. But even in the misery of the final miles, I knew I was passing an internal milestone. I made a commitment as I ran along the banks of the Vltava River to give up on the perfectionism that had plagued me since childhood. I would embrace the mess.

Chapter 3. Together and Alone: My Own Vision Quest, September 2003–June 2007

It would be almost four years, with plenty of messes to embrace, before I would run my next marathon and fully engage in the quest to run on every continent. I had some things to attend to back home. For one thing,

I needed to sort through what it meant to be a woman on the eve of midlife without the backdrop of the institutions of church and marriage to tell me what to value. When we got back from Prague, I started looking for a place of my own. It was time for me to emerge from my tiny rented studio apartment and to buy a home of my own. Before I had looked for a perfect life; now I would find a good enough life and it would need to include a home that would serve as a sacred place for the healing I had to do.

I bought a condominium in Seattle and painted the walls bright blues and purples and put my red furniture wherever I wanted it to go without negotiating with anyone. This was gratifying and healing and helped me to know I was fully in charge of my own life. I stayed there for two years. During this time, Bill and I talked and dreamed about the idea of running seven marathons on seven continents. Although we discussed it constantly, we didn't make plans for another race. It wasn't time.

Within the space of those two years, I also started my own business and fell in love with Bill. This time I wouldn't have any institution looking over my shoulder to tell me what partnership should look like. Bill and I would define the relationship any way we wanted to. We took careful stock of how we wanted our relationship to function and, as was becoming our style, running helped us along.

We ran together as we made plans for a wedding celebration. During these runs, we were in harmony and Bill ran patiently beside me, cheering me on. I felt it was a good omen for our relationship, but I never forgot what I learned in Prague: Nothing is perfect.

After we'd been married for a year, on a dark, rainy day, as we ran a half-marathon in Vancouver, B.C., in training for our next long-awaited intercontinental marathon, our individual needs began to compete. In a torrential storm, Bill wanted to run faster to finish the race quickly; and he wanted me to hurry up, too. I couldn't oblige him.

We had an uncomfortable conflict as we ran, and I let some unflattering parts of myself run the show. But I knew now to embrace the chaos and imperfection, even in my relationship with Bill. It was there to teach me something. It was there to teach me that it was time for me to own my journey as a runner and release Bill from his role as my champion. Just as in relationship it is critical to maintain flexible roles with one another, so it is in running.

We were training for this next marathon, and I decided we would have to run it separately. We would arrive at the starting line together and join up at the end, but we would run at our own paces. Together *and* alone, with *and* without! I was learning that even though I had a new partner, my life was still my responsibility alone.

Chapter 4. Australia: The Mudgee Nudge, August 2007

By the time we arrived in Australia for our second international marathon, we knew we were on a course to run a marathon on every continent of the world, and I knew I was on a personal quest to listen to the marathon as I would a great teacher. I was finding a place of personal strength in running, and I wanted to continue to break through cultural, religious, and familial expectations and roles to live into a personal knowledge of self that would actually work for me. It was a midlife rite of passage of my own making. It was a vision quest to find my truth, as opposed to "the truth" of a particular theological perspective. How could running teach me how to be an authentic person? And how could the values I held in my life inform the way I trained and the place running had in my life?

As we traveled only a couple of hours outside of Sydney, Australia, and encountered the lovely laid-back Australian culture, I drew closer to the start of my second marathon, the first one I would do absolutely alone. This marathon had only 31 participants, so I would not only be running it without Bill, but I would be at the back of a very small pack, where I might see no one but the occasional cockatiel or, if I were lucky, a kangaroo. Two days into our time Down Under, jet-lagged and haggard, I got on my mark and started the long, slow slog to the finish line. Each solitary kilometer reminded me of my existential isolation in this life, and how I was okay being alone, even inside of a marriage, even on the winding roads beside Australian vineyards. These were the longest five hours of my life, alone with my thoughts, and smells and sights I had never encountered before. They were full of moments when I felt lost and anxious about being without guidance or help, but gradually I rested in a tentative confidence that I would find my way.

As I crossed the finish line, while I was duly overjoyed to see Bill's tired face, I was also thrilled and gratified at how I had navigated the course on my own, in my own company, a complete person who could trust in herself. I was finally learning to be in a relationship and an individuated person at the same time, a confusing lesson we all need to grasp at some point. Some of us just take the long way.

Chapter 5. Back of the Pack: Finding Community

Along with the an increased love for Australian wine, I came away from the land of the Outback with a deeper appreciation for solitude and for the kind of runner I was becoming—a back of the packer. My pace was slow and I understood that I would likely always be running at the tail end of any group of runners. I was ready to make friends back there. I was ready to own my own glory and to find a way to celebrate myself and the few others who trailed along with me. This was in contrast to my previous life, when celebrating oneself was considered selfish and to be avoided.

I was in a new community now, with Bill in the little town where he lived about 90 miles north from Seattle. I needed to build relationships for myself and the long-distance running community was a good place to start. In years past I would have only allowed myself to connect with those who shared my dogma; now I would look for people wherever I could find them and open myself up to the gifts they might offer me. I was moving from a small-minded, cloistered way of life to an open space where anyone could be welcome.

As I trained for my next marathon, a local run that was to be my North American continental race, a runner in our town reported being raped. I had just embraced running alone and now, suddenly, I felt afraid to run on the trails around our home. Two things happened as a result of this. First, I did much of my training by joining community running events, and thereby met and ran with other back-of-the-packers who patiently chugged along at twelve minutes a mile. Second, I attended a race organized in response to the rape. Six hundred runners and walkers showed up to "take back our trails." Here I saw that I had moved into a compassionate and socially conscious community. Maybe I could sink in here, something I hadn't dared to let myself do much in my life—to offer my gifts and talents, to open my heart to whomever the universe brought my way.

In a strange twist, it was later uncovered that the woman who said she had been raped had actually made up the story. Many in the community felt shocked and betrayed, and I shared their sadness and confusion, but remained grateful to have seen the character of my new town.

Chapter 6. North America: The Whidbey Island Grind, April 2008

I was ready to run my North American race. It would be the first marathon Bill would not be involved in. He'd already run several local marathons and had North America ticked off his list. This race would be all mine. I'd chosen a race in Washington State, on beautiful Whidbey Island. This course promised views of the San Juan Islands and pleasant breezes, but it also promised some of the most ass-kicking hills I'd ever seen. I was a slow, easy plodder as a runner, not a hill-climbing superhero.

As I ran the Whidbey Island course, I felt myself complaining and worrying about whether or not I would be able to complete the task. It was the most physically difficult run I had ever attempted. In the midst of my despair, I sidled up next to Mel. Mel was seventy-five years old and was on his 333rd race. He was running with a broken hip bone, and he was smiling his way through the run at about thirteen minutes a mile. Mel put my self-pity to shame. He also helped me put something important into perspective: Every task we do in life should proudly be done at each person's ability level and celebrated freely. Whether it's a marathon or work of art or day at work, we have the right to have pride in our own accomplishments.

It may sound strange, but this concept was just occurring to me. There were a lot of messages in my old mindset that insisted I think of myself as unworthy of love without redemption (something no one could ever be good enough for or "earn"). But Mel was totally confident in his pace and as proud as could be of his marathon story. Why shouldn't I follow his example? Why shouldn't everyone, no matter what their "race" is?

As I came to the finish line that day, the porta-potties were being removed and the award ceremony was long over. There were no more bananas or orange slices in the recovery area. No one but Bill cheered for me as I ran over the finish line, but I thought of Mel (still behind me at that point) and remembered that I carried with me my own internal locus of celebration. Hurray for me! And for every one else, too!

Chapter 7. Powerful and Vulnerable: Tales from a Sub-Continental Race

We were serious now about completing the seven continents as soon as we could afford to do so. Bill and I made a plan to run in Asia the following January and then in June to hop from South America over to Africa.

We would also get on the waiting list for the Antarctica race. To pull off three marathons in a year, I would have to be in the best shape of my life. After the Whidbey race, I decided to keep my miles up. After April, I continued to run long courses on the weekends; and then an odd thing began to happen: I got faster.

I knew I would never be a competitive runner, but I was surprised to notice how good I felt after running eleven or even ten minutes a mile. Since I was in such good shape I figured, *Why not find another marathon to run?* Bill and I located a marathon in Panama City that fit perfectly into our vacation schedule. I had never intended on running *more* than our seven marathons when we started this whole journey, but I was finding now that I was falling in love with running—after six years of doing it faithfully!

The race in Panama changed my life. In five hours and twelve minutes I became a hero in my own eyes. I ran the first three hours without incident, feeling solid and even on course to finish my first sub-five-hour race. But three hours in, I looked down and saw that I was bleeding down my legs. Apparently, one perimenopausal symptom is excessive blood flow during one's time of the month, and this was kicking in for me the morning I was running the Adidas International Panama City Marathon. With nowhere to go for privacy (and upon discovering that the humidity had ruined my spare tampon anyhow), I ran on—bloody. I had been spending the last many years sorting through cultural narratives about women, accepting some, rejecting others. Here was my chance for a strange declaration. I was a woman, and women bleed. I was going to keep going, come hell or high water.

It would be high water that day. After what happened next, I'll always be convinced God is of a feminine persuasion. The skies thundered and opened wide to dump monsoon waters down on me (and on everyone else, of course) to wash me clean. Meanwhile, a lovely Panamanian man took pity on me and purchased me some maxi-pads with wings, delivering them to me along the course. For the first time in my forty-one years, I felt self-admiration. I felt strong and victorious. I believed in myself. I could take on anything life threw at me. Or so I thought.

The marathon was quickly followed by Bill getting sick and yet another life-changing experience as I both blew his illness out of proportion and realized how fragile life is—and how love can make you crazy.

Chapter 8. Asia: The Tateyama Trek, January 2009

Bellingham has a Sister City in Japan with a well-attended marathon. Bill and I both have several ties to Japan and so we decided that we would fulfill our Asian marathon here. While it is impossible to know exactly what lessons the great teacher will give me in each of the next four trips, I have found that they are always plentiful and universal.

Chapter 9. Getting Ready for the Long Haul

We will prepare to run two marathons on two continents in three weeks, and hopefully climb a mountain. One of my goals for this preparatory period is to adjust my eating habits to give me the most energy possible. I expect this to be a challenge, as I am a dyed-in-the-wool, committed junk food lover.

Chapter 10. Africa: Killer Kilimanjaro, June 2009

Our plan is to run the Mt. Kilimanjaro Marathon, rest, and then climb the mountain (which is actually more of a long, rigorous, guided hike than a skilled mountain climb). This race takes place on the last Sunday of June each year.

Chapter 11. A Brief Reprieve

Since there will be such a short time between our African and South American marathons, we will have to be very careful to rest, eat well, and get some good sleep. The trick is, we'll be traveling and sleeping in strange beds. This chapter will chronicle this period of time.

Chapter 12. South America: Sao Paulo Celebration, June 2009

Again, the vision quest requires that we watch for the lessons life offers rather than prescribe them, but we do know that we will reconnect with a family Bill lived with in Brazil when he was a high school exchange student. The dates for this race are not yet released, but in 2008 it happened June 1.

Chapter 13. Resting and Recuperating: Preparing for Antarctica

Preparations for Antarctica are more complex than other races. We are on the waiting list for the 2010 race, which will happen in March of that year.

Chapter 14. Antarctica: South Pole Shout Out, March 2010

We will take a ship from the tip of South America to a little island off the coast of Antarctica's mainland, where we will run one of only two marathons available on this continent.

Chapter 15. Reflections: How to Prepare a Midlife Vision Quest

Reflections on the lessons and growth and a challenge to readers to invent their own meaningful adventure vision quests.

Author Biography

I grew up in the Seattle area in a chaotic, blue-collar family. The craziness of my childhood drove me to look for solidity and structure outside of my family. I found what I was looking for in church. There I learned the rules about being a woman in a patriarchal institution, and there I was dutifully married as a virgin at age twenty-three. For many years I hid, closing my mind to questions that were bubbling under the surface of my religious smile. Questions about my role as a woman, about the sadness I saw in the world, and about the legitimacy of asking for happiness remained dormant until they could be still no more.

In an attempt to answer my questions, I went to graduate school to earn my master's degree in marriage and family therapy from Seattle Pacific University. This is when I began my work as a psychotherapist. I found my passion in supporting people coming to terms with losses in their lives and discovering new and empowering aspects of themselves. Through working with my clients and holding their grief and their stories with deep respect, I eventually began to ask myself some of the most difficult questions of my own life: What did I want? What was I, as a woman, allowed to want? Who could I be if I were free from the structure of my religious beliefs? How could I change my life? The collision of my personal and professional journeys culminated in a divorce, the discovery of running as a great teacher, and, ultimately, a new perspective on life that I now share with others in therapy and in lectures.

Since graduating in 2000, I have used my therapeutic skills and the lessons I've learned in my personal life to work with many populations of people looking for healing and growth. I have a special interest in helping women going through transitional periods create experiences that will help them live more authentically and freely. For me, that experience has been the quest to run a marathon on every continent in the world.

I began running to catch my breath, and now I run between twenty and forty miles a week as part of my own commitment to self-discovery. I belong to the Greater Bellingham Running Club, and I participate in races as short as five kilometers and as long as 26.2 miles, always running at the back of the pack with my head held high.

I am a Licensed Marriage and Family Therapist. My practice is located in Bellingham, Washington, where I live with my husband, Bill Pech, and our dogs and cats and lizards.

Target Audience

In 2007, approximately 407,000 people completed a marathon in the United States. This is up by 2.3% in spite of the extreme weather conditions that prevented over eight thousand completions in the Chicago Marathon and the windstorm that prevented many from even showing up for the Boston Marathon last year. Of the marathon finishers from last year, 21% of them finished in times between five and six hours, right alongside little old me near the back of the pack. Of these 407,000 people who completed a marathon in 2007, 39.9% of them were women averaging 36.5 years of age. This means a potential readership of 162,393 for *In the Long Run: One Woman's Midlife Quest to Run a Marathon on Every Continent* right off the bat.

Besides marathoners, there are the hundreds of thousands of women and men who run shorter races with the same personal goals in mind that the marathoner has. A half-marathoner is no slouch. Neither is a 10K-er, or anyone who runs around the block for fitness or to clear the mind.

And even for those who do not run, there is a lot to be found in the pages of *In the Long Run*. This book is about running, but it is also about a woman's post-divorce journey at the cusp of midlife, out of patriarchy and into self-knowledge. This is a universal story, even for those who may never run a marathon or travel to another continent. Each of us will come up against ourselves in a difficult challenge that will require more than we knew we had to give.

Those who will love this book are:
- People in the running community across the United States and Canada.
- People who have struggled to re-invent their lives after divorce.
- People who enjoy travel and adventure in exotic places.
- Women in midlife transitions.
- Women and men who recognize that patriarchal religious values do not provide the richness and complexity in their spiritual lives that they desire.
- People who are looking for inspirational truths about life and life's struggles.
- Anyone who would like to take on an adventurous quest in order to discover truths about themselves or about life.

Marketing Strategies

The following is a list of my local contacts and the possible groups in which I have some influence. Let me say for the record that I am willing to travel anywhere or make myself available to any group or organization willing to invite me.

- *Greater Bellingham Running Club*

I am a member of the Greater Bellingham Running Club, a group 600 members strong who support one another in their running pursuits and their commitment to running in our county. I will attend planned events and meetings and promote my book in our community as an encouragement to (especially) women runners.

- *Bellingham Fit*

Bellingham Fit is the local chapter of USA Fit, an organization that encourages people of all fitness levels to exercise and move their bodies. I will offer myself as a motivational speaker and seek invitations to promote my book among their members.

- *Girls On the Run*

The local chapter of Girls On the Run, a national program encouraging girls in the third to fifth grades to build self-confidence through running, is an active chapter. I will offer lectures and support to this organization and promote my book among the coaches and parents of participating girls.

- *Western Washington University and Seattle Pacific University*

I have numerous connections at both of these universities. I will contact professors and offer to give guest lectures on fitness, running, self-confidence, travel and writing. I will also seek to get my book in both university book stores. In addition, Western Washington University chooses one book at the beginning of each year it requires all incoming students to read. I will submit my book for this option.

- *Village Books*

One of the best bookstores in the state is right here in Bellingham. I will seek an invitation to offer readings and book signings to promote my book at this independent bookstore known for supporting local authors.

- *Runner's World and Running Times*

I have had contact with editors from both *Runner's World* and *Running Times*. Both have shown interest in my story. I will pursue these venues as I continue to build my platform and promote my book.

- *Marathon Expos around the state/country*

I will attend any Marathon Exposition I can get a booth at for book signings and sales.

- *7marathons7continents.blogspot.com*

This is my personal blog. I send email updates with each new entry to an ever-expanding readership. I have also acquired a permanent website address and am in the process of building a permanent website, the content of which will be to promote ideas for how others can create their own adventurous vision quests.

- *Local Running Shoes Stores*

Running stores are an excellent place to market my book. I know the owners of the three local stores in Bellingham and will ask them to carry *In the Long Run*. In addition, I will make contact with other running stores in the Pacific Northwest and request that they carry my book.

- *Whidbey Island Writers Association*
Whidbey Island Writers Association is known for supporting its members and promoting its members' works. I have been a member of this organization since 2006. I will submit a proposal to provide a session at their annual conference. Books of presenters are sold through an on-site book store provided by Village Books (see above).

Competitive Titles

- *Ultramarathon Man: Confessions of an All-Night Runner*, Dean Karnazes, Penguin Books, Ltd., 2005. *Ultramarathon Man* is an amazing story of an amazing runner. Dean Karnazes has inspired me to run with and to follow my heart. I read his book while I was training for my third marathon on Whidbey Island, Washington, and was encouraged by the way running took Dean to greater depths in his life and healed him from the loss of his sister years earlier. I was so encouraged by his book that I made a point of meeting Dean when he was in my town for a race. Athletically, I will always pale in comparison to Mr. Karnazes (as will we all), but in terms of personal growth, I believe it is time for the story of a woman's midlife vision quest, an almost universally expressed need by women in America, to get some air time. In my book, women who run and women who don't will see what it means to really challenge oneself and reach for deeper truths that require us to change what we think of ourselves. As Dean Karnazes did in his book, I also write about coming to the end of living a less-than-vibrant, passionate life, but in *In the Long Run* I will show how an average woman can decide to do something extraordinary to change her life. You don't need to be blessed with perfect biomechanics or all-night stamina to face up to yourself and feel like a hero. Readers of *In the Long Run* will see themselves in my story and will take away inspiration to craft their own fabulous life-changing challenges.

- *Crossing to Avalon: A Woman's Midlife Quest for the Sacred Feminine*, Jean Shinoda Bolen, HarperCollins, 1995. Jean Shinoda Bolen hit on the need for her own midlife pilgrimage during a difficult transitional time in her life. For Dr. Bolen, her quest took her to several sacred sites in Europe, such as the Chartres Labyrinth, that represented the Divine Feminine experience through history. She shared her journey in her poignant, powerful book, *Crossing to Avalon,* and gave me the gift of knowing I was not alone in needing to search for that which was divine and powerful inside of me. *In the Long Run* takes the reader into the Divine Feminine in a different way. My path is through the body and the labyrinth that is the Marathon. *In the Long Run* will appeal to those who would search for self in a grittier, more visceral way than some, through hard physical testing and endurance.

- *What I Talk About When I Talk About Running,* Haruki Murakami, Alfred A. Knopf, 2008. Haruki Murakami is a remarkable acclaimed novelist. His short memoir, *What I Talk about When I Talk about Running,* takes the reader around the world as he describes the importance of running in his life as a writer, and how running and writing inform one another. Mr. Murakami, like me, does not race at the front of the pack, and like me, he runs for deeply personal reasons. *In the Long Run,* however, approaches running from a somewhat different perspective. It is the story of a woman runner and a woman writer who has reflections that will be universally understood and relatable by those who are neither runners nor writers but who are simply on a quest to find a deeper sense of authenticity in their lives.

- *Women Who Run with the Wolves,* Clarissa Pinkola Estes, Ballantine Books, 1992. *Women Who Run with the Wolves* is both a landmark book on the inner worlds of women and my favorite book. Dr. Estes looks at several myths and fairy tales through the lens of the female psyche and encourages her readers to embrace their creativity, verve, and power. *In the Long Run* will make Dr. Estes proud. It is the operationalization of her principles and truths, an example of how a woman can reclaim her wild soul, one step at a time.

- *Standing Tall: A Memoir of Tragedy and Triumph,* C. Vivian Stringer & Laura Tucker, Crown Publishers, 2008. Ms. Stringer is truly one of today's sports heroines. In *Standing Tall,* she writes of the trials of her daughter's illness, her husband's sudden death, and her own fight with cancer. Through it all, basketball and her role as head coach of the Rutgers University women's basketball team served to keep her steady. She coached her team into victory and through the unfortunate situation spurred on by Don Imus's insensitive comments. She is a powerful woman whose book encourages other women to overcome their own unique obstacles. My book, *In the Long Run*, is about an everyday woman who finds hidden strength and personal power. Women who read *Standing Tall* will find similar encouragement in *In the Long Run* to look inside themselves to find a heroine.

- *The Dance of the Dissident Daughter*, Sue Monk Kidd, HarperSanFransisco A Division of HarperCollins, 1996. Sue Monk Kidd is one of today's favorite novelists, but I first fell in love with her memoir, *The Dance of the Dissident Daughter*. In this eloquent, powerful book she writes about her awakening from a life lived in patriarchal religious traditions to an experience of the Divine Feminine. This book shook me and invited me to look at my own religious experience in a new way that revolutionized my concept of God. The one thing I was left longing for after reading her memoir was a description of the way Ms. Kidd must have agonizingly changed her personal, internal scripts that were informed by all those years in patriarchy's shadow. In *In the Long Run*, I take the reader on a very messy, very imperfect journey from viewing myself as one required to respond to the demands of a male god and his church to one who learns to make and live by her own rules. In *In the Long Run*, you will see the sweat and snot and tears and blood all shed in the process of shedding that old religious skin. You'll come along with me as I put on the running sneakers that capably carry me into a new and powerful sense of the Divine Feminine.

- *The Crowd Sounds Happy: A Story of Love, Madness and Baseball*, Nicholas Dawidoff, Pantheon Books A Division of Random House, 2008. In *The Crowd Sounds Happy*, Mr. Dawidoff, a best-selling author and finalist for the Pulitzer Prize, tells of how baseball inspired and changed him. Never a professional himself, he was a devoted fan and player during his youth when he needed the stability baseball offered him. *In the Long Run* is another story of how a sport can save a person and bring needed stability. While baseball saw Mr. Dawidoff through his chaotic childhood with a mentally ill mother, *In the Long Run* describes how running saw me through my divorce and showed me how to grow up and create a new and improved life. Both of these books are stories of "sport as teacher." In *In the Long Run*, readers will additionally be encouraged to engage in adventure in their own lives as a path to learning life-changing lessons.

- *My Life on the Run: The Wit, Wisdom and Insights of a Road Racing Icon*, Bart Yasso, Rodale, 2008. With more than one thousand competitive races under his belt, Mr. Yasso is a man after my own heart, although he's ahead of me in the running pack. In his book, *My Life on the Run*, he describes his adventures running in exotic locations and touts the advantages of taking part in adventure for the purposes of personal growth. In my book, *In the Long Run*, I take Mr. Yasso's philosophy one step further than he does. I not only take the reader to all seven continents on earth, but I also trace the journey through a woman's inner terrain as I inch into my midlife years. Whether they are athletes or merely people experiencing transition in their lives, my readers will see themselves in my journeys, my races and in the lessons they teach me.

- *No Need for Speed: A Beginner's Guide to the Joy of Running*, John "The Penguin" Bingham, Rodale, 2002. John Bingham is the king of the back-of-the-packers in the running world. His book, *No Need for Speed*, is an excellent guide for the average person who wants to run for fitness or other personal reasons without the competitive edge. His book has encouraged many (present author included) to start right where they are and give it a try. *In the Long Run* is the story of a living model of his philosophy. I tell the story of a non-runner starting out with a walk/run routine and never really moving forward very far in any given pack of runners, but still plodding along. *No Need for Speed* is the philosophy; *In the Long Run* is the result of putting it into practice.

Some Additional Titles:
The following books bear some similarity to mine in that they represent stories of individuals who took on finite quests for some definite period of

time and then wrote about their learnings and challenges. I recognize the market for such books as a trend that *In the Long Run* will fit into at this time and expect it to draw a similar readership.

- *Animal, Vegetable, Miracle: A Year of Food Life*, Barbara Kingsolver, Camille Kingsolver & Steven L. Hopp, HarperCollins, 2007.
- *Eat, Pray, Love: One Woman's Search for Everything Across Italy, India and Indonesia*, Elizabeth Gilbert, Viking, 2006.
- *Tales of a Female Nomad: Living at Large in the World*, Rita Golden Gelman, Random House, 2001.

Length and Delivery
This book will be approximately 80,000 words in length and will include fifteen chapters, plus an introduction and an afterword when completed. The completion date will be one month after the running of the final marathon, which will occur in March 2010. The final manuscript will be completed by the end of April 2010.

Young Readers' Nonfiction

I had the pleasure of working with Loree Griffin Burns on this book proposal. It was during the proposal process that she realized she was writing the wrong book for the wrong audience and she shifted her focus slightly. The result was a publishing contract from Houghton Mifflin. In fact, she received a phone call from the publisher within minutes of his having received the proposal, letting her know a contract was on its way. They kept her title and changed the subtitle to: "Flotsam, Jetsam, and the Science of Ocean Movement."

Note Griffin Burns's method of introducing her sidebars in the chapter summaries (outline) section.

This author was savvy enough to realize that there were at least two categories of books related to the book she proposed—texts exploring oceanic principles and those highlighting the work of oceanic scientists. She did a comparative analysis for both types of books. And she did a thorough job of listing potential markets and outlets for this book (Houghton Mifflin, 2007).

Tracking Trash:
Oceanography and the Science of Floating Objects

by

Loree Griffin Burns, Ph.D.

Approximately 12,500 words

Synopsis

Tracking Trash: Oceanography and the Science of Floating Objects is a book about the ocean, how it moves, and *what* it moves. Readers are given the basics: a thorough overview of the principles underlying ocean movement, the techniques used by the men and women who study this movement, and the importance of ocean movement in the lives of marine animals and humans. Unlike more traditional ocean science texts, however, *Tracking Trash* presents these facts in the context of a real-life scientific drama. Shipping mishaps, mysterious floating objects, choked marine life—these elements lend intrigue and accessibility to this middle-grade science book.

Since 1991, Dr. Curt Ebbesmeyer, a Seattle-based oceanographer, has been conducting one of the most unique ocean research programs in the world. Dr. Ebbesmeyer tracks trash. Through the Beachcombers' and Oceanographers' International Association, a group he founded in 1996, Dr. Ebbesmeyer has tracked the whereabouts of thousands upon thousands of man-made floating objects adrift on the world's oceans. The majority of this flotsam can be traced to shipping accidents, and Dr. Ebbesmeyer estimates that more than ten thousand shipping containers fall from cargo ships annually. *Tracking Trash* delves deeply into the ramifications of this statistic, highlighting the advantages a spill of this magnitude provides ocean researchers as well as the devastating effects of cargo spills on the health of our world ocean.

Tracking Trash will appeal to young readers on many levels. The narrative opens with the first major cargo spill to capture Dr. Ebbesmeyer's attention: the accidental dumping of 68,000 sneakers into the Pacific Ocean. Readers follow the evolution of Dr. Ebbesmeyer's research chronologically, beginning with encouragement from his mother and ending with the publication of his results to the scientific world. Further spills, including the loss of 28,000 rubber duckies, 34,000 hockey gloves, and four million plastic LEGO pieces, serve as an introduction to the ecological impact of cargo spills. The story moves to the Eastern Garbage Patch, a plastic-ridden wasteland in the middle of the Pacific Ocean where much of this cargo-turned-trash ends up. Readers meet Captain Charles Moore, another researcher who tracks trash, and learn of his tireless efforts to define and address the issue of marine trash. The convergence of Dr. Ebbesmeyer's work with that of Captain Moore closes out the story and provides a stunning example of the age-old scientific method at work in our twenty-first century society.

Tracking Trash will be approximately 15,000 words in length. Each of the seven chapters will contain multiple sidebars with anecdotal and accessory information. The book will provide suggestions for further reading as well as information on how to follow the work of Dr. Ebbesmeyer and Captain Moore. The format and content of the book make it a good fit for Houghton Mifflin's "Scientist in the Field" series of science books for middle readers.

The primary market for *Tracking Trash* will be schools and libraries, as the book will provide an excellent curriculum tool for teachers covering either the scientific process in general, or ocean science in particular. The widespread media attention given to both cargo "spills of opportunity" and to ocean ecology will make this book a good candidate for bookstore sales to the general public as well.

Promotional Notes

Books that make science accessible and relevant to children will always be of interest to teachers and parents. While textbooks can provide an important introduction to a topic, it is the creative telling of nonfiction that will build on this introduction in a way that can entice and encourage young readers. One need only look as far as the latest Newbery Honor book, *An American Plague*, by Jim Murphy, for proof of this. *Tracking Trash* is intended to fulfill a similar mission: intrigue child readers with a riveting true-life story while providing scientifically accurate information.

National Science Standards dictate that students in grades five through eight study the structure of the earth system, including oceanography. *Tracking Trash* is written for just this audience and should be a useful resource for earth science teachers throughout the country. I plan to contact professional teaching organizations, including the National Science Teachers Association and the National Earth Science Teachers Association, to suggest they review the book for their members. Both organizations maintain websites and distribute newsletters to their members, ensuring such reviews would reach science teachers throughout the country.

I also propose to submit the book for review in those review resources of use to school and public librarians: *School Library Journal, Kirkus Review* and *Horn Book* magazine.

Since the book will also appeal to adults with an interest in ocean science, or who are aware of its subject matter as a result of reports in the popular press, I propose to seek coverage by those media outlets that have reported in depth on spills of opportunity in the past, including National Public Radio, *Smithsonian* magazine, *US News & World Report* and *Natural History* magazine.

I also look forward to promoting *Tracking Trash* through signings and speaking engagements at schools, libraries and bookstores. I will, of course, promote the book on my website, which is scheduled to launch early in 2005.

Other smaller and more specific marketing venues exist for this book. These include:

1. Aquarium bookstores. A portion of the book focuses on marine pollution and the approaches scientists are taking to remedy it. I plan to contact major aquariums nationwide with a request that they offer *Tracking Trash* at their gift shops and bookstores.

2. Beachcomber's and Oceanographer's International Association quarterly newsletter, "Beach Alert!" This newsletter (circulation 800) is written and edited by Dr. Curt Ebbesmeyer, one of the scientists profiled in the book. I plan to ask Dr. Ebbesmeyer to review and promote the book in his newsletter.

3. Algalita Marine Research Foundation newsletter, "Coastal Perspectives." The AMRF was founded by Captain Charles Moore, the marine conservation scientist whose work is highlighted in *Tracking Trash*. I plan to ask Captain Moore to review the book in his newsletter and to consider promoting the book on the AMRF website (www. algalita.org).

4. The First Years company, manufacturers and distributors of the thousands of bathtub toys that were lost at sea and are described in the book, has maintained a special web page devoted to tracking the lost ducks. The company may have an interest in marketing the book on their website.

Finally, a note on jacket copy and potential current events tie-ins. Dr. Curt Ebbesmeyer and Dr. W. James Ingraham, Jr. are the world's leading experts in flotsam tracking and their work is discussed at length in *Tracking Trash*. I have spoken with both men and believe they would be willing to help promote the book by providing testimonials and jacket quotes and also by alerting me to any relevant media attention. For example, a media frenzy like that surrounded the landing of tub toys along the Atlantic coast of the United States during the summer of 2003 could greatly increase visibility of the book.

Market Analysis

Through extensive market research, I have identified two types of ocean science books for middle readers. The first group consists of ocean science texts that relate known oceanographic principles to its readers. Although many of these books, including those listed below, are excellent resources for children and teachers in need of an introduction to ocean science, the dry recitation of facts is unlikely to interest children outside of curriculum assignments. Also, while some of these books make passing mention of cargo spills, none capitalizes on the child appeal of these spills of opportunity in any detail, or highlights the problem of marine debris in a way that brings the problem home to child readers. In fact, I was unable to identify any published book that focuses on these topics in the way *Tracking Trash* does.

1. *The Restless Sea: Savage Waters*, by Carole G. Vogel (Franklin Watts, 2003)

   The Restless Sea: Human Impact, by Carole G. Vogel (Franklin Watts, 2003)

These are two in a series of five books recently released by Franklin Watts. They are well written and thorough in their coverage of ocean science and will be included in the Recommended Reading section of the book proposed here. They will not compete directly with *Tracking Trash*, as they are broader in scope and textbook-like in nature.

2. *Waves, Tides and Currents*, by Daniel Rogers (Bookwright Press, 1991)
This book is a detailed introduction to ocean movement that reads very much like a textbook. As such, it will not compete directly with *Tracking Trash*.

3. *Ocean Currents: Marine Science Activities for Grades 5-8*, by Lawrence Hall of Science (University of California Berkeley, 2001)
This is a National Association of Science Teachers (NAST)-endorsed curriculum resource for teachers. This title is one of the first books to appear when one searches for books on ocean currents in library or online book catalogs. One of the seven activities included in the manual contains a detailed summary of the Nike sneaker spill. Although *Tracking Trash* would clearly be a nice supplement to this activity, the books will not compete directly.

4. *Bill Nye the Science Guy's Big Blue Ocean*, by Bill Nye (Hyperion, 1999)
Although less dry than traditional ocean science texts, this book covers a very broad range of ocean science topics, making it unlikely to compete directly with *Tracking Trash*.

The second group of ocean science books I identified includes books that examine the work of ocean scientists. These books, which include the series listed below, provide a wonderful introduction to careers in the marine sciences. However, neither series contains a title that details the science of a working oceanographer. *Tracking Trash* will fill this void.

1. *Once A Wolf*, by Steve Swinburne (Houghton Mifflin, 2001)
This is one title in a series of "Scientist in the Field" books. There is not yet a title in this series highlighting an ocean scientist.

2. *A Whale Biologist at Work*, by Sneed B. Collard III (Franklin Watts, 2000)
This is one title in a series of books for the Wildlife Conservation Society. Each title explains in detail the life and works of a particular scientist.

The scope and format of the series is similar to that of *Tracking Trash* and of Houghton Mifflin's "Scientist in the Field" series. The series also does not contain a title about an ocean scientist.

In summary, *Tracking Trash* will distinguish itself from the competitive works listed here by relating an intriguing tale of the scientific process in action. Young readers watch an ocean science story unfold, see the data accumulate, predict the outcome of experiments, and are left, in the end, with a more complete understanding of the ocean, how it moves, and what it moves.

About the Author

Loree Griffin Burns received a Bachelor of Science degree from Worcester Polytechnic Institute in 1991 and a PhD in biochemistry from the University of Massachusetts in 1997. She spent ten years pursuing academic research in the fields of biochemistry, genetics, and molecular biology, resulting in publications in peer-reviewed journals such *The Journal of Biological Chemistry, Molecular and Cellular Biology*, and *Nature*. During this time, Loree also wrote articles for *Centerscope*, a publication of the University of Massachusetts Medical Center. (Clips of her articles are available on request.) Since leaving academic research, Loree has taught science at the collegiate level and worked as a scientific curator for a private biotechnology company. Both positions have utilized her extensive scientific background and her writing and organizational skills.

Loree began to follow the work of Dr. Curt Ebbesmeyer during the summer of 2003. As a member of the Beachcomber's and Oceanographer's International Association, she receives detailed accounts of the status of lost cargos and trash being tracked in the world oceans. As a member of the Algalita Marine Research Foundation, she receives regular updates on the status of the marine environment and the Foundation's work to define and address the problem of plastic pollution in the ocean.

Loree has been a member of the Society of Children's Book Writers and Illustrators since 2003. Her fiction has been cited in *ByLine* and *TWINS* magazines and published in *New England Writer's Network*. *Tracking Trash* is her first nonfiction book proposal.

Outline

Chapter 1   "A Spill of Opportunity"

In May of 1990 a cargo ship encountered a vicious storm in the North Pacific Ocean. By the time the seas subsided, the ship had lost twenty-one cargo containers overboard. Although shipping accidents of this nature are not unusual, this particular accident was unique in that remnants of the lost cargo—80,000 Nike sneakers—floated around the Pacific Ocean for many years. Hundreds of them washed ashore on beaches along the Pacific coasts of the United States and Canada, inciting a beachcombing extravaganza and capturing the imagination of one curious oceanographer. With a little detective work and a lot of networking, Dr. Curt Ebbesmeyer was able to track the sneakers as they traveled around the Pacific Ocean and, as a result, became the first person to recognize the Nike spill as something more than free shoes. Dr. Ebbesmeyer had stumbled upon the largest oceanographic drift experiment of all time.

> Sidebars:
>
> *Longitude & Latitude*, an introduction to how global location is recorded
>
> *Messages in Bottles*, a brief history of these intriguing floatables
>
> *One Ocean*, a reminder that the world's oceans are inextricably linked

Chapter 2   "Ocean Motion"

Anyone who has ever seen the ocean can be sure of one thing: the ocean moves. In addition to the highly visible motion caused by waves and tides, harder-to-see ocean currents move huge volumes of water on the surface and in the depths. In this chapter, readers learn that it is oceanic surface currents that played the major role in moving the floating sneakers. The major surface currents at work in the world's oceans are examined, with particular attention given to what is known about the currents at play in the area of the sneaker spill.

> Sidebars:
>
> *The Gulf Stream*, a brief history of the most famous ocean surface current
>
> *Eddies*, an introduction to oceanic whirlpools

Chapter 3   "OSCURS"

In order to more accurately determine the path of the floating sneakers, Dr. Ebbesmeyer called on his friend and colleague, Dr. W. James Ingraham. Dr. Ingraham specializes in modeling surface currents in the Pacific Ocean with a computer program called the Ocean Surface CURrent Simulator (OSCURS). By feeding his sneaker data into the OSCURS computer program, Dr. Ebbesmeyer was able to predict the exact path of the sneakers through the Pacific Ocean. Furthermore, the OSCURS results highlighted the importance of seasonal variability of surface currents, information of crucial importance to fishermen, sailors and marine biologists. Drs. Ebbesyemer and Ingraham presented their findings to the scientific world in 1992 and, recognizing the usefulness of their unique research, readied themselves for the next great cargo spill.

Sidebar:

The Science Behind OSCURS, a technical look at how this computer modeling program works

Chapter 4   "The Big Test"

In early 1992, Dr. Ebbesmeyer learned of another cargo spill: 29,000 bathtub toys had been tossed into the Pacific Ocean during a storm. Dr. Ebbesmeyer activated his network of beachcombers and oceanographers and waited for the rubber ducks, turtles, beavers, and frogs to make their way ashore. By the end of the year, hundreds of the toys began beaching along the western coast of North America. Surprisingly, the toys washed ashore six months earlier than OSCURS predicted they might, launching Drs. Ingraham and Ebbesmeyer on an investigation into the effect of wind on the movement of flotsam. The two scientists followed the travels of the bathtub toys over the next fourteen years on a journey that extended, quite literally, halfway around the world.

Sidebar:

Windage, an extended definition of the term and a look at the varying roles it played in the travels of the sneakers and the bathtub toys

Chapter 5   "Current Events"

Tracking trash is clearly fascinating work. Dr. Ebbesmeyer is in contact with beachcombers constantly and hears about all manner of strange floating objects. He travels the world investigating their origins. As an added bonus, Dr. Ebbesmeyer organizes the tracking data and teases from it oceanographic insights. But what is the real use of this information? Why is it important to know that floating objects can move faster than the underlying current? What is the significance of annual surface current variations? The simple answer is this: because they affect the lives of humans and marine animals every day. From planktons to fish migrations to larval drift, this chapter highlights the biological importance of surface currents.

Sidebar:

Plankton, a definition of the word and a look at the creatures it describes

Chapter 6   "The Garbage Patch"

In 1997, Captain Charles Moore, the founder of the Algalita Marine Research Foundation, took a trip across the eye of the North Pacific gyre. What he and his crew discovered there was startling: miles and miles of trash. "There were shampoo caps and soap bottles and plastic bags and fishing floats as far as I could see. Here I was in the middle of the ocean, and there was nowhere I could go to avoid the plastic." The area, which is the size of Texas, has since been dubbed the "Eastern Garbage Patch," and remains one of the most polluted regions of the world ocean.

Sidebar:

Stuck in a Gyre, an explanation of why gyres collect flotsam

Chapter 7   "A Synthetic Sea"

Captain Moore and his crew of volunteer scientists have vowed to define the extent of the pollution in the Eastern Garbage Patch. Their results have shocked ocean scientists around the world. For every pound of naturally occurring zooplankton in the Eastern Garbage Patch, they found six pounds of floating plastic. The impact of these findings is still being recorded as scientists begin to investigate the effect of floating plastics on marine life.

Sidebars:

Plastic is Forever, a look at the limited degradation of plastic in the ocean

Chapter 8   "The Future"

This chapter provides a summary of where things stand today. Though Dr. Ebbesmeyer still tracks trash, the utility of his work (oceanographically speaking) is decreasing as satellite tracking technology advances and becomes more fiscally available to scientists. He remains the world's foremost expert on flotsam and its origin and continues to work with Captain Moore to identify the extent and scope of the plastic problem, and to propose solutions. Dr. Ingraham continues to develop and expand the OSCURS program as oceanographers around the world develop and test other approaches to modeling ocean currents.

Endpages will include: "Glossary," "Websites," and "Further Reading."

First Novel

This is a sample query letter for C. Hope Clark's first novel, *Lowcountry Bribe*. You'll notice that she identifies the genre early on in her pitch and she includes writing credits as well as her background with the theme of her story. And she mentions Book Two. Publishers are usually pleased to know that an author has more than one book in them. If the publisher likes working with the author and the book is doing well, he's likely to eagerly publish any subsequent books, as well.

Clark's book was accepted by Bell Bridge Books and published under the author's original title in 2012.

Dear

A by-the-book agriculture bureaucrat reluctantly becomes a crime solver in this Southern mystery wrought with fraud, murder, kidnapping and a particularly attractive federal agent whose specialty is none other than agricultural crime. LOWCOUNTRY BRIBE, a 100,000-word contemporary mystery suspense, takes place in the Toogoodoo area of Edisto Island in South Carolina.

One employee commits suicide and another disappears during Carolina Slade's first year as federal agriculture manager in Charleston. Crime tape and blood splatters still decorate her small government office when hog farmers Jesse and Ren Rawlings strut in with a truckload of hog carcasses and a bold bribery offer, money in exchange for falsifying papers. Two special agents swoop in, and Slade's world evolves into professional pandemonium as Jesse proves slick, twisting suspicion back around on her. Slade and Special Agent Wayne Largo clash as longtime client Jesse Rawlings escalates into a serious threat, one worse than bribery. Law enforcement, however, turns its back on Slade, leaving her at the mercy of the farmer, her malicious boss, and a deviant ex-husband. Her agency questions her motives with the farmer, placing her job on the line. Finally, her children kidnapped, Slade realizes operating "by the book" can have mortal limitations, and a woman needs gut instinct to fight for her family, her career, and her life.

C. Hope Clark is the founder of FundsforWriters.com, a thirteen-year-old weekly newsletter service reaching 42,000 members. *Writer's Digest* recognized the site in its annual "101 Best Web Sites for Writers" for the past twelve years. She's published in *The Writer* magazine and *Writer's Digest* as well as many trade publications. Hope speaks at several conferences a year. She's a member of South Carolina Writers Workshop, Sisters in Crime, and Mensa. Hope hold a BS in Agriculture from Clemson University and has 25 years' experience with the US Department of Agriculture, enabling her to talk the talk of Carolina Slade.

The second book in the Carolina Slade Mystery series, TIDEWATER MURDER, takes place in the tomato fields of coastal Beaufort, South

Carolina. Slade discovers slavery and drugs while investigating her best friend Savvy Conroy, suspected of fraud with a tomato farmer who mysteriously dies on his shrimp boat. Agent Wayne Largo reappears. He takes over the investigation, clashing once again with Slade over case details, methods and authority. Shoved aside, Slade grabs longtime friend and peer from her headquarters, Monroe Prevatte, and snoops on her own, only to learn he has feelings for her. The case becomes more than saving a best friend's job as kidnapping, murder, and voodoo warn Slade to walk away. Trust is the theme of TIDEWATER MURDER as Slade judges how to trust her friends while routing out the hidden evil among tomato farmers, an evil that is infiltrating and eroding the historic Gullah population of St. Helena Island.

Please advise if you would like to read LOWCOUNTRY BRIBE and I thank you in advance for your time.

Sincerely,
C. Hope Clark

INDEX

ALLWORTH PRESS
NEW YORK

Books from Allworth Press

The Author's Toolkit: A Step-by-Step Guide to Writing and Publishing Your Book, Fourth Edition
by Mary Embree (6 x 9, 240 pages, paperback, $16.99)

Branding for Bloggers
by Zach Heller (5 ½ x 8 ½, 112 pages, paperback, $16.95)

Business and Legal Forms for Authors and Self-Publishers, Fourth Edition
by Tad Crawford, Stevie Fitzgerald, and Michael Gross (8 ½ x 11, 176 pages, paperback, $24.99)

The Business of Writing
Edited by Jennifer Lyons; foreword by Oscar Hijuelos (6 x 9, 304 pages, paperback, $19.95)

The Fiction Writer's Guide to Dialogue
By John Hough, Jr. (6 x 9, 144 pages, paperback, $14.95)

Promote Your Book: Over 250 Proven, Low-Cost Tips and Techniques for the Enterprising Author
by Patricia Fry (6 x 9, 224 pages, paperback, $19.95)

Publish Your Book: Proven Strategies and Resources for the Enterprising Author
by Patricia Fry (6 x 9, 264, paperback, $19.95)

Starting Your Career as a Freelance Writer, Second Edition
by Moira Anderson Allen (6 x 9, 304 pages, paperback, $24.95)

Starting Your Career as a Freelance Editor
by Mary Embree (6 x 9, 240 pages, paperback, $19.95)

Talk Up Your Book: How to Sell Your Book Through Public Speaking, Interviews, Signing, Festivals, Conferences, and More
by Patricia Fry (6 x 9, 320 pages, paperback, $19.95)

The Writer's Legal Guide
by Kay Murray and Tad Crawford (6 x 9, 352 pages, paperback, $19.95)

To see our complete catalog or to order online, please visit *www.allworth.com.*